The Economics of German Unification

Dedication

Unseren Eltern, Horst und Rosemarie Lange
sowie Tom und Ruby Pugh
in Dankbarkeit zugeeignet

To our parents, Horst and Rosemarie Lange
and Tom and Ruby Pugh

The Economics of German Unification:

An Introduction

Thomas Lange
Professor of Economics and Director of the Centre for International Labour Market Studies, Robert Gordon University, Scotland, UK and Contract Professor of Managerial Economics, Polytechnic University of Bucharest, Romania

Geoffrey Pugh
Principal Lecturer in European Economics, Staffordshire University Business School, UK and Visiting Professor at Warsaw University, Poland and Tirana University, Albania

Edward Elgar
Cheltenham, UK • Northampton, MA, USA

Published by
Edward Elgar Publishing Limited
8 Lansdown Place
Cheltenham
Glos GL50 2HU
UK

Edward Elgar Publishing, Inc.
6 Market Street
Northampton
Massachusetts 01060
USA

A catalogue record for this book
is available from the British Library

Library of Congress Cataloguing-in-Publication Data
Lange, Thomas, 1967–
  The economics of German Unification : an introduction / Thomas
Lange, Geoffrey Pugh.
  Includes bibliographical references and index.
   1. German—History—Unification, 1990—Economic aspects.
  2. Germany (East)—Economic conditions—1990– I. Pugh, Geoff.
  II. Title.
  HC286.8.L33 1998
  330.943'09'049—dc21   97-38249
                          CIP

ISBN 1 85898 090 9

Printed and bound in Great Britain by Bookcraft (Bath) Ltd.

Contents

Figures

Tables

Introduction and Acknowledgements

> the experience of all revolutions, which from the very point of view of the development of productive powers had a powerful positive influence, shows that this development was bought at the price of ... destruction of these powers. (N. Bukharin, *Economics of the Transformation Period*, pp. 105–6)

Following German Unification in 1990, East Germany's 'socialist' command economy was abolished and replaced with West Germany's 'social' market economy. By the middle of the 1990s, western Germany had provided more than one trillion Deutschmarks to support economic reconstruction. It is likely that at least this amount again will be needed if eastern Germany is to catch up with west German productivity and living standards. The purpose of this book is to explain these events as well as their consequences and associated policy issues. To this end, the following are among the topics that we discuss at length:

- the relative backwardness of East Germany's economy;
- how Unification was implemented as an economic process (that is, how the socialist economy of East Germany was integrated into the social market economy of the West);
- why the initial impact of monetary and economic integration was so devastating (and so different from the consequences of monetary and economic reform in 1948);
- restructuring and privatization;
- labour market and industrial policy;
- prospects for catching up with western Germany; and
- repercussions for German competitiveness and the wider European economy.

A summary of each chapter is given below.

Politically, the Unification of Germany was a triumph. Forty years of East–West division were overcome in less than a year. The first democratic elections in the German Democratic Republic (DDR) took place on 18 March 1990, and opened the way for economic, monetary and social union with the German Federal Republic (BRD). The terms of German Economic, Monetary and Social Union (GEMSU) were detailed in the State Treaty between the governments of the two German states and took effect on 1 July 1990. From that date, the BRD's Deutschmark (DM) became the sole legal tender in the DDR and the DDR's command economy was replaced with the legal and institutional framework of the BRD's 'social market economy'. On 3 October 1990, political union was brought about by the accession of the five reconstituted Federal States of the DDR to the BRD under Article 23 of the Basic Law (or German Constitution, which makes provision for such accession).

The economics of Germany Unification is a very different story. This starts with the relative economic backwardness of the DDR, which undermined the political legitimacy of the socialist regime. In turn, this helped to set in motion the political process that culminated in Unification. Economic backwardness and associated lack of political legitimacy also determined that the West would set the terms of Unification. These terms offered immediate benefits to east Germans as consumers, thereby easing the political process of Unification. However, economic and monetary union imposed huge costs on east Germans as producers: output and employment collapsed on a scale unprecedented in the history of industrial capitalism. This is the source of the intractable costs and problems of Unification as an economic process. No other developed market economy has been confronted with economic problems both so large and so unexpected.

We believe the economics of German Unification to be of interest from a variety of perspectives and thus for a variety of readers.

- From the perspective of business intelligence and strategic planning, Unification means the enlargement of Europe's largest market: population increased by a quarter, to almost 80 million; geographical size increased by about half, to 138,000 square miles; and eastern output, accounting for 6.9 per cent of total current price German GDP in the second half of 1990, reached 10.9 per cent in the second half of 1995 (*Bundesbank Monthly Report*, October 1995, p. 49). Inward investment on an unparalleled scale is renewing productive capacity. The development of eastern Germany is thus creating both opportunities and threats for business throughout the single European market and beyond.
- There is scope for comparison and contrast with the reform process elsewhere in the old Soviet bloc. German Unification enforced the first transition – albeit accelerated and under financially more favourable circumstances than elsewhere in Eastern Europe and the Soviet Union – from a command to a market economy.
- German Unification is testing economic policies and providing information for policy discussion elsewhere. This applies, for

example, to active labour market policy in response to mass unemployment as well as to the relative costs and benefits of 'low-wage, low-tech' and 'high-wage, high-tech' development strategies. Both of these issues are discussed at length.

- German Unification provides a case study on the fiscal consequences of economic and monetary integration.
- International trade and financial linkages have transmitted unification effects to the economies of the European Union. The external repercussions of German Unification figure prominently in the development of the European economies and, in particular, of European monetary cooperation in the 1990s.
- Feedback effects of Unification on western Germany – for example, on public sector finances and competitiveness – must be of concern to Germany's partners and competitors in the European Union and beyond.

In keeping with this variety of potential interests, we have tried to keep the book accessible to readers with a business or social science background, hence with some conceptual but not necessarily much technical background in formal economics. With the exception of a few equations and diagrams, technical material has generally been confined to appendices. The contents and structure of the book are as follows.

Chapter 1 explains the measures that made up GEMSU together with the 'social market' philosophy that informed these diverse measures and gave them coherence. In particular, we consider the sudden or 'shock therapy' character of GEMSU and the reasons for its speed of implementation. Next, GEMSU is compared with the reform process in Eastern Europe. This helps to identify the reasons why GEMSU had such a devastating impact on the eastern economy – industrial output down by two-thirds and employment down by as much as 45 per cent. The image of the J-curve is used: often in a process of economic reform, things tend to get worse before they get better – hence, the downward movement along the 'J-curve' of economic reform. The output and employment effects of GEMSU led to a dramatic deterioration of public finances. These fiscal consequences are discussed in relation to the convergence criteria of the Maastricht Treaty. Finally, these outcomes of GEMSU are contrasted with government expectations and promises. The position of the government from the beginning of the Unification process had been to minimize the potential costs. Soon, however, the short- to medium-run outcome of GEMSU belied the optimistic expectations of the government. This had economic consequences, because the initial political benefit of overly optimistic expectations – maximum support for GEMSU and immediate Unification – was secured at the cost of worsening the conditions for economic reconstruction in eastern

Germany and for controlling public expenditure. There would have been a better chance of public support for improving economic conditions by wage restraint and higher taxes if the costs – for both easterners and westerners – had been made clear from the beginning. Political opportunism, we argue, has been the enemy of coherent economic strategy.

From Chapter 1, readers who follow with Chapters 2 and 3 will gain additional insight into the impact phase of GEMSU – the downward slide along the J-curve. This is obtained first in Chapter 2 from analysis of the East's 'socialist' economy (which began as an alternative to capitalism but ended in hand over to the West for reconstruction) and, second, in Chapter 3 from comparison with the 1948 currency and economic reforms (which established West Germany's social market economy as a successful alternative to both central planning and unfettered capitalism). Readers who prefer to skip this background can continue with Chapter 4, which discusses reconstruction in the medium to long run – the upward movement along the J-curve – together with privatization.

Chapter 2 describes and analyses the economic weaknesses of the DDR that were exposed by GEMSU. Prior to Unification, the DDR economy had been the best performer among COMECON (Council for Mutual Economic Assistance) economies. However, when measured against the performance of Western economies, problems of weaker technological development and lagging product innovation were increasingly apparent. The missing (or misinterpreted) incentive system was partly to blame. However, there are other more fundamental reasons for the poor economic performance of the DDR. In this chapter we try to establish the link between central planning and economic backwardness. We elaborate the notion that planned (or command) economies perform relatively weakly because they are less able than market economies to handle complexity in production. In an appendix to this chapter, we use a formal model – based on work by Banerjee and Spagat – to deepen this analysis.

Chapter 3 compares and contrasts GEMSU with the 1948 currency and economic reforms. Analysis of the 1948 reforms is motivated by two considerations. First, comparison reveals that similar measures may have opposing outcomes if applied in circumstances as different as those of 1948 and 1990. In brief, while 1948 realized economic potential, 1990 exposed economic weakness. Second, the 1948 reforms were a factor in 1990, because popular memory of 1948 influenced expectations about the outcome of GEMSU. In 1990, comparisons made by politicians with the 1948 reforms contributed to unrealistically optimistic expectations about the outcome of GEMSU which, in turn, exerted an adverse influence on policy-making. Such comparisons were informed by a substantially mythologized account of the 1948 reforms and their effects. The aftermath of GEMSU illustrates the harm that can be caused when policy is guided by myth rather than by assessment of actual conditions.

Chapter 4 continues the analysis of GEMSU beyond the impact phase; that is, the first two years or so characterized by collapsed output and employment and only faint signs of recovery. This chapter deals first with the preconditions and initial problems of reconstruction in eastern Germany and, second, with the Treuhand as the agency of privatization and restructuring.

- The construction of a competitive traded goods sector in eastern Germany depends upon inward investment. First, private sector investment is the means of restructuring at the level of the firm – as existing firms introduce new processes and products and new firms set up in response to market opportunities and pressures. Second, as competition guides the investment decisions of firms, so the economy as a whole is restructured – with respect to the sectoral distribution of output, the regional location of production and the trade pattern. Investment, then, is the key to restructuring and growth. Accordingly, we estimate the investment needs of eastern Germany in the immediate aftermath of GEMSU. Next, we discuss the initial obstacles to investment as well as the incentives that contributed to overcoming these obstacles. In an appendix to this chapter, we use a more formal analytic framework, based on the new investment theory associated with Avinash Dixit, to deepen insight into why investment was initially lower than expected as well as why it eventually picked up. This analysis suggests that investment in transitional economies be encouraged by policies that either reduce uncertainty or increase reversibility of investments.
- Taken together, there were powerful incentives to invest in eastern Germany. However, because virtually all the land and capital stock had been state property in the DDR, investment was inextricably linked with privatization. Accordingly, most of this chapter focuses on the work of the privatization agency, the Treuhandanstalt. The privatization programme was completed within five years of GEMSU.

By the mid-1990s, eastern Germany's economic problems were no longer those of transition but more those of a relatively backward region in a developed market economy. Accordingly, in Chapters 5 and 6 we discuss policies for promoting employment and output growth. In particular, we focus on investment promotion and wage policy. Subsidized investment powers productivity increase and will continue to be necessary. In the case of wage policy, however, we take a more differentiated approach. We argue that in the first phase of Unification (say, 1990–91) high wages, together with currency conversion, were an instrument of 'creative destruction'.

Wage increases helped to ensure that east Germany's existing productive capacity would not be viable. This, in combination with subsidized investment, was necessary to ensure that eastern development would replicate the high-wage, high-tech development path of west Germany. We argue that only *after* this initial phase did wage restraint become necessary to allow productivity to rise faster than wages in order for profitability to rise. Increased profitability of eastern enterprises is a necessary condition for domestically generated investment finance which, in turn, is the key to a convergence process that is self-sustaining rather than dependent on external support.[1]

Chapter 5 analyses the labour market consequences of GEMSU together with active labour market policy in eastern Germany. The process of Unification has had far-reaching implications for the labour market in both east and west Germany. The DDR belonged to the centrally planned economies in which the role of the market in labour allocation was very limited. Over recent decades, structural unemployment has been identified as one of the main problems for West European labour markets. By contrast, East Germany (along with all other planned economies) experienced severe labour shortages. With the introduction of market principles and demand-led production, this situation changed dramatically. This chapter takes stock of these changes and describes the respective labour market policies that have been tried out in eastern Germany in an attempt to reduce mass unemployment. We assess government training programmes and publicly financed work creation schemes and highlight their limited effectiveness in combating unemployment. Our alternative solutions to the problem of east German joblessness focus on real capital investment and appropriate wage policies. We also highlight the spillover effects for west German regions by examining whether the process of German Unification was the sole source of, or simply a catalyst for, attempted and partly realized changes in the German welfare system.

In *Chapter 6* we elaborate our position on the role of wages and wages policy in the catch-up process. Here, we tend to see more justification for the strategy actually implemented than do most mainstream economists. We argue that initially the prevailing strategy of high wages plus investment subsidy precluded a low-wage, low-tech development path in eastern Germany while creating the *potential* for a high-wage, high-tech development. However, by the mid-1990s wages were already high by the standards of developed industrial economies and it became necessary to restrain further wage growth in order to *realize* this potential. In the first phase of Unification, the unique advantage of western investment finance and fiscal transfers enabled high and rising wages to play a positive role in east Germany's development strategy. However, this initially positive role turned into its opposite. This defines a second phase of the Unification process in which wage restraint is the key to self-sustaining development.

Our approach differs from Sinn and Sinn, who argue that *from the beginning* low wages and increases strictly in line with productivity would have been beneficial to the catch-up process. Our approach qualifies Sinn and Sinn's. Instead of a single, low-wage strategy for the entire period of catch-up, we develop a case for a *dynamic strategy*; that is, one that can change over time. In our model, the Unification process has two phases to which correspond directly opposite wage strategies.

- *Phase 1*, from economic and monetary union until, at the latest, the completion of the privatization process at the end of 1994, is the period which saw not only the elimination of much of the productive apparatus of eastern Germany but also massive investment and a substantial beginning to the reconstruction of the eastern economy. This was a process of creative destruction. In this phase, we argue that high wages *in combination with* investment subsidy were defensible as an instrument of an industrial policy designed to preclude a 'low-wage, low-tech' development path in favour of a 'high-wage, high-tech' strategy. While high wages were an instrument of destruction with respect to the low-tech productive apparatus of eastern Germany, investment subsidy – the essential condition or requirement for this strategy – provided the creative instrument for renewing the capital stock and constructing a new, high-tech industrial base in eastern Germany. From an eclectic but consistent theoretical basis we argue that in this initial phase of Unification the costs of this strategy were outweighed by two benefits. First, high-tech output is subject to more rapidly rising demand than low-tech output. And, in turn, expanding markets enable expanding output, which favours productivity growth. Second, high-tech industries maximize 'learning-by-doing' and thus productivity growth. Accordingly, for both demand-side and supply-side reasons, a high-wage, high-tech strategy has the potential to generate a higher rate of growth than a low-wage, low-tech strategy. In the long run, therefore, initial costs consequent upon high wages are potentially recoverable from the benefits of higher growth.
- *Phase 2*, beginning, at the latest, with the completion of the privatization process, has been a period of declining growth rates and renewed pessimism about economic development in eastern Germany. We argue that the benefits of high wages as an instrument of creative destruction were subject to diminishing returns and probably maximized at an early stage. Even by 1991, as wages rose to more than 50 per cent of western levels, more than 90 per cent of industrial workers were employed by enterprises that could not cover even their variable costs. Given this, it is unlikely that further substantial

rises above the rate of increase of productivity were necessary to secure the benefits of precluding low-wage, low-tech development.

Although we cannot date the onset of Phase 2 with precision, it signifies the onset of a period in which continued wage increase entailed additional costs that were no longer offset by additional benefits, either actual or potential. Instead, increasingly high wages not only were an obstacle to low-tech output but also curtailed the growth of high-tech output and employment. In Phase 2, therefore, the need is for strategic reorientation with respect to wages. A prolonged period is necessary in which wages rise more slowly than aggregate productivity growth. Over time this will raise aggregate profitability, thereby securing investment and employment. This is necessary to realize the potential created in Phase 1.

Chapter 7 considers how long it will take for eastern Germany to catch up with western levels of productivity and living standards (measured by per capita output). Eastern Germany is often compared with Italy's Mezzo-giorno. On the one hand, the comparison is misleading in that the first five years of Unification established a convergence dynamic very different from that of postwar Italy. Yet, on the other hand, this largely reflects the scale of inward fiscal transfers. In the long run, the comparison will prove misleading only if investment and growth become self-sustaining, thereby allowing the steady reduction of fiscal transfers. In turn, this is conditional on establishing conditions for profitable production in eastern Germany. In a continuation of the argument of Chapter 6, we show that the aggregate difference between productivity (value added per worker) and wages is too small to fund investment from retained earnings. Hence, a precondition for self-sustaining convergence is prolonged wage restraint allowing sustained increase in profitability in the eastern enterprise sector. If Germany's 'social partners' prove capable of delivering the necessary consensus, then historical and comparative data suggest that a convergence period of 20–30 years is possible. During this period, inward fiscal transfers to support consumption and investment will continue but on a diminishing scale.

Chapter 8 deals with the consequences of Unification for the rest of the EU and for German competitiveness.

- First, expenditure associated with Unification constituted an enormous fiscal expansion. In turn, increased demand led to current account deterioration equivalent to about 5 per cent of German GNP as well as inflationary pressure. From the point of view of Germany's EU partners, these developments led to offsetting spillover effects. On the one hand, expenditure generated by Unification led to a step increase in the level of imports from

Germany's EU partner countries. On the other hand, the Bundesbank countered inflationary pressure with higher interest rates. In turn, because of the Exchange Rate Mechanism of the European Monetary System, higher interest rates in Germany caused interest rates throughout the EU to be higher than they otherwise would have been and, hence, exerted a deflationary effect throughout the EU. High interest rates in particular had serious consequences for Germany's EU partners and for monetary cooperation within the EU. This experience demonstrates that a fixed exchange rate regime with no possibility of realignment cannot survive major asymmetric shocks.

- Second, we argue that the Bundesbank's tight money stance in the aftermath of Unification has contributed to a substantial appreciation of the DM. However, this does not establish, as is often asserted, that the DM is overvalued. To assess whether or not and, if so, to what extent the DM is overvalued, we present a simple method for estimating the equilibrium level of exchange rates over time. It is applied to the DM with respect to the currencies of Germany's three major trading partners. We find that by 1995 the DM was overvalued by between 10 and 20 per cent. This implies a major loss of price competitiveness for German producers of internationally traded goods.

Chapter 9 presents our conclusions. In particular, we discuss the emerging possibility that increasing flexibility in eastern Germany with respect to wage rates and working conditions not only favours wage restraint and cost reduction, identified in Chapters 5, 6 and 7 as the main precondition for self-sustaining growth and convergence, but is also a catalyst for institutional renewal throughout the German labour market. If so, this could be a source of renewed dynamism in the whole German social market economy.

Chapters may be read independently. None the less, they are related not only by dealing with successive phases or aspects of the Unification process but also by the linked themes of productivity and wages.

Transition in eastern Germany was concluded with privatization. Yet transition is not the same as convergence. The transformed economy is not yet *competitive*. In the aggregate, the output of eastern producers does not have a combination of price and quality capable of generating sales sufficient to sustain the current standard of living while balancing the value of imports with exports.[2] Nor yet are eastern producers, in the aggregate, able to generate sufficient profit to finance the investment necessary to reduce costs and prices and/or increase quality of output. Consequently, eastern producers still lack the independent means to enhance competitiveness and so deliver improving and self-sustaining living standards. The aim of competitiveness is synonymous with the aim of *self-sustaining* convergence: that is, a process which brings eastern Germany closer to west German living standards while fiscal transfers are progressively eliminated. However defined, the task requires productivity increase at the most rapid possible rate.

Productivity increase comes from innovation: this means

- finding ways to produce more of existing products with fewer resources – above all, less labour time; and
- even more important, improving existing products and introducing new ones that command higher prices.

Singly or together, these innovation effects increase value added per period of working time and are the ultimate source of competitiveness. Accordingly, the economics of German Unification resolves largely into productivity-related issues. We discuss the 'socialist' command economy of the DDR by addressing the problem of why productivity systematically and increasingly lagged behind western levels. In turn, this is the point of departure for analysing the collapse of eastern industrial output after GEMSU. The productivity gap explains why at the time of Unification unit labour costs – wage and non-wage costs per unit of output – were twice the western level and why, therefore, the majority of eastern enterprises were rendered uncompetitive. In turn, if eastern Germany is to remain a high-wage economy, and if fiscal transfers are to be reduced over time, then productivity growth will determine eastern Germany's chances of creating a core of internationally competitive firms and, hence, of convergence with western Germany. Thus productivity is discussed as the true long-run objective of policy.

Finally, this book is intended for English-speaking undergraduate and postgraduate students within the broad field of European studies, economists interested in transition or new developments in Germany's social market economy, other social scientists with interests in contemporary Germany, and readers with strategic business interests in Germany. Of course, the German-reading specialist will be familiar with much of the material.[3] Yet we do not offer the book *only* as a round-up and synthesis of existing material for the benefit of English-speaking readers. We have also tried to 'add value' to existing work by incorporating material from our own research. Of course, there is a continuum rather than distinct borderlines between descriptive material that is more or less a simple synthesis of the sources, more analytic work drawing on secondary sources but offering an individual interpretation, and new work that can be dignified as research findings. Yet these categories help to characterize the contents of the book. In the main, this book is not a research monograph. Chapters 1 and 4 – but not the appendix to Chapter 4 – are the closest to simple synthesis. Yet these chapters, describing and analysing the transformation process and, in particular, the privatization of the eastern economy, are indispensable for the non-specialist. Chapters 2 and 3, on the DDR economy and comparing the economics of Unification with the reforms of 1948, attempt individual interpretations of material known to the specialist. It is mainly in the latter half of the book that we incorporate new work: on active labour market policy in Chapter 5, on the catch-up process and strategic policy in Chapters 6 and 7, and on the consequences for German industrial competitiveness in Chapter 8.

ACKNOWLEDGEMENTS

We owe a great deal to our teachers, colleagues and critics without whom our work, its change and progress over time, would have been impossible. They include Nick Adnett, Bob Beachill, John Bridge, Wendy Carlin, David Carr, Emil-Maria Claassen, K.H. Domdey, Yannis Georgellis, Jens Hölscher, Grant Lewis, Val Lintner, Mehrdad Emadi-Moghadem, Keith Maguire, Wolfgang Nicolai, Spiridon Paraskewopoulos, Dieter Schmidtchen, Hilmar Schneider, J.R. (Len) Shackleton, Eric Owen-Smith, Johannes Stephan and Chenggang Xu. Likewise, we make a collective acknowledgement to colleagues at the Institut für Arbeitsmarkt- und Berufsforschung (IAB) der Bundesanstalt für Arbeit in Nürnberg, the HWWA-Institut für Wirtschaftsforschung, Hamburg, and the Institute for German Studies, Birmingham University, who have been generous in sharing knowledge and data. Both authors have gained information and, most important of all, insights from participants in conferences and seminars. In particular, we would like to thank the organizers and participants of 'The German Currency Union of 1990' (University of Wales, Swansea, March 1995) and 'The German New Länder in Locational Competition' (Institute for German Studies, Birmingham University, June 1996). Finally, both authors would like to thank Lynn Frances for her excellent support in preparing the manuscript.

NOTES

1. Convergence takes place if per capita income or product grows faster in eastern than in western Germany. We use this term as synonymous with a process of catch-up, which is completed as eastern per capita income or product begins to approximate western levels.
2. The characteristic outcomes – hence, indicators – of national competitiveness are discussed by Dunn (1994, pp. 304–5 and 307).
3. Such readers will easily detect omissions from our list of sources. However, the literature is vast and every specialist will have his or her own list of 'glaring' omissions. Moreover, we make no claim to be encyclopaedic in the coverage of our subject. In the course of researching and writing, the list of such omissions was at least reduced by the generous advice of those friends and colleagues acknowledged below.

Abbreviations

BRD	Bundesrepublik Deutschland (the Federal Republic of Germany or FRG)
CDU	Christlich-Demokratische Union Deutschlands (German Christian Democratic Union)
DDR	Deutsche Demokratische Republik (German Democratic Republic or GDR)
DM	Deutsche Mark (German mark or Deutschmark)
GEMSU	German Economic, Monetary and Social Union
PDS	Partei des Demokratischen Sozialismus (reformed SED)
SED	Sozialistische Einheitspartei Deutschlands (German Socialist Unity Party, the governing party of the DDR)
SPD	Sozialdemokratische Partei Deutschlands (German Social Democratic Party)
THA	Treuhandanstalt

Note When referring to the pre-Unification period before 1 July 1990, East Germany refers to the DDR and West Germany to the BRD. In the post-Unification period, east(ern) and west(ern) Germany refer to regions within the enlarged BRD.

1. GEMSU – Switching from Socialism to Capitalism

1.1 THE COLLAPSE OF 'REAL EXISTING SOCIALISM' IN EASTERN EUROPE AND THE DDR

Ironically, the unconditional surrender of the Soviet bloc's most successful command economy to Western Europe's most successful (social) market economy accords with Karl Marx's view that social, economic and political institutions are ripe for overthrow when they prove unable to develop the 'forces of production'. In the then USSR, the reaction to the 'stagnation years' of the Brezhnev era was a reform process whose failure unleashed revolution. Part of this process was the removal of the Soviet guarantee for the ruling parties of Eastern Europe which, once supported only by their own reserves of power and authority, soon succumbed to popular contempt. In the then DDR, the crisis and demise of 'state socialism' was driven by the increasingly unfavourable contrast between, on the one hand, the manifest costs imposed by the regime on its citizens – a relatively low and stagnating living standard, the denial of human and democratic rights, and environmental deterioration – and, on the other, the perceived benefits of the West German 'social market economy'. Once released from the Soviet grip, the gravitational pull of West German economic success and political rights persuaded the majority of East Germans to demolish the Wall – at first as a physical barrier but soon after as the symbol of an alternative form of society.

Economic and political integration between nations is a long process fraught with frustrations and setbacks: more than three decades after the Treaty of Rome (1957) EU members are still uncertain about progress towards monetary union, while political union is still scarcely on the agenda. Compare, then, the process within a nation – Germany – when the opportunity, long denied, is presented: not quite 11 months from the opening of the border (9 November 1989) to economic, monetary and social union (1 July 1990) and political Unification (3 October 1990).

The rest of this chapter outlines the measures that comprised German Economic, Monetary and Social Union (GEMSU), the 'social market' philosophy that informed these measures, GEMSU as a strategy of 'shock therapy', why GEMSU was introduced so rapidly, and how GEMSU compares with economic reform in Central and Eastern Europe. It concludes with an explanation of why GEMSU had such a devastating initial impact on the eastern economy – industrial output down by two-thirds and employment down by 40 per cent. The image of the J-curve is used: often in a process of economic reform, things tend to get worse before they get better – hence, the downward movement along the 'J-curve' of economic reform. This outcome is contrasted with Government expectations and promises.

1.2 GEMSU – THE STRUCTURAL ASSIMILATION OF THE DDR

Against the step-by-step approach favoured by the Bundesbank, members of the government including Finance Minister Theo Waigel, leading German economists and EC experts, the policy of Chancellor Helmut Kohl was for economic and monetary union and then political union as soon as possible (see Section 1.9, below). The dangers were known: extending the West German monetary system to the East with a 1:1 conversion rate between the Deutschmark (DM) and the DDR's mark could boost inflation for the West (by increasing money supply to a greater extent than output) while exerting a massive deflationary influence in the East (via the output and employment effects of suddenly forcing Eastern producers to set prices and pay current costs in DM) (OECD 1990, p. 47). None the less, on 18 March, elections in the DDR brought to power a Christian Democrat-led coalition which, in mid-April, pledged support for GEMSU. On 18 May the State Treaty was signed for monetary, economic and social union to come into effect on 1 July.

The State Treaty abolished 'socialism' and reconstituted the DDR as a 'social market economy' (Treaty of 18 May 1990, 1990, pp. 65 and 68). The Treaty involved no compromise between the BRD and the DDR but, rather, the abolition of central planning and the assimilation of the Eastern economy into the economic structures of the West. The measures comprising GEMSU liquidated the DDR's command economy while establishing the basic rules and institutions within which the transition to a social market economy could proceed.

1. *Monetary union* The DM became the only legal means of payment in the DDR. The conversion rate for wages and pensions as well as for amounts of savings varying according to age was 1:1, while the rate for financial assets and liabilities was 2:1. Accordingly, the Bundesbank became the central bank for the whole of Germany.

2. *Social union*   This was an essential complement to monetary and economic union, because without a social dimension the pain of adjustment entailed in monetary and economic union would have provoked renewed migration as well as social and political unrest. Accordingly, the welfare system was restructured along West German lines and finance provided for raising pensions (to DM 495 per month) and paying unemployment benefit (at an average rate for a worker with one child of DM 650 per month – a sum based on the West German unemployment benefit system of 68 per cent of the previous net wage). It was for social reasons, moreover, that during a transition period the prices of a number of basic, non-traded goods – above all, rents – remained heavily subsidized and controlled.

3. *Economic union*   This meant the structural assimilation of the East German economy into the West German social market economy. Privatization of state-owned enterprises within a liberalized and open economy reconstituted the previously planned economy of the DDR on the basis of two fundamental principles.

   a. *Private ownership of the means of production*   However, within the social market philosophy the principle of private ownership is tempered by 'the notion of an economically *and* socially efficient enterprise' (Owen-Smith 1994, p. 300, original emphasis). Accordingly, private ownership was introduced into east Germany under the constraints of labour market law (including codetermination at board level, wage determination through collective bargaining, and the right to strike) as well as competition policy.

   b. *Free competition* – secured by

     - creating independent firms – by breaking up into separate firms and, hence, demonopolizing the existing state owned 'Kombinate' (or industrial groupings);
     - freedom of economic activity – that is, free movement of labour, capital, goods and services – thereby allowing market entry as a source of competitive pressure;
     - free prices – requiring the abrogation of both price controls and the heavy subsidies applied generally to basic goods under the command economy – thereby allowing markets and the price mechanism to operate without massive distortion;
     - creating an open economy – an end to currency inconvertibility and the state monopoly of foreign trade and, consequently, the liberalization of trade and capital

movements – thereby exposing the economy of the DDR to competition from 'foreign' (that is, Western) producers;
- reform of the East German banking system along West German lines – thereby creating a capital market and subjecting the allocation of capital to the competitive process; and
- reform of the East German tax system along West German lines (Treaty of 18 May 1990, 1990; and OECD 1990, p. 53).

The key institution for securing private ownership and competition – hence, the transition to a market economy – was the Treuhandanstalt (THA). The THA – a trust fund or state holding company (the world's largest) – was set up by the government of the DDR early in 1990 to take charge of state-owned enterprises. With GEMSU it became a privatization agency whose task was not just to transfer existing firms into private ownership – as in the West – but to create the necessary conditions for privatization by restructuring the DDR's state enterprises into independent firms capable of being privatized. (Privatization and the work of the THA are discussed in Chapter 4.)

1.3 GEMSU – THE UNDERLYING PHILOSOPHY

The concept of the 'social market economy' has come to refer to the actual economic order in the BRD. Originally, however, the 'social market economy' was the economic philosophy that inspired the economic and currency reforms of 1948 as well as subsequent economic policy in the BRD. Accordingly, it is the underlying philosophy of the 'social market' that gave the particular measures of GEMSU an overall coherence.

The ethical foundation of the social market – or 'socially responsible free market economy' – is the social-Christian principle that individuals have comprehensive personal and social responsibilities (Grosser et al. 1990, pp. 9 and 12). Responsibility means making choices, which presupposes freedom. Accordingly, the creation of private property and a competitive environment in eastern Germany is dictated not only by considerations of economic efficiency but also because these are the means of decentralizing decision-making and enabling individuals to take responsibility and exercise initiative. Private property compels individuals to take responsibility: it is 'the institutional device by which decisions can be decentralized and microeconomic costs and benefits are related to the specific producer' (Siebert et al. 1991, p. 2). At the same time, private property gives incentives to owners that favour an efficient allocation and use of resources: decentralized decision-making motivated by private profit gives rise to competition, requires effective control of managers, and encourages risk-taking.

The social market is distinguished from the unqualified free market by a dense system of law, regulation and associated institutions, which not only provides the framework within which competitive markets operate but is designed also to impose 'social responsibility' on the market.[1] Accordingly, property rights – hence, individual responsibility and initiative – are constrained and qualified. First, in east Germany a liberalized and open economy subject to the legal framework of competition and labour law was created *prior* to privatization. This accorded with the principle that competition and law must constrain the devolved economic power of owners and managers to direct it towards a continuous increase in economic performance rather than the exploitation of consumers and workers (Härtel et al. 1995, p. 16). Second, responsibility is not only individual but also social. The social dimension of responsibility is reflected in commitment to social justice and solidarity along with economic transformation. A fundamental principle of the social market concept is that neither the market nor the social principle may be subordinated to the other (Grosser et al. 1990, p. 12). This is apparent in the official title of the reform process: German Monetary, Economic and Social Union (*not* German Economic and Monetary Union – the truncated form used by many Anglo-American commentators).

The social market philosophy recognizes conflicting aims within society; for example, between capital and labour, and different regions. However, social conflicts are not to be allowed to proceed unchecked and threaten the legitimacy of the free market. Instead, they are to be reconciled by institutions designed to counteract concentrations of power, promote social justice and build consensus; for example, codetermination (industrial democracy) in industry and a high degree of fiscal equalization among the Federal States. Accordingly, GEMSU incorporated eastern Germany not only by way of competition and private property but also by way of principles and institutions through which social conflict is ameliorated in a social market economy.

Of course, general principles do not furnish solutions to particular problems. For example, while the principle of private property requires privatization, how actually to proceed has been fraught with difficulties and policy disputes: issues included whether to return property to former owners ('restitution') or simply to provide compensation as well as the appropriate balance of market forces and structural policy in the privatization process. Likewise, while the German Constitution requires 'adherence to the uniformity of living conditions' (Gröner and Baumann 1994, p. 4) this still leaves to the judgement of policy-makers decisive problems such as the extent and nature of fiscal transfers and wages policy for east Germany.

1.4 GEMSU – SHOCK THERAPY

The social market economy was introduced into West Germany in stages between 1948 and (arguably) 1958 (Owen-Smith 1994, pp. 25–28). In contrast, the totality of the measures that assimilated eastern Germany into the western economy together with the speed with which GEMSU and subsequent privatization were implemented, rejected a gradual, step-by-step approach to transformation in favour of a strategy of 'shock therapy'. On the one hand, this avoided the problem of destroying central control and planning mechanisms more rapidly than market institutions and the price mechanism could be brought into operation. In particular, extending west Germany's financial institutions and capital market to east Germany constituted a new mechanism for allocating finance and factors of production (see Section 1.6.1). On the other hand, the very totality and speed of GEMSU left east Germans with little of their own to contribute to the united Germany or even the transformation of their own land. The social–psychological and political consequences of this have been profound: for example, the widely reported arrogance of '*wessis*', '*ossi*' perceptions of having been 'colonized', and the continued electoral success of the PDS. However, these observations lead beyond the confines of this book. Instead, we focus on the unprecedented and overwhelming shock to which GEMSU subjected the economy of the DDR.

The impact of GEMSU on the Eastern economy will be explored more fully below in Sections 1.7 and 1.8. In brief, replacing the non-convertible (Eastern) mark with the DM suddenly opened the Eastern economy to Western goods – and, hence, to prevailing world market prices for traded goods. Consequently, the relatively backward productive apparatus of the East succumbed to massively superior competitive pressure from which, hitherto, it had been sheltered by a non-convertible currency and a state monopoly of foreign trade. Moreover, state-owned enterprises and cooperatives were cut off from their usual sources of credit, the government – subjected to a tight budget constraint by GEMSU – could not provide finance, and Treuhand liquidity credits were insufficient to maintain liquidity throughout the entire traded goods sector. The result was a rapid descent of the economy into depression.

So why shock therapy rather than a step-by-step approach? There were economic arguments but political considerations were decisive.[2]

1.5 GEMSU – WHY SO RAPID?

In the rapid move to Unification, politics was in command. Overriding political priorities drove the process, and decisions were taken without regard to their economic consequences. In this respect, pressure from below and policy from above were mutually reinforcing: from the point of view both of the mass opposition in the East and of the Federal government monetary and economic union were simply part of the process of political Unification. From the East, among the main slogans of the mass demonstrations, which undermined the old regime, was 'D-Mark jetzt!' (DM now!) and 'Kommt die D-Mark nicht zu uns, gehen wir zur D-Mark' (if the DM does not come to us, we will go to the DM). For the Federal government there were likewise compelling reasons for action sooner rather than later. While official reasoning stressed the need for action to control migration, political considerations also suggested rapid implementation of GEMSU.

First, a step-by-step approach was unlikely to have had sufficient impact upon expectations to diminish mass migration from the East to the West (240,000 in the final quarter of 1988 and continuing at a peak annual rate of 344,000 in 1989). In a Federal election year, the government was scared of the potential impact of migration on both western unemployment and housing (Hoffmann 1993, p. 10). To influence expectations sufficiently to persuade people in the East not to migrate, dramatic measures were seen as necessary to promote the conviction that acquiring the DM would more or less rapidly lead to acquiring a West German standard of living. (A mythologized version of West Germany's 1948 economic and monetary reform and subsequent 'economic miracle' helped inform this conviction; see Chapter 3.) The 1:1 mark/DM conversion rate had an immediately beneficial impact on Eastern consumption – especially on consumer durables and foreign holidays – before the deflationary effect was felt with full force (see below, 1.6.2). Not only GEMSU itself, however, but even the conversion rate was politically determined. The Bundesbank proposal for a 2:1 conversion in April provoked a storm of protest: banners appeared in the demonstrations demanding 1:1 and even a general strike was threatened. Responding to this pressure, the State Treaty incorporated the 1:1 rate, thereby maximizing the initial value of wages and social benefits.[3]

Second, denying an extended period of step-by-step adjustment to the state-owned enterprises of the East meant avoiding 'half-baked measures and potentially counterproductive compromises' (OECD 1990, p. 48). In particular, even while the DDR remained an independent state, GEMSU and its consequences – the crippling effect of Western competition and incipient illiquidity – ruled out experiments with 'third-path' or market–socialist reforms. (A 'third path' between capitalism and 'real existing socialism', rather than assimilation into the Western model, was favoured not only by the PDS – the reformed SED – but also by parts of the New Forum which had helped inspire mass opposition to the old regime.) In this way, the ground was cleared – unambiguously – for market structures and private ownership and, hence, the most rapid possible assimilation of East Germany into the Federal Republic.

Third, West Germany, and Chancellor Kohl in particular, had invested more heavily in Mikhail Gorbachev than had any other G7 country. In turn, Gorbachev's renunciation of the 'Brezhnev doctrine' with respect to Eastern Europe and, later, his initial lack of opposition and eventually favourable attitude towards Unification dissolved the cardinal Cold War determinants of German division. Consequently, nervousness about the domestic position of Gorbachev, and the possibility of a hard-line successor less favourably disposed towards German unity, also inclined Chancellor Kohl towards urgency.

Criticism of the speed of GEMSU is misdirected. GEMSU was driven by the revolutionary transformation of a whole society and the expectations this aroused. Moreover, the alternative – a strategy of economic convergence culminating in monetary union (as in the EU) – was not credible. The transitional regime in the East would have been – at best – a regime of crisis, undermined by currency, demographic and political instability.

GEMSU took place not only rapidly but also in the absence of any historical precedent or theory of transition from which policy guidance might have been sought. Of course, changes could not remain pending while the theory was worked out! However, lack of historical example or theory of transition from command to market economy does not mean that it was impossible to anticipate the nature or likely scale of the problems associated with GEMSU.

There was no lack of economic intelligence on the state of the Eastern economy available to the Federal government (indeed, overwhelming economic superiority was a constant refrain in the 'competition between the systems'). Using available information, economists and others were able to warn that GEMSU would cause the collapse of much of the East's economy, that the East's backwardness could not be made up in a few years, and that the process of reconstruction would place unprecedented strain on public finances (Priewe and Hickel 1991, pp. 59 and 75 and Hoffmann 1993, p. 10).[4]

The costs of GEMSU are the price of political judgements and priorities. In this case, if there was no politically feasible alternative, then criticism of GEMSU and the speed of implementation is beside the point. A more reasonable criticism is that foreseeable consequences of GEMSU were ignored or systematically downplayed (see Section 1.9). For this reason, public policy often appeared as a mixture of political opportunism and crisis management. This compounded the lack of historical precedent or theory and undermined the coherence of economic strategy. In turn, this increased the costs of Unification. Lack of coherence in economic strategy was evident in the following examples of failures in policy design, each of which delayed and/or increased the costs of Unification:

- the radical underestimation of the costs of Unification and its financial consequences, leading to a series of *ad hoc* policy reversals uncharacteristic of German public policy (see 1.9);
- embracing the principle of 'restitution' of property expropriated after 1948, only to loosen it upon finding it a major obstacle to privatization and inward investment (see Chapter 4);
- ambivalence in the Treuhand's role with respect to privatization and restructuring (see Chapter 4); and
- in labour market policy (see Chapter 5).

1.6 GEMSU AND ECONOMIC REFORM IN EASTERN EUROPE

1.6.1 Similarities: economic reform in general

Transition from a command to a market economy requires fundamental reform in three broad areas. This much is common to GEMSU and reform in Eastern Europe.[5]

1. *Property and property rights* The marginalization of advocates of a 'third way' – based on theories of market socialism – meant that the 'property question' was reduced to the transformation of state property into *private property*. This required not only privatization but also the prior transformation of the economic constitution. The *economic constitution* of a market economy must include the legal foundations of private ownership, production and exchange – contract and company law together with means of enforcement. In addition, the distinction between public and private sectors must be secure – requiring, for example, a two-tier banking system separating the Central Bank from commercial banking.
2. *Macroeconomic stabilization* The macroeconomic priority is *currency stability* – with respect to both the domestic price level and external convertibility. This is the *sine qua non* for a functioning price mechanism and efficient resource allocation. In turn, currency stability requires control of public sector and current account deficits.
3. *Microeconomic reform* The microeconomic priority is *competitiveness*. In turn, competitiveness requires price deregulation and competition. *Price deregulation* reveals the actual competitive position of firms. With administered prices in a command economy, actual costs and actual revenue-earning potential are unknown – in which case, actual profitability and thus firms' real competitive position are likewise

unknown. To make firms competitive requires *competition*. The pressure of competition that forces firms to be efficient and innovative was systematically precluded in command economies. Both internal and external liberalization, however, create competitive pressure. First, the break-up of producer monopolies into competing firms and, second, abolition of the state monopoly of foreign trade confront domestic firms – for the first time – with both domestic and foreign competition. Finally, if competitive pressure is to enforce the restructuring of the economy along the lines of competitive advantage, then goods market liberalization has to be accompanied by capital and labour market liberalization to facilitate the redeployment of factors of production.

1.6.2   Differences: Particular Problems of Economic Reform in Eastern Germany

Eastern Germany acquired the legal and institutional basis of a market economy together with macroeconomic stability through unification with Europe's most successful market economy. This provided huge advantages not enjoyed by the rest of the old Soviet bloc. However, transition by means of GEMSU also entailed some unique problems.

GEMSU was introduced overnight. GEMSU thus constituted a more radical 'shock therapy' than undertaken in Eastern Europe (where, for example, trade is being liberalized only gradually and combined with currency devaluation). GEMSU suddenly exposed the inability of eastern producers to compete in free markets: they were defeated on the terrain both of price and of non-price competition (to a large extent, goods were produced of such low quality that, in a free market, they were unsaleable at virtually any price). Hence, the sudden disordering of economic life in eastern Germany triggered economic breakdown (see sections 1.7 and 1.8).

Eastern Germany endured the most radical 'shock therapy' of all the reforming economies. It also enjoyed some uniquely favourable conditions for recovery.

Economic reform imposes costs before it yields benefits. In a democracy, therefore, economic recovery in the medium to long run depends not only on the persistent application of market principles but also on continued political stability. In eastern Germany, political stability is ensured by assimilation to the political institutions and processes of the Federal Republic. In turn, this assimilation is underpinned by fiscal transfers. Uniquely, reform in eastern Germany is being supported by a western patron obliged to reduce the pain of adjustment by financing the introduction of its own social security system as well as much of the cost of reconstruction. The scale of this obligation is apparent from the dominant role of fiscal transfers in financing eastern Germany's absorption–output gap.

In the first full year of Unification, for example, domestic absorption in eastern Germany (that is, total expenditure by households on consumption, firms on investment, and by Land and local governments) was estimated at DM 333 bn. The value of output, in contrast, was only DM 182 bn (JG 1991, p. 160). This gap between absorption and production was covered by an excess of imports (DM 204.5 bn) over exports (DM 53.5 bn) – a trade deficit of DM 151 bn and equivalent to 83 per cent of eastern GNP. Table 1.1 displays this data as well as similar data for the years 1992–95. In each year, inward transfers have been in excess of three-quarters of eastern output and have imposed a financial burden on western Germany typically in excess of 7 per cent of western output. This has been the scale of inward transfer which enabled consumption to rise (by about 25 per cent between the second half of 1990 and the second half of 1991), *Länder* and Municipal spending to rise, and an investment boom to begin even while output and employment were collapsing (JG 1991, pp. 160 and 163).[6]

Table 1.1   Eastern Germany's absorption–output gap, 1991–1995 (1994 – estimate; 1995 – forecast) (DM bn in constant 1991 prices)

	1991[*]	1992	1993	1994	1995
Output (GDP)	182	222.10	235.00	258.00	281.5
Absorption	333	408.32	429.07	461.5	492.5
Output–absorption [†]	–151	–186.22	–194.07	–203.5	–211
Exports [‡]	53.5	51.69	54.55	63.5	74.5
Imports [‡]	204.5	241.61	253.77	276.5	295.5
Trade deficit [†]	–151	–189.92	–199.22	–213	–221
Output–absorption gap:					
• Percentage of east German GDP	83	84	83	79	75
• Percentage of west German GDP		6.9	7.3	7.5	7.6

Notes

* In 1990 (second half) prices; output refers to GNP. (The difference in 1991 between east German GNP – DM 182 bn – and GDP – DM 171.5 bn – is probably accounted for by employment income remitted from migrants back to families in east Germany.)

† In the case of GNP, equal by definition (absorption not covered by domestic output requires *either* an excess of imports over exports *or* net receipts of factor income from outside the territory of east Germany). GDP does not include net receipts of factor income; hence the small discrepancies between the output–absorption gap and the trade deficit for the years 1992–95.

‡ Including from and to western Germany.

Sources: JG 1991, p. 160 and 1994, p. 11 (own calculations).

Eastern Germany's absorption–output gap was and remains possible because of fiscal transfers from western Germany. The full record of fiscal transfers is presented in Table 1.2. In round terms, since Unification east Germany has benefited from the inward transfer of about 5 to 6 per cent of total German national income. For eastern Germany, therefore, fiscal transfers have eased the pain of a uniquely rapid reform process. Consequently, whatever political and social tensions have arisen from Unification, reform in eastern Germany is not seriously threatened by fears of national disintegration or social conflict.

Table 1.2   Public financial transfers to east Germany (DM bn)

	1991	1992	1993	1994	1995
Financial transfers of central, state and local government[1]	112.0	133.0	154.5	146.5	161.5
• German Unity Fund	35.0	36.0	36.5	36.0	–
• Central government spending arising out of Unification (net figure)[2]	66.0	85.5	106.5	99.5	113.5
• Redistribution of VAT receipts among Federal states	11.0	11.5	11.5	11.0	–
• New system of inter-state financial compensation	–	–	–	–	48.0
Transfers from social insurance institutions	21.5	29.0	24.0	33.5	32.5
• Transfers from west to east unemployment insurance	21.5	24.5	15.0	19.5	17.5
• Transfers from west to east pensions insurance	0.0	4.5	9.0	14.0	15.0
Total financial transfers	133.5	162.0	178.5	180.0	194.0
Memo item:					
• Borrowing by the Treuhandanstalt	19.9	29.6	38.1	37.1	–
Public financial transfers to east Germany as a percentage of total German GDP					
• Excluding Treuhandanstalt borrowing	4.7	5.3	5.7	5.4	5.6
• Including Treuhandanstalt borrowing	5.4	6.2	6.9	6.5	–

Notes
1. Excluding
   a. administrative aid by state and local government;
   b. reduced revenue in west Germany due to entitlement to tax allowances for investment in the new *Länder*;
   c. spending by the Treuhandanstalt and the subsidization of interest payments on ERP (European Recovery Programme) loans.
2. In 1995 including interest payments on the debts incurred by the Treuhandanstalt to the end of 1994.

Sources: Economic Bulletin, November 1995; JG (1995, pp. 6 and 347); and own calculations.

As well as political stability, GEMSU meant that eastern Germany enjoyed immediate advantages associated with the credibility of an irreversible regime change and an enduringly stable and convertible currency. Together, these secured two of the three dimensions of the reform process.

- *Private property* was guaranteed by adoption of the West German legal and regulatory system. Once provided, the legal framework was applied without question. This, as Kaser explains, was 'a short cut to the protection of property and contracts and to the prudential and regulatory provisions which cost other states much time and effort and through the interstices or inadequacies of which crime and fraud penetrated'. Firms trade and invest 'with foreknowledge of the protection available... predictability – so important for investment – was also assured, for example, of tax regimes and profit convertibility' (1995, p. 5). This was the precondition for private ownership of the means of production to be extended and secured by rapid privatization (see Chapter 4).

  Social responsibility is imposed on the market by law and regulation (see Section 1.3). However, western and eastern Germany acquired the elements of the contemporary social market in contrasting ways: in west Germany these developed over a 40-year period, whereas in eastern Germany they were imposed all at once. Accordingly, the German legal and regulatory framework has been criticized as inappropriate for an economy whose priority is rapid growth and job creation. In particular, labour market regulations and institutions such as employment protection and centralized collective bargaining have been widely criticized as bureaucratic and costly in slowing the pace of business formation. Yet, against this must be set the avoidance of several years of chaos and corruption (a very un-German 'wild East'!). In addition, the legitimacy of the market economy and, hence, political stability in eastern Germany was strengthened by establishing uniform conditions throughout unified Germany (rather than first class in the west and second class in the east). In turn, this limited the appeal of 'reform socialism' and so eased the extension of west Germany's political system to the east.

- *Macroeconomic stabilization* was secured by the introduction of the DM. First, the size of the overall stock of DM was large enough to minimize the inflationary potential of an East German monetary overhang (Pugh and Carr 1993, pp. 118–19). Second, acquiring one of the world's hardest currencies solved the problem of external convertibility. And, third, Unification solved the problem of external debt as well as – to a large extent – public sector debt (with budget deficits of the new eastern public authorities being partly assumed by western transfers).

In turn, this meant that the *sequence of reform* was less of an issue than elsewhere in the old Soviet bloc.[7] For the DDR, the pace of the Unification process overtook concerns about the sequence of reform: instead of sequencing, GEMSU introduced reforms immediately and simultaneously. Together, certainty over property rights, macroeconomic stability, massive inward transfers and the absence of conflict over the sequencing of reforms all make the environment more conducive to inward investment and privatization than elsewhere in the ex-Soviet bloc.

The third broad area of the reform process, however, was *not* immediately secured by GEMSU. It is here that problems have arisen that are different from those experienced in Eastern Europe.

- *Microeconomic reform* GEMSU was implemented before significant restructuring of the eastern economy. Yet, by the standards of developed market economies, the productive apparatus bequeathed by the DDR was utterly uncompetitive. Consequently, GEMSU subjected the command economy of the DDR to an unprecedented and overwhelming competitive shock. The result was a rapid descent into depression (see Sections 1.7 and 1.8). The problem was that while GEMSU secured reform – including price reform and competitive pressure – it simultaneously undermined the potential of eastern Germany to secure the intended benefits of reform; that is, a competitive economy. In particular, the terms of currency conversion meant, in effect, a massive appreciation of the East's currency (in Eastern Europe price competitiveness has been defended by devaluation), while unification of labour market institutions enforced higher wages (again, in contrast to Eastern Europe). These effects of GEMSU are an obstacle to privatization and inward investment.

In two dimensions of the reform process – legal and institutional framework and macroeconomic stability – east Germany has a decisive advantage over the rest of the ex-Soviet bloc. With respect to macroeconomic stability, west Germany's currency and financial support have been decisive. In the other dimension – microeconomic reform – east Germany has suffered some disadvantage. However, in concluding that 'it is not at all obvious whether, 20 years from now, east Germany will indeed have won the race for prosperity among the former communist states', Sinn and Sinn (1992, pp. 28–9) underestimate the effect of west German financial support. In particular, investment incentives – which, in part, are additional to the fiscal transfers accounted for in Table 1.2 – have generated inward investment on an entirely different scale from central and Eastern Europe. Table 1.3 gives data on total and German direct investment in east Germany and the Visegrad countries (Poland, Hungary and Czechoslovakia – since the beginning of 1993, the Czech and Slovak Republics).[8]

Table 1.3   Inward direct investment in eastern Germany and the Visegrad countries (net flows – total and from Germany) (DM bn at 1991 prices)

	1989	1990	1991	1992	1993	1994	1995	Total 90/95
Czechoslovakia* Czech / Slovak Republic		0.33	0.99	1.60	1.05	1.31	3.34	8.62
• from Germany	−0.001	0.0021	0.807	0.5570	0.7731	1.1267	1.182	4.45
Hungary		0.63	2.42	2.23	1.90	4.44	5.99	17.61
• from Germany	0.08	0.21	0.416	0.832	0.890	0.911	1.678	4.94
Poland		0.15	0.19	0.43	1.35	0.84	1.54	4.50
• from Germany	0.0032	0.0083	0.0680	0.1655	0.4529	0.4021	0.7575	1.85
East Germany [†]	–	–	92	118	134	156	171	671

Notes
* Data for Czechoslovakia up to end of 1992; thereafter for the Czech Republic and the Slovak Republic combined. (Most of the combined figures is accounted for by the Czech Republic: the Czech: Slovak ratio of inward investment varies from 22:1 to 8:1 in the case of German investment and from 14:1 to 5:1 for total inward investment.)
[†] Gross fixed capital formation DM bn at 1991 prices for the whole economy.

Sources: For German direct investment to the Visegrad countries – JG (1993, p. 53; 1995, pp. 37 and 455; and 1996, pp. 35, 337 and 423); and own calculations (nominal data is deflated by the west German price index for investment goods); total foreign direct investment in the Visegrad countries – Gowan (1995, p. 41) and Citibank database (nominal US dollars converted at annual average exchange rates and deflated by the west German price index for investment goods); East German data from Chapter 7, Table 7.3.

According to proponents of shock therapy, this strategy best creates the institutional conditions for inward foreign direct investment through which transitional economies will gain 'the new technologies, managerial talent, organizational methods and financial capital needed to overcome the dismal economic legacy of the past 40 years' (Jeffrey Sachs, *Poland's Jump to the Market Economy*, cited in Gowan 1995, p. 9). Table 1.3 provides no obvious confirmation of this hypothesis in the case of Poland or the other Visegrad economies. However, in east Germany the changes wrought by shock therapy have allowed subsidies to stimulate an unprecedented level of investment. In Chapter 7 we compare investment in east Germany with historical and contemporary examples of countries with unusually high rates of investment. Here we draw attention to the entirely different magnitude of investment in east Germany and the most developed of the former communist states – DM 500 bn within the first five years of Unification compared to less than DM 10 bn in the same period.[9] In the 'race for prosperity', east Germany not only starts from a higher basis as the most developed of the communist economies but the advantages of fiscal transfers and western investment should ensure a higher growth rate. Table 1.4 shows that in the three years beginning with 1992 – the earliest that post-Unification investment could have had a significant effect on output – east Germany growth was the highest and rising. Since 1994, however, the growth rate has fallen both relatively and absolutely.

Table 1.4   GDP growth in eastern Germany and the Visegrad countries
            (percentage change over the previous year) (1991 prices)

	1991	1992	1993	1994	1995	1996[*]
Czechoslovakia	−16.0	−7.0				
Czech Republic			−0.9	2.6	4.8	5.0
Slovak Republic			−3.7	4.9	7.4	5.5
Hungary	−11.9	−3.0	−0.8	2.9	1.5	1.0
Poland	−7.0	2.6	3.8	5.2	7.0	5.5
East Germany	−8.8 [†]	7.8	8.9	9.9	5.3	2.0

Notes
* Estimates.
† Second half 1990 to second half 1991.

Source: JG (1993, p. 6; 1994, p. 40; and 1996, pp. 22 and 33).

For eastern Germany the problem of transition is the creation of a competitive economy in which growth is sustained by investment financed from domestic savings. Up to 1994, rising inward investment and fiscal transfers secured rapid growth. As these levelled off, transition to self-sustaining growth was obstructed by lack of profitability, hence lack of investment financed by retained earnings. In Chapter 6 we discuss the growth effects of inward investment as well as the policy changes needed to secure a return to high growth and rapid convergence. Meanwhile, Sections 1.7 and 1.8 outline the consequences of exposing the uncompetitive eastern economy to unfettered competitive forces (that is, the downward section of the 'J-curve'). Chapters 4 and 7 discuss longer-term prospects (the upward section of the 'J-curve').

1.7 SHORT- TO MEDIUM-TERM CONSEQUENCES OF GEMSU: COLLAPSE IN THE EASTERN ECONOMY (DOWNWARD MOVEMENT ALONG THE J-CURVE OF ECONOMIC REFORM)

The immediate impact of GEMSU on the uncompetitive economy of the DDR was to trigger an unprecedented slump in output and employment. In this section, we outline the magnitude of the slump. We discuss causation in Section 1.8.

1.7.1 Output

Figure 1.1 displays the J-curve of output. For 1989, East German output was valued in 1991 DM and should be treated as indicative. None the less, unlike official series that generally begin in 1991, beginning our output

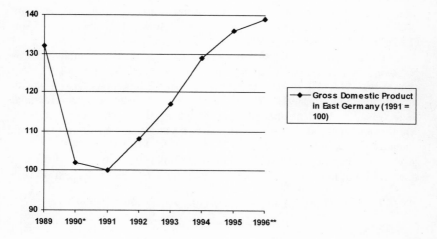

Notes
* Second half.
** Estimate.

Sources: 1989 estimate of East German GDP in 1991 DM prices from the DIW, Berlin and communicated to the authors by Johannes Stephan of the Institute for German Studies, Birmingham University; 1990–95 data from Bundesbank *Monthly Reports*; and JG (1996, p. 72).

Figure 1.1   The J-curve of East German national output (GDP at 1991 prices) (1991 = 100)

index in 1989 makes clear the extent of the slump in eastern output. The downward movement lasted from 1989 to the end of 1991: industrial production in the east fell by about two-thirds and 'national' output (GDP) by about one-third (Priewe and Hickel 1991, p. 12). Moreover, while the incidence of decline varied between sectors, output contracted in *all* sectors. Upward movement along the J-curve began in 1992, sustained largely by expansion in building and services. However, there was still no sign of a 'broad and self-sustaining expansion' (JG 1992, p. 69). Only by 1995 did output exceed the 1989 level. The extent to which recovery by then had become 'broad and self-sustaining' is analysed in Chapters 6 and 7.

1.7.2 Employment

The impact of GEMSU on employment has been devastating. Before GEMSU, in 1989, the labour force was about 9.7 million and there was virtually no unemployment.[10] According to data and estimates published by the Council of Economic Experts, during the course of 1990 and 1991 the labour force declined by almost 20 per cent to less than 8 million (7,970,000) (JG 1991, pp. 107 and 163; own calculations).

In the second half of 1991, the number of registered unemployed was just over one million (1,030,000) – an unemployment rate of about 10.5 per cent of the 1989 labour force or 13 per cent of the labour force as it was in the second half of 1991. However, as well as registered unemployment there was also 'hidden' unemployment: namely, those who, in effect, were wholly unemployed but in work only because of short-time working extended for up to 18 months (1,335,000) (WB, 11 October 1990, p. 586) or work creation schemes extended to the end of 1992 (300,000). If we sum registered and hidden unemployment, then rates of unemployment of 10.5

Table 1.5   Unemployment in eastern Germany (second half of 1991)

1989 Labour force ('000s)	9,700
1991 (Second half) Labour force ('000s)	7,970
1991 Removed from workforce	1,730
1991 Registered unemployed	1,030
1991 Hidden unemployment	1,635
1991 Registered + Hidden + Removed from 1989 workforce	4,395
1991 Registered unemployment rate	13%
1991 Registered + Hidden unemployment rate	33.4%
1991 Registered + Hidden + Removed from 1989 workforce (as percentage of 1989 workforce)	45%

Source: JG (1991, p. 163); own calculations.

and 13 per cent become, respectively, 27.5 and 33.4 per cent. Table 1.5 summarizes the main data.

In terms of the pre-GEMSU 1989 labour force, registered and 'hidden' unemployment (2,665,000) together with those removed from the labour force (about 1,700,000) give an unemployment rate of 45 per cent. In other words, between GEMSU and the second half of 1991 about 45 per cent of the labour force lost their jobs (JG 1991, p. 108; own calculations). Alternatively, by the second half of 1991 the rate of unemployment in the reduced eastern labour force was more than one-third.

1.8 THE MECHANISMS OF COLLAPSE

The collapse in output and employment was caused by changes both on the demand and on the supply side.

1.8.1 Demand side

Demand conditions changed dramatically. Customers moved away from east to west German products both on the home market and in traditional COMECOM export markets (Härtel and Krüger et al. 1995, pp. 42 and 302; see also Table 6.10 below and the following discussion). Simple multiplier effects amplified the fall in aggregate demand, forcing eastern producers to cut production and shed labour while surviving on credit.

1.8.2 Supply side

The fundamental cause of collapse in output and employment lies in supply-side weakness. GEMSU precluded – by definition – devaluation as a means of rapid adjustment. Consequently, the combined lack of both price and non-price competitiveness was so severe that all but a few eastern producers were rendered unable to sell their goods at prices which would cover even variable costs. *Only Treuhand loans and subsidies have allowed eastern producers to stay in business.*

GEMSU precipitated economic collapse not only by exposing eastern producers to competition – that much was inevitable – but also through the terms of the mark/DM conversion rate and the ensuing wage rises. Together, GEMSU, the 1:1 conversion rate, and the impact of these events on the eastern labour market subjected eastern producers to a catastrophic *price–cost squeeze*.

- *Prices* Elsewhere in the old Eastern bloc, restructuring packages have included massive devaluations. GEMSU, in contrast, not only deprived east Germany of the exchange rate as an instrument of adjustment to competitive forces, but also delivered a catastrophic blow to price competitiveness.

GEMSU required east German producers to set prices as well as cover current costs – including wages – in DM. The 1:1 conversion rate, in effect, imposed a currency revaluation of more than 300 per cent (based on the estimated average expenditure by DDR industry in 1989 of 3.73 OM to earn DM 1 from exports to the West; Akerloff et al. 1991, p. 17). Consequently, GEMSU suddenly exposed eastern producers to competition but did so on terms that rendered them utterly unable to compete on price.

- *Costs* In addition, GEMSU exposed eastern producers to an increasing gap between existing productivity levels and rising real wages. In circumstances of falling output and employment, nominal wages rose by 42 per cent between the first quarter of 1990 and the following October. During 1991, wages in east Germany reached about 50 per cent of west German levels.

The following mechanisms ensured that wages would rise whatever the actual competitiveness and long-run viability of eastern producers.

i. *Parity between the OM and the DM.* This alone meant wages too high for competitiveness. None the less, wages did not subsequently fall under competitive pressure but continued to rise.

ii. *The nature of wage bargaining in the aftermath of GEMSU.* Bargains were struck with the help of experienced western unions on the one hand while, on the other, the existing managers – reckoning on either continued soft-budget constraints or their own demise – had little incentive to bargain for lower wages. Moreover, because unemployment benefits are based on terminal wages, widespread expectation of unemployment and short-time working gave powerful incentives to increase wages.

iii. *Government complicity.* Unions and government both argued that high wages are necessary to prevent a more massive emigration.

GEMSU, therefore, squeezed eastern producers between falling prices and rising wage costs. The most authoritative study of this price–cost squeeze and its implications for the short-run viability of eastern industry was undertaken by Akerloff et al. (1991). For each sector and each *Kombinate*, the short-run average variable cost (SRAVC) of output in DM was compared with its DM price on the world market. If the 'expense ratio' of SRAVC to earnings was less than one, then variable costs were less than revenue and the firm was viable in the short run. However, 'the majority of firms currently have short-run variable costs between one and two DM per DM earned'. When this conclusion is expressed in employment terms, the catastrophic impact of GEMSU is apparent: 'only about 8 percent of the industrial workforce is employed in viable *Kombinate*, those with expense ratios below unity... In the absence of massive productivity improvements or substantial subsidization, most Eastern industry will have to close down' (Akerloff et al. 1991, pp. 27–8).

We conclude this chapter by establishing that the short- to medium-run outcome of GEMSU belied the optimistic expectations of the government. This matters, because the initial political benefit of overly optimistic expectations – maximum support for GEMSU and immediate Unification – was secured at the cost of worsening the conditions for economic recovery.

1.9 UNREALISTIC EXPECTATIONS, FISCAL CONSEQUENCES AND TIGHTENED CONSTRAINTS ON RECOVERY

Throughout Eastern Europe, political revolution aroused expectations of rapidly improving living standards, and nowhere more so than in the DDR, where the introduction of the DM and economic reform were generally expected to inaugurate a new 'economic miracle'. Expectations were magnified, moreover, by government promises not remotely in accord with the real supply-side condition of the east German economy.

Heightened expectations maximized support for Unification in both East and West Germany. The government took full advantage of this to secure both GEMSU and political Unification, and then victory in the general election of December 1990. The government, however, was manufacturer as well as beneficiary of heightened expectations. In particular, the government resisted public recognition of the economic and financial downside of what, politically, had been a wholly successful Unification process. The position of the government from the beginning of the Unification process had been to minimize the potential costs and condemn those who suggested otherwise: 'Mr. Theo Waigel, the Finance Minister, said in the Bundestag debate that... it was an illusion to start talking about "hundreds of billions" in economic aid' (FT, 30 November 1989). Similarly, in two speeches on the first day of GEMSU (1 July 1990), Chancellor Kohl promised east Germans that 'for nobody will it be worse than before', while assuring westerners that 'nobody will have to do without anything because of German Unification' (quoted by Priewe and Hickel 1991, p. 86). In spite of mounting evidence to the contrary, government leaders supported these promises with unrealistic forecasts of economic recovery. As late as March

1991, Economics Minister Jürgen Möllemann 'echoed Chancellor Kohl in predicting that it would take five years to achieve the economic and social equalization of the two parts of the country' (FT, 13 March 1991).

Yet from the beginning there were dissenting voices. As an alternative to the immediate 'shock therapy' of GEMSU, a step-by-step approach was favoured by leading German economists and EC experts, leading figures in the opposition SPD, the Bundesbank, and even members of the government (including Finance Minister Waigel) (Roth 1990, p. 10; OECD 1990, p. 47; and Priewe and Hickel 1991, p. 84). For example, on the very day – 6 February 1990 – that Chancellor Kohl declared for the rapid introduction of currency union, Bundesbank President Karl Otto Pöhl condemned publicly the idea of immediate GEMSU as 'premature ... a wild idea' (FT, 11 June 1990). There was no lack of economic intelligence on the state of the Eastern economy available to the Federal government: indeed, overwhelming economic superiority was a constant refrain in the 'competition between the systems'. Using available information, economists and others were able to warn that GEMSU would cause the collapse of much of the East's economy, that the East's backwardness could not be made up in a few years, and that the process of reconstruction would place unprecedented strain on public finances (Priewe and Hickel 1991, pp. 59 and 75). To quote Herr Pöhl again: 'I find it bizarre not to tell the population that helping east Germany will have a real cost' (FT, 13 November 1990).

By early 1991, however, the real cost was becoming apparent. In eastern Germany, unemployment left virtually no family unscathed, while westerners were confronted with the effects of a dramatic deterioration of public finances. Eventually, it had to be admitted that government optimism had not been based on a realistic view of the initial condition or potential of the East's economy: Otto Schlecht, state secretary at the economics ministry, for example, admitted that 'we deceived ourselves about the size and depth of the restructuring crisis' (FT, 29 April 1991).

GEMSU placed and will continue to place unprecedented pressure on German public finances. At first, however, the government's 'prime concern was to avoid calling into question the tax-cutting policies it pursued between 1986 and 1990' (*Economic Bulletin*, February 1995, p. 8). Instead, officially promulgated optimism supported plans to meet the expenditure commitments in the State Treaty as well as later costs of Unification through 'off budget' special funds – the largest of which was the German Unity Fund. This fund was intended to operate only for the five years 1990–94 and to have DM 115 bn at its disposal for expenditure in eastern Germany. All but DM 20 bn of this planned expenditure was to be financed through borrowing (Priewe and Hickel 1991, p. 136). Table 1.6 shows the time path of expected expenditure arising out of GEMSU together with the anticipated balance between borrowing and direct allocations from the budget.

Table 1.6   German Unity Fund (DM bn)

	Credit authorization	Direct allocations	Total
1990	20	2	22
1991	31	4	35
1992	24	4	28
1993	15	5	20
1994	5	5	10
Total	95	20	115

Source: Priewe and Hickel (1991, p. 136).

The government's initial expectation, therefore, was that Unification costs would be short-lived and minimal (amounting to about 1.3 per cent of total GNP in 1991 and declining thereafter). In this case, Unification could be financed through the capital market without increased taxation. According to the Council of Economic Experts, the financial policy presented in November 1990, 'rested on the assumption that the boost to growth triggered by German Unification would generate sufficient additional tax revenue to cover a large part of the associated extra expenditure'. Even by the beginning of 1991, however, this had proved 'unrealistic' (JG 1991, p. 130). Just how unrealistic can be gauged by comparing annual totals in Table 1.6 (anticipated expenditure arising from Unification) with annual totals in Table 1.2 (actual expenditure arising from Unification). Not only has actual expenditure been much larger than anticipated but also, far from expenditure reaching an early peak and then declining, the discrepancy grew larger in each successive year: from 1991 to 1994, the ratio of anticipated to actual expenditure rose from less than 4:1 to 18:1.

The early refusal to account honestly for the likely costs of Unification is reflected in an *ad hoc* approach to mounting pressure on public finances. Instead of the early restructuring of public expenditure and indirect taxation proposed by the Council of Economic Experts, the government reacted with a series of partial adjustments.[11]

In every year since Unification, fiscal transfers occasioned by GEMSU have been running at about 5–6 per cent of German GNP (see Table 1.2, above). The public sector deficit remains high partly because of cyclically determined expenditure: because the economy is producing at less than capacity, income and taxation are less and expenditure – especially arising from unemployment – more than when production is at capacity. Figure 1.2 depicts the consequent deterioration in public sector finances. The public sector debt series is defined in the note to Figure 1.2: it is not complete, because it omits both the social insurance system (in surplus in most years) and the borrowing of public enterprises – above all, the Treuhand from

1990 to 1994 as well as the Bundespost (post and telecommunications) and Bundesbahn (railway). However, it shows clearly enough that by 1989 fiscal retrenchment had reduced the deficit to a little more than 1 per cent of GDP but that, subsequently, Unification-related expenditure raised deficits back into a range of about 3.5 to 4.5 per cent of GDP. The structural deficit is added for comparison. This is defined as that part of the deficit which, when the economy is at capacity output, persistently exceeds borrowing for investment (JG 1995, p. 323). Initially, this tracked the public sector deficit but by 1994 had been reduced to about 1 per cent (the typical level for the late 1980s).

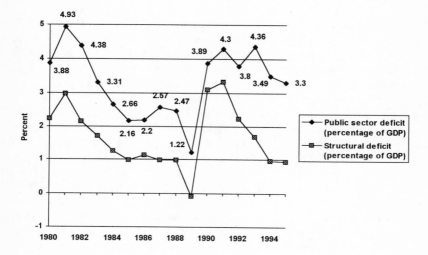

Note: The data are financial statistics and refer to West Germany (1980–90) and Germany (1991–95; 1995 estimated). Note that the inclusion of east German GDP reduced the debt:GDP ratio. The public sector deficit depicted here is the combined deficit of all three levels of government (Federal, eastern and western *Länder*, and eastern and western municipalities), two funds originating in West Germany's post-war reconstruction which were relatively small before 1990 (the *Lastenausgleichsfonds* – Equalization of Burdens Fund – and the European Recovery Programme fund), contributions to the EU, the German Unity Fund and the Debt Management Fund (*Kreditabwicklungsfonds*).

Source: JG (1995, pp. 324, 404, 140 and 378) (own calculations).

Figure 1.2   The fiscal consequences of Unification, 1980–1995 (public sector deficits as a percentage of GDP)

The dimensions of Germany's fiscal problems are further illustrated by Figures 1.3 and 1.4. Respectively, these show a rising debt:GDP ratio and, as a corollary, an increasing tax burden together with rising interest payments.

Figure 1.2 showed that by 1994 and 1995 the increase in public sector deficits towards 5 per cent of GDP caused by Unification had been contained and reduced. However reduction of the public sector deficit towards the 3 per cent of GDP prescribed by the Maastricht Treaty still leaves the problem of total debt increasing and, in the presence of low rates of growth of nominal GDP, a rising debt:GDP ratio. Figure 1.3 shows that the ratio of public sector debt on the wide definition to GDP has risen by nearly 30 per cent since 1989. Only by attributing Treuhand, railway and postal service debt to the corporate sector will Germany be able to satisfy the Maastricht debt:GDP ceiling of 60 per cent.

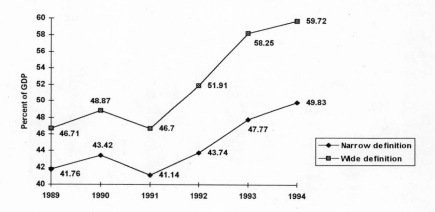

Definitions

- Narrow – central, state and local government, the social insurance system, German Unity Fund, *Kreditabwicklungsfonds*, ERP Special Assets.
- Wide – narrow definition plus Treuhandanstalt, railways and postal service.

Source: *Economic Bulletin*, September 1995, p. 22.

Figure 1.3   German public sector debt (percentage of GDP) (current prices)

The effect of Unification has been to increase the role of government as proxied by the share of national income accounted for by public spending. Figure 1.4 shows that over the period 1989–95, total expenditure increased more than GDP, rising from 45.8 per cent of GDP in 1989 to a little more than 50 per cent in 1995 (*Economic Bulletin*, September 1995, p. 22). The deficit has been contained by increasing taxation and social insurance contributions (the latter account for more than 20 per cent of public sector revenue) (JG 1995, p. 139). In 1991, within three months of a pledge by Chancellor Kohl not to raise taxes in association with Unification, the Government increased tax and social insurance by DM 31.65 bn – more than 1 per cent of GNP – and by a larger sum (DM 40.35 bn) for 1992 in order to stem the public sector deficit (FT, 4 February 1991; in detail, Priewe and Hickel 1991, pp. 154–6). Altogether, increases to finance Unification took taxes and social security contributions to 41 per cent of gross earnings – a record level (FT, 13 June 1992). In the three years after 1992, total income tax was increased by, respectively, 4.3, 3.3 and 7.0 per cent (JG 1995, p. 148).

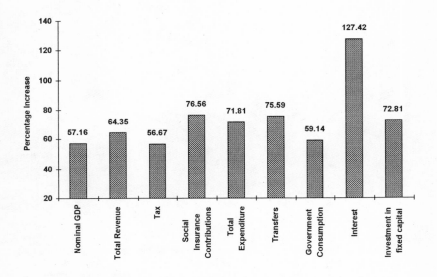

Source: *Economic Bulletin*, September 1995, p. 22.

Figure 1.4 Nominal GDP and the German public sector budget, 1989–1995 (percentage increase)

Figure 1.4 also shows that interest payments on public sector debt display a higher rate of increase than any other category of public spending. Interest payments accounted for 12 per cent of total public expenditure in 1989, more than 18 per cent in 1995 and, even on optimistic assumptions, will account for nearly 22 per cent by 1998 (*Economic Bulletin*, February 1995, p. 6). Increasingly, if tax rates are not to be raised further, interest payments will crowd out other forms of expenditure – public capital spending in west Germany has already been squeezed (*Economic Bulletin*,

February 1995, p. 4) – and reduce the scope for fiscal expansion during recession. Moreover, the higher are interest payments, the more vulnerable become public finances to financial market instability causing exchange rate and interest rate fluctuations.

Currently, there are conflicting pressures to reduce the tax burden and to reduce deficit spending. This tends to increase pressure for reduced social security spending, which runs counter to the ethos of the 'socially responsible market economy' and could threaten political and social stability. Against this fiscal background, increased support for east Germany is unlikely. Even maintaining current levels of support may become politically untenable.

Finally, we conclude that Germany's fiscal problems as well as some of the major constraints on east Germany's convergence result from initially excessive optimism and the associated decision to finance Unification through borrowing rather than taxation. By not confronting the costs of Unification at the beginning, when national sentiment could have been harnessed to create a willingness to sacrifice, the government has since had the self-inflicted problem of convincing west Germans of the need for even moderate contributions to pay for Unification. This enforces deficit spending and rising interest payments that put downward pressure on spending, including spending on eastern Germany. In addition, the 'great tax lie' – as it was labelled by the unions – has contributed to political disaffection. It has also fuelled wage militancy which, for example, resulted in settlements of 5.4 per cent for public sector workers and 5.8 per cent for engineering workers in May 1992 (well above the 4 per cent urged by the Council of Economic Experts).[12] Similarly, unrealistic expectations propagated by the government in the early stages of GEMSU made it hard to convince eastern workers of the need for wage restraint. There would now be a better chance of public support for higher taxes and wage restraint if the costs – for both easterners and westerners – had been made clear from the beginning. Political opportunism, therefore, has been the enemy of coherent economic strategy.

NOTES

1. This is most apparent in the labour market with respect to, for example, social insurance, employment protection and industrial democracy (codetermination).
2. The Bundesbank view was that monetary union should follow a process of economic convergence (as with monetary union in Europe). The counter-argument was that an independent DDR would be unstable and that the Federal Republic would have to bear the cost of stabilization even without Unification. This discussion, together with associated plans for transitional regimes in the DDR, was rendered superfluous by political considerations.
3. To be more precise about the conversion rate, it is useful to distinguish between flow and stock conversion. 'The *conversion rate for flows* was important for determining the D-Mark

amount above all of wages and rents ... the decisive factor for the international competitiveness of the East German economy immediately after monetary unification. After a heated debate a 1:1 conversion rate was adopted ... For monetary policy the more important question was the *conversion rate for financial stocks* ... The public resistance of East Germans against a 2:1 rate was simply too strong. As a result, for a limited amount of deposits a 1:1 conversion was granted, while a general conversion rate of 2:1 was adopted for all other deposits, currency and for bank credits. This led to an average conversion rate of 1.6:1 for the GDR money stock' (Bofinger 1997, pp. 205–10, original emphasis).

4. In April 1990, the Treuhand estimated that 50 per cent of East German enterprises required 'thorough restructuring' if they were to be competitive after monetary and economic union while 20 per cent faced 'almost inevitable bankruptcy'. Two months later, 30 per cent of enterprises themselves reported that they were in danger of bankruptcy (Fischer et al. 1996, p. 30).

5. More extended comparisons of transformation in eastern Germany with Central and Eastern Europe are to be found in Sinn and Sinn 1992, pp. 23–9 and Kaser 1995, pp. 5–6.

6. One number neatly illustrates the increase in consumption: in 1991, east Germans purchased more than 800,000 of both cars and video recorders.

7. Identifying the broad areas of reform does not solve the problems of timing and sequencing. 'It is now widely accepted that the institutional infrastructure has to be established without delay. But controversies persist on whether large-scale privatization should proceed quickly because it proves the basis for other reform steps, or rather be postponed until after macro stabilization has been achieved and micro reforms have been implemented' (Siebert et al. 1991, p. 3).

8. We do not take the comparison beyond 1995 because, already by 1994, investment activity by eastern affiliates of west German firms was making it increasingly difficult to distinguish west German investment from indigenous investment in east Germany (JG 1994, p. 61).

9. Table 1.3 also demonstrates two further points: (1) the substantial share of direct investment in the Visegrad economies coming from Germany; and (2) German fears of investment being displaced from high-wage Germany to low-wage Central and Eastern Europe are so far not supported by comparison at the aggregate level of direct investment in these locations compared to investment in either east Germany or the German economy as a whole.

10. In January 1990 the number of unemployed workers was 7,400 (with 158,600 vacancies) (Akerlof et al. 1991, p. 8).

11. This theme is discussed at length by Priewe and Hickel (1991, see pp. 15, 91, 117–18, 127–31 and 138).

12. Formal evidence of the impact of tax increases on wage behaviour in west Germany is cited by Carlin and Soskice (1997, p. 14).

2. The DDR Economy Revisited

2.1 INTRODUCTION

Like other Central and Eastern European economies, the German Democratic Republic (Deutsche Demokratische Republik, or DDR hereafter) was under rigid political and economic control. The levels of output, employment and prices were all determined by the central administration based at the economic ministry in East Berlin and its regional subsidiaries. The inefficiency of planning cumulated as any market history receded. Allocative and dynamic inefficiencies coincided with the ignorance of imperfect information, which is endemic to economic planning.

Competitiveness depends largely on low transaction costs, continuous developments and product innovation 'defined broadly, to include both improvements in technology and better ways and methods of doing things' (Porter 1990, p. 45). The DDR's poor economic performance can be explained by reference to the lack of a proper price mechanism and, hence, a missing (or misinterpreted) incentive system (allocative efficiency). However, another major reason for the DDR's declining ability to export profitably to the West was its relatively weaker pace of technological development and innovation (dynamic efficiency). Eastern producers lagged behind in research and development and, above all, in the application of new technologies to processes and products alike. For example, while the microelectronics industry was given priority in the DDR, the technology was not integrated into new products on the broad basis characteristic of the developed market economies. For example, Praktica cameras used to be competitive in terms of their non-price characteristics (for example, the introduction of through-the-lens metering in the late 1960s), but went out of production in October 1990, because lack of innovation, especially in sophisticated electronic features, meant loss of non-price competitiveness and an increasing inability to export profitably.

A number of factors, usually byproducts of dynamic and allocative inefficiency, accelerated this process of economic decline: an increase in underutilization of productive capacity (Hitchens et al. 1993), overmanning (see Chapter 4), the lack of investment in capital with a high-technology content, the malfunctioning of the physical infrastructure and the lack of organized business services (Beintema and van Ark 1993) culminated in a relatively low productivity performance. However, there are other more fundamental reasons for the poor economic performance of the DDR. In this chapter we provide a more detailed analysis of the causes of the productivity gaps which arose during the four decades of central planning.

In Section 2.2 we discuss a number of arguments on central planning to shed light on the reasons for economic backwardness of the East German economy. In Section 2.3 we introduce a formal analytical framework within which reasons for poor productivity performance and low economic growth can be explored. Section 2.4 provides an overview of comparative productivity in the DDR and the Federal Republic prior to Unification, drawing heavily on work on the East and West German manufacturing sectors by Beintema and van Ark (1993). Section 2.5, finally, pulls the threads together and concludes this brief, scene-setting chapter.

2.2 INNOVATION, PRODUCTIVITY AND ECONOMIC GROWTH

At the time of its 40th anniversary – 1989 – the DDR was an industrial country with the highest productivity and living standard in the COMECON group. However, is a planned economy better equipped than a market-led economy when it comes to promoting innovation and stimulating economic growth? This question has figured prominently in the debate about the pros and cons of socialism. It is also at the heart of our discussion of economic backwardness of the German Democratic Republic and its subsequent failure to measure up to western standards.

Socialist economists usually argue that the intrinsic conflict between private ownership and socialized production and between individual capitalists' benefit and social welfare will lead to overproduction and economic crisis. Capitalist economies, it is claimed, cannot adjust to rapid innovations and common (socialist) ownership will emerge. However, the history of socialist economies over the past several decades shows that all centralized economies have done poorly, in general, in technological innovation (Quiang and Xu 1990) and factor productivity (Bergson 1978) compared with decentralized market economies. According to Balcerowicz (1990) the problem of the impact of an economic system upon innovativeness can be reduced to two questions, 'What types of technical projects are selected under a given economic system?' and 'How effectively can the chosen projects be executed?'

To find potential answers to these questions, we have to address three basic characteristics of the Soviet-type economic system which are interrelated and give thus rise to a number of derivative features. These are:

1. *The command-rationing mechanism at the central level*, that is planning targets, administrative allocation of inputs, and the material balances that are meant to harmonize the first two instruments. All this is expressed in a comprehensive and relatively detailed central plan. In its coordinating and allocative functions the command-rationing mechanism replaces a product market as known in western economies.

2. *Information limitations* Given the inevitable human information limitations, the command-rationing mechanism requires a strictly determined organizational system. Its principal features consist of the hierarchical subordination of the managers of enterprises, banks and so on, to the state and party officials by means of the *nomenklatura* mechanism; a highly developed central and intermediate administration; and an extreme organizational concentration (irrespective of the industry) combined with the merging of plants into bigger units, by way of both vertical and horizontal integration. Other features are prohibition of diversification (that is, assigning enterprises to specific branches), prohibition of independent ties between different organizations, and elimination of enterprises through administrative procedures rather than through bankruptcy. This centralization of organizational rights precludes the spontaneous evolution of the organizational system and ensures that it preserves the basic features necessary for the operation of the command-rationing mechanism.

3. *Centralization of monetary resources* Massive centralized redistribution of monetary resources between enterprises via the specific bureaucratic institutions is a necessary supplement to the two features discussed above and a substitute for the capital market. These institutions include a disintegrated financial system for enterprises (exemplified through many different purpose-specific 'funds') and a non-commercial monobank, which distributes credit according to the stipulations of the central plan rather than criteria of financial viability.

A number of commentators have elaborated on these issues, and we need not recapitulate at length. The points on information limitations could provide a rationale for the *Kombinate*-type organizations in the DDR to ensure coordinated supply of whole packages of products to other enterprises. Vertical concentration within *Kombinate* was used to ensure a largely self-contained production process, which was to remove continuous supply bottlenecks. Similarly, in the Soviet Union, some companies' strength was in being able to supply the full package of products required for major construction projects. In other words, the *Kombinate* form was not just for planners' convenience but ironically – in the context of a command economy – in customers' interests.

The consequences of these basic characteristics of the Soviet-type economic system were, first, that the sectoral structure of the economy and its trade were increasingly backward and uncompetitive by the standards of international markets. And, second, that central planning selected projects directed primarily towards expanding the output of the existing industrial base rather than towards new processes and products. On both counts, the economy underwent minimal restructuring and suffered from under-developed specialization and division of labour. Lack of specialization and division of labour was apparent at both the enterprise level and in the economy as a whole.

- *The elimination of independent producers*   The *Kombinate* of the DDR were characterized by an extraordinary degree of vertical integration (see Priewe and Hickel 1991, pp. 73 and 79). A major development in this respect was the enforced incorporation, in 1972, of previously privately owned and independent small- and medium-sized firms (SMCs) into the vertically integrated *Kombinate*. This denied the DDR what, for the BRD, is a generally recognized source of competitive strength: that is, the existence of fiercely competitive SMCs capable of responding quickly and flexibly to demand. This contributed significantly to the characteristic shortages of specific components, which typically hindered investment and innovation in the DDR. (In the BRD, in contrast, SMCs have played a crucial role in innovation and the upgrading of quality; see Porter 1990, pp. 373–5.)

- *Lack of specialization and integration into the international division of labour*   The state monopoly of foreign trade and an inconvertible currency protected the DDR's producers from the competitive pressures of the world market. The benefit was secure employment and stability. The cost, however, was lack of structural change and hence – compared to developed market economies – a distorted sectoral structure. By 1989, 47 per cent of employment in the DDR was in agriculture, energy, mining and manufacturing (37 per cent in the BRD), while employment in manufacturing had increased from 2.9 to 3.2 million since 1970 (in the BRD, reduced from 10 to 8.7 million). Conversely, this bias was reflected in a relatively undeveloped service sector (Siebert 1991). Moreover, employment was relatively concentrated in sectors that in developed market economies have been in decline: altogether, 16 per cent of the DDR's workforce were employed in agriculture, forestry and fishing, mining, clothing and textiles (6.4 per cent in the BRD) (Siebert et al. 1991a, p. 14).

On the one hand, lack of competition deprived producers and planners alike of the most potent *incentive* to allocate resources to their most productive use and to innovate. On the other hand, there were systemic *obstacles* to an efficient allocation of resources and innovation.

The complexities of centralized planning together with a strategy of import substitution meant that *foreign trade was conducted according to a 'residual principle'*: that is, output was planned according to existing capacity and foreign trade was used to secure products that could not be produced domestically. It was not possible to allow foreign firms to compete with domestic producers or to allow domestic producers to seek out more profitable markets abroad, because this would have contradicted the planning of domestic output (impossible with enterprises subject to competition) and its use (for example, as inputs into other enterprises). Furthermore, the allocation of resources was subject to arbitrary *political intervention*, which was often economically disastrous in its consequences.

Finally in this section, we comment further on the selection and implementation of investment projects.

2.2.1 Project selection

In a command economy, there are markets and prices but no price mechanism. This means that impersonal market forces – demand and supply – do not determine market prices and thus do not govern the allocation of resources. Moreover, command economies lack an effective alternative means of enforcing allocative and dynamic efficiency. Accordingly, an explanation for the poor economic performance of centrally planned economies, which has gained in popularity amongst commentators, is that of ineffective project selection, driven by so-called *'soft budget constraints'* (Kornai 1980, 1986, 1990) – that is, a relaxed financial discipline imposed upon enterprises by the state. This means that markets and prices have no allocative function. Freeing prices on its own does not introduce a market economy unless budget constraints bite. In the Western world, firms that cannot cover their variable costs in the short run and their variable and fixed costs in the long run go bankrupt and resources will be reallocated.

It has been argued that the promotion of innovation in a given system depends critically on screening mechanisms that terminate inefficient projects. Screening mechanisms are in turn closely related to the financial constraints imposed upon innovators by the economic system. Information imperfection and centralization of credit, however, may cause commitment problems, which relax financial constraints and thus disable the screening capability of a centralized economy. This may lead to the continuation of inferior projects.

Quiang and Xu (1990, p. 13) note that

> in the presence of sunk costs in the early stages of investment, it is impossible for the state-bank in subsequent periods not to refinance bad projects ... in order to avoid

financing too many bad projects, the central bank may rely on administrative procedures, using the limited prior information available to improve its project portfolio at the beginning. As a result, not only are innovative projects delayed by the pre-screening process, but because of the poor quality of prior information, many promising ideas are rejected from the very beginning and many bad projects are refinanced.

Command economies, therefore, do not have an effective alternative to the price mechanism for enforcing an efficient allocation of resources. In addition, central administration combined with soft-budget constraints may result in a complete lack of competition among suppliers. There are two necessary conditions for this competition to exist: first, the demand for goods must be able to move freely among alternative suppliers; and, second, a drop in demand should generate the threat of financial sanctions on the affected supplier. Neither condition is met under central planning. The hierarchical organizational system, the centralization of organizational rights and administrative allocation of inputs rule out the first condition. And the soft-budget constraint prevents the second one.

2.2.2   Project implementation

Turning to the execution of projects, innovations, as distinct from mere continuation, require qualitatively new inputs, and – on average – the more so, the more efficient they are to be. However, obtaining increasingly sophisticated inputs under the conditions of command-rationed mechanisms requires much more additional effort (and, hence, imposes higher costs upon the enterprise) than is the case with market clearing and free access to resources – that is, informational requirements increase and transaction costs rise. It is this mechanism that led ultimately to the collapse of the DDR economy.

Compared with the developed market economies of the OECD, the DDR's economic development lagged by perhaps 20 years. In comparison with West Germany, its productive apparatus was obsolete and characterized by low productivity, low quality and – most fundamentally – the lack of any kind of dynamic with which to close the gap. Economically, the East was utterly unable to compete with the West. Unification, therefore, had a catastrophic impact on the eastern economy: sudden exposure to overwhelmingly superior competition had an impact on eastern producers – and, hence, on output and employment in the east – that has been likened to the supposed change in cosmic environment that brought to an end the era of the dinosaurs. Ultimately, in the competition between the two systems, it was the relative economic weakness of the DDR that led to Unification on the terms of the west. There are many dimensions to relative economic strength. However, in so far as any one indicator proxies economic strength and enables comparison, productivity is the best guide. This is because, ultimately, higher real wages can come only from higher productivity: higher productivity means producing more in the same time, thereby having either more to consume or the same to consume while spending less time on production – or, of course, some combination of the two. Productivity, then, is the key to the standard of living.

Consequently, the production process and associated measures of productivity figure prominently in this debate. It is for this reason that some commentators have concentrated on the issue of increasingly complex production processes as a potential source of the economic backwardness of command economies. Levine (1982, p. 164) points out that as a result of an economy growing in size and sophistication 'centralised planning and control become more difficult and errors have more of an effect. The centralised supply system ... intensifies these problems by reducing the ability of decision-makers at the periphery to respond flexibly to errors and imbalances in the economy'.

In what follows, we present a simplified version of Banerjee and Spagat's productivity model (1991), which can be used to demonstrate why Soviet-type economies became increasingly inefficient relative to Western economies and, as a result, why in the light of increasing global competition the market system emerged as victor over central planning.

2.3 PRODUCTIVITY AND COMPLEXITY IN COMMAND AND MARKET ECONOMIES

Since Adam Smith we have known that the wealth of nations depends on the extent of division of labour and that, consequently, growth entails increasing complexity. The price mechanism on the one hand and planning on the other are organizing principles for dealing with complexity. A common explanation of the superior performance of the market-based system is that the price mechanism is better at handling complexity than planning agencies in command economies. This is explored and formalized by Banerjee and Spagat (1991), who argue that increasing complexity – defined as the increasing number of intermediate goods (input) used in final goods production – causes productivity growth to be less than in market economies. In large part, the following is a simplified version of their work.

The argument in detail rests on three assumptions:

1. Technical change generates two effects which, potentially, are in conflict:
   a. higher productivity; and
   b. a requirement for more intermediate products.

2. The greater the disturbances in the supply (that is, delivery to firms) of intermediate goods, the more the productivity benefits of technical change are offset by the costs of increased complexity. Supply disturbances refer to both under- and oversupply in terms of *quantity* and to varying, hence unreliable *quality* of supply.

3. Command economies are relatively more prone to supply disturbances than market economies, because they are relatively less able to deal with the growth of intermediate products. As an economy grows, and plants and products grow more numerous, coordination becomes more difficult (while principal–agent problems and incentive structures make it hard to ensure reliable information and conformity to directions). Consequently, command economies are particularly prone to supply disturbances – that is, less reliable or more variable supplies of intermediate goods. Moreover, because technical progress continually generates new intermediate products, the problem is something of a vicious circle; that is, it worsens over time.

The notion of complexity adopted by the authors is that, as the economy matures, it takes increasing numbers of intermediate products to produce a final, more sophisticated product. Consequently, it is assumed that M, the number of inputs used in final goods production increases over time.[1] As M increases, labour productivity falls *ceteris paribus*. Note that increased complexity – that is, a greater number of intermediate goods – generates a directly proportionate increase in supply disturbances. This follows from the rule that the variance of the sum of two random variables (X and Y) is equal to the sum of their variances plus twice their covariance: $\text{var}(X + Y) = \text{var}(X) + \text{var}(Y) + 2\text{cov}(X,Y)$. Given that intermediate goods are defined as independently and identically distributed random variables, it follows that the covariance of two or more intermediate goods is zero – that is, $2\text{cov}(X,Y) = 0$. In this case, supply disturbances – that is the variance of the supply of intermediate goods – grows in proportion to the number of intermediate goods, M.

Moreover, downward fluctuations in the supply of intermediate products inflict more damage on production (and, hence, productivity) than upward fluctuations contribute. In the case of a downward fluctuation, labour and capital will be underutilized (or, even if labour can be laid off instantly, capital will be underutilized). In the case of an upward fluctuation, there will be insufficient labour and capital to utilize fully the additional intermediate goods (even if labour can be hired instantly, there are productivity-reducing adjustment problems such as the implementation of training programmes). If downward and upward fluctuations are equally likely, then – on average – unreliable deliveries generate lower productivity than reliable deliveries (that is, the expected value of productivity is lower).

Figure 2.1 illustrates this assumption as a concave relationship between the quantity of intermediate goods and productivity.

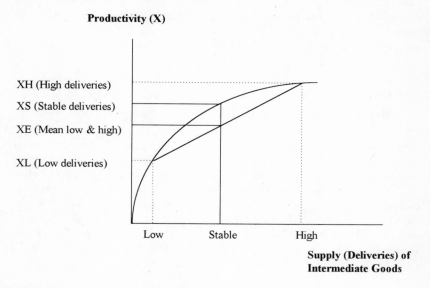

Figure 2.1 Productivity and supply of intermediate goods

Figure 2.1 shows how productivity is affected by supply disturbances. It is drawn for a given level of technology and assumes fixed quantities of labour and capital. It compares the productivity level when supply of intermediate goods (that is, deliveries to firms) undergoes fluctuations of equal size and equal probability between low and high levels together with the productivity level when supply is stable. When supply fluctuates (XE), productivity with stable – that is, predictable – supply (XS) is greater than average productivity (that is, the expected value).

In general, the more producers are affected by supply disturbance the lower the level of productivity for a given level of inputs and technology. To the extent that supply disturbances are greater under central planning, productivity will be relatively low in command economies (even in the case of similar technology and inputs). Over time, technical progress tends to increase complexity and thus increase the downward pressure on productivity relative to market economies. Consequently, the benefit of such technical progress as can be achieved under central planning tends to be limited by the associated increase in complexity.

In summary, the flexibility of market mechanisms appears to be sufficiently prepared to deal with the increase in product sophistication and supply of intermediate products. Conversely, under central planning the significant degree of bureaucratization and related costs will cause productivity to decline relative to market economies. Although there is no way to point to a particular feature of central planning as the single most important factor behind chronic shortages and supply disturbances of intermediate products, there appears to be little doubt that the responsible factors are systemic (Kornai 1980; Gomulka 1986; and Soos 1984).

2.4 PRODUCTIVITY IN EAST AND WEST GERMANY BEFORE UNIFICATION

Having analysed potential sources of productivity gaps between different economic systems we now present some empirical findings in support of our thesis. Although it is generally accepted that the productivity level in East Germany was considerably below that of West Germany prior to Unification,[2] there is also some evidence which suggests that the comparative productivity performance differed significantly between sectors. Our results are based on work by Beintema and van Ark (1993) who estimated relative productivity levels for the former East and West Germany, on the basis of comparisons of value added and labour input by manufacturing industry in 1987.[3]

If our above assumptions and modelling results are applicable, then the costs of supply disturbances will increase with increasing complexity and the productivity gap between centrally planned and market economies should be largest in the most complex industries. It comes as no surprise that the study by Beintema and van Ark (1993) reveals that for the manufacturing sector as a whole, value added per hour worked in East Germany was 28.6 per cent of the level in West Germany in 1987. One has to bear in mind, however, that the measurement and international comparison of productivity levels is still fraught with difficulties, which are compounded when trying to compare across different economic systems.

The most direct approach is via disaggregated data on physical output, which enables comparison of output per working hour of similar products. Such ease of comparison is rarely possible, however, because the products tend not to be precisely similar (in particular, when comparing products produced by economies of different regimes and/or levels of development). Products will differ according to their quality as well as how up to date they are – typically, products were still produced in the DDR that had long been discontinued or updated in the BRD (see WB, 5 April 1990, p. 172). For this reason, it is also necessary to consider labour productivity from the point of view of the value produced per working hour in similar industries.[4]

To put the results into perspective, Table 2.1 gives an impression of comparative levels of value added per hour worked in manufacturing in 1987 across countries.

Table 2.1   *Comparative levels of census value added per hour worked in manufacturing, 1987 (as a percentage of the USA and West Germany)*

	United States = 100%	West Germany = 100%
India	5.7	6.9
Czechoslovakia	16.2	19.8
Korea	18.2	22.1
East Germany	23.2	28.2
Brazil	28.4	34.6
United Kingdom	58.0	70.6
Japan	67.5	82.2
France	73.3	89.2
West Germany	82.2	100.0
United States	100.0	121.7

Source: Beintema and van Ark (1993).

What is interesting to observe, is that the comparative productivity performance in industries characterized by less complex production processes (such as food products, beverages and leather products) is well above this average, while the productivity levels in industries characterized by production complexity and increasing sophistication (such as machinery and equipment) is less than 20 per cent of the West German level. Although the authors admit that comparisons based on data collected and processed prior to Unification have to be looked at with some caution, a clear productivity pattern emerges that supports our assumptions in Section 2.3. Beintema and van Ark's data support the hypothesis that a generally low level of labour productivity can be explained by the larger amount of intermediate inputs per unit of output in East Germany, which appeared to be the major source of inefficiency. Table 2.2 illustrates these productivity levels in complex and less complex East German industries.

Table 2.2   Census value added per employee and per hour worked in manufacturing, East Germany, 1987

	Census value added per person employed	Annual hours worked		Census value added per hour worked
		East Germany	West Germany	
Food products, beverages and tobacco	45.3	1,806	1,817	45.6
Textiles, wearing apparel and leather	34.9	1,644	1,617	34.3
Chemicals, rubber and plastic products	42.9	1,712	1,644	41.2
Basic metals and metal products	37.4	1,784	1,620	33.9
Machinery, electrical engineering and transport equipment	21.4	1,753	1,586	19.4
Other manufacturing branches	26.7	1,713	1,641	25.6
Total manufacturing	30.5	1,735	1,627	28.6

Source: Beintema and van Ark (1993).

Productivity can also, of course, be defined more broadly so as not only to determine price competitiveness but also to reflect *non-price competitiveness*. In this case, productivity is defined as 'the value of the output produced by a unit of labour or capital' (Porter 1990, p. 6). Now, productivity and competitiveness depend not just on efficiency of production but also on quality – that is, all the non-price features of products that influence demand (and, hence, the price they command): reliability, durability, technical sophistication, delivery times, after-sales service, and so on.

Throughout the 1980s, in spite of increasing subsidies to maintain price competitiveness, DDR producers lost ground in Western markets because of weakening non-price competitiveness – the consequence of producing goods of relatively lower quality.

The weakening competitiveness of the DDR can be tracked in the one arena where its products were subject to competitive markets: that is, foreign trade with the West. Two types of evidence may be quoted.

- While, between 1985 and 1988, proceeds from the exports of new makes of products to the rest of the Soviet bloc rose by 30 per cent, those to the West – that is, those subject to competition – fell by 25 per cent (Hofmann and Stingl 1990, p. 78). Moreover, the problem was worsening during the 1980s.

- There is no direct measure of quality and non-price competitiveness. A plausible proxy, however, is the value of exports per kilo within particular commodity groups: thus, for example, the value per kilo of BRD exports of capital goods was 3.5 times higher than that of the DDR in 1980 but 5.2 times higher by 1987 (Hofmann and Stingl 1990, p. 79).

At the time of Unification, eastern producers lacked the ability to compete on either price (through lower costs) and/or on non-price characteristics. To a large extent, goods were produced of such low quality that, in a free market, they were unsaleable at virtually any price.

2.5 CONCLUDING REMARKS

The DDR was a command economy, meaning that resources were allocated by centralized administration – in accord with political priorities – rather than by markets and the price mechanism. In a market economy, information and incentives – to consumers and producers alike – are provided through the price mechanism. Consequently, compared to a command economy, economic decision-making in a market economy is decentralized. In turn, decentralized decision-making enables complexity and dynamism (in response to, for example, changing patterns of demand and technological opportunities). In contrast, centralized decision-making requires a minimum of complexity and change in order to render feasible the task of collecting information and issuing instructions. This creates an inherent bias against innovation and restructuring.

In the DDR, the imperatives of centralized decision-making required the number of enterprises to be reduced while the number of planning targets multiplied. By 1988, the whole of centrally controlled manufacturing industry had been organized into 126 '*Kombinate*' – each with between 20 and 40 plants and an average of more than 20,000 employees – subject to about 200 planning targets (Cornelsen 1990, p. 73).

In addition to an essential bias against innovation and change, this system imposed incentives and structures that exerted an adverse effect on economic performance. At the broadest level of the motive for economic activity – for continued effort towards maximum output, quality and innovation – the DDR authorities did away with the profit motive but were unable to develop alternative 'socialist' incentives. (Under conditions of dictatorship, appeals by the leadership to ideals wider than personal gains were met with a cynicism and indifference that undermined leaders and ideals alike.) At the level of the operation of the economic system, the greatest enemy of economic performance was monopoly and the corresponding absence of competition. In particular, lack of competition meant lack of economic stimulus to the constant *restructuring* – at the level of both the firm and the economy as a whole – increasingly characteristic of developed market economies.

The market mechanism is far from perfect. Hardly a day goes by without witnessing some form of market failure. Still, an economic comparison between plan and market mechanisms will always point to the market as the victor over command regimes. It is the combination of both allocative and dynamic inefficiency that results in the decline of a planned economy. The lagging economic performance of the DDR compared to developed market economies was thus apparent in two respects: first, with respect to the traditional criterion of an efficient, static allocation of resources (that is, the situation in which competition enforces the welfare-maximizing use of existing resources – which means specialization in only the most profitable productive activities); and, second, with respect to mechanisms promoting innovation and change.

NOTES

1. Gallik et al. (1979) report on statistics based on Soviet input–output tables and note that 'one of the striking features of the economy highlighted by these statistics is the high and increasing proportion of intermediate output in total production ... the increasing rate of growth in intermediate output in the Soviet economy relative to final demand is undoubtedly due in part to shifts in relative importance of individual industries and to increasing specialization, but it also suggests some decline in production efficiency' (p. 429).
2. A number of studies have assumed a level of labour productivity in East Germany of about one third of that in West Germany: Statistisches Bundesamt (1993a); Hitchens et al. (1993); Lange (1993); and OECD (1993a).
3. 'East German output was converted into Deutschmarks with purchasing power parities (or 'unit value ratios') which take account of differences in relative price levels for individual industries' (Beintema and van Ark 1993).
4. It should be noted that in a number of other studies productivity estimates are somewhat higher (see Deutscher Bundestag 1987; Görzig and Gornig 1991; and Görzig 1991). This is largely because these estimates were often based on gross output in East Germany per person. However, as we implied in Section 2.3, gross output under central planning may be relatively high because of the larger share of intermediate inputs. We thus decided to use a study whose results are based on census value added.

APPENDIX 2A   A FORMAL MODEL OF PRODUCTION COMPLEXITY

Following Banerjee and Spagat (1991) we are able to model the above assumptions by assuming that an economy produces one final good, Y, in a symmetric, strictly concave, strictly increasing, constant returns to scale technology setting:

$$Y = Y(Q_1 \ldots Q_M) \tag{2A.1}$$

with $Q_1 \ldots Q_M$ = number of M intermediate goods. Furthermore, we assume that the amount of each intermediate goods is equal to the production of the final good: that is, for reasons of simplicity we do not include stocks of intermediate goods in our model.

The production of each intermediate good can now be modelled by using the inputs of capital, C, and labour, L, together with the assumption of random shocks to supply, λ_i, identically distributed across all suppliers.

$$Q_i = F(C_i, L_i, \lambda_i) \tag{2A.2}$$

The supply shocks are likely to occur in both a market and a Soviet-type economy. However, we make the crucial assumption that the distribution of the random shocks in a market economy differs from that under central planning. That is to say, we assume that the supply of intermediate goods in a market-led environment is more reliable than the supply in a Soviet-type economy. We also note that in our model input-producing industries are identical which implies an equal distribution of resources across industries.

Under the assumption of optimally allocated resources and F being constant returns to scale in L and C we arrive at the expected output of Y in the market economy:[1]

$$E(Y^m) = E_{\lambda 1}{}^m \ldots {}_{\lambda M}{}^m \{Y [F(C_1, L_1, \lambda_1{}^m), \ldots, F(C_M, L_M, \lambda_M{}^m)]\} \tag{2A.3}$$

which can be rewritten by taking into account that $L_i = \overline{L}/M$ and $C_i = \overline{C}/M$, yielding

$$E(Y^m) = E_{\lambda 1}{}^m \ldots {}_{\lambda M}{}^m \{Y [\overline{L}/Mf(\overline{C}/\overline{L}, \lambda_1{}^m), \ldots, \overline{L}/Mf(\overline{C}/\overline{L}, \lambda_M{}^m)]\}. \tag{2A.4}$$

Factoring out $\overline{L}/M$ and dividing the expression through by the supply of labour provides us with the level of productivity per unit of labour; that is, with labour productivity in terms of intermediate goods M:

$$1/\overline{L} \, E(Y^m) = (1/M) \, E_{\lambda 1}{}^m \ldots {}_{\lambda M}{}^m \{Y [f(\overline{C}/\overline{L}, \lambda_1{}^m), \ldots, f(\overline{C}/\overline{L}, \lambda_M{}^m)]\}. \tag{2A.5}$$

Finally, by defining the random variable $\tilde{Q}_i^m = f(\overline{C}/\overline{L}, \lambda_i^m)$ we can write the expression for the labour productivity of the final goods industry in the market economy as

$$\text{Prod}^m = E\,[Y(\tilde{Q}_1^m, \ldots, \tilde{Q}_M^m)]\,/\,M. \tag{2A.6}$$

A similar line of argument will produce the expression for the labour productivity of the final goods industry under central planning:[2]

$$\text{Prod}^{cp} = E\,[Y(\tilde{Q}_1^{cp}, \ldots, \tilde{Q}_M^{cp})]\,/\,M \tag{2A.7}$$

All we need to note is that $\tilde{Q}_i^{cp}$ is defined in exactly the same way as $\tilde{Q}_1^m$, except that it depends upon λ_i^{cp}, the random supply shock under central planning, and that we assume the supply of intermediate goods under central planning to be less reliable than the respective supply in a market economy.[3] As complexity grows ($\Delta M > 0$), therefore, Prod^{cp} falls more rapidly than is the case under market conditions.

NOTES

1. The superscript *m* stands for the association with a market economy.
2. The superscript *cp* denotes the variables corresponding to central planning.
3. For some early theoretical and empirical models describing these supply disturbances, see Brada (1978), Manove (1971) and Powell (1977).

3. The 1948 Currency and Economic Reforms in Comparison with the 1990 Economic and Monetary Union

3.1 INTRODUCTION

In post-war German history the years 1948 and 1990 are associated with the defining moments of division and unification. Currency and economic reforms in 1948 led to the foundation of the German Federal Republic (BRD) and contributed to the division of Germany. Similar measures in 1990 were agreed by the German Democratic Republic (DDR) as part of German Economic, Monetary and Social Union (GEMSU). This chapter argues that the different circumstances of 1948 and 1990 dictated that similar measures – currency reform coupled with free prices – would have not only opposing political outcomes but also radically different economic consequences.

In 1990, comparisons made by politicians with the 1948 reforms contributed to unrealistically optimistic expectations about the outcome of GEMSU which, in turn, exerted an adverse influence on policy-making. Unfortunately, such comparisons were informed by a substantially mythologized account of the 1948 reforms and their effects. The aftermath of GEMSU illustrates the harm that can be caused when policy is guided by myth rather than by actual conditions.

To most contemporary observers in 1945, Germany's economic potential appeared to be shattered (Kramer 1991, p. 17). Yet by the mid-1950s recovery to pre-war levels of output and, above all, continued growth of the German economy – being both spectacular and unexpected – was described and experienced as an 'economic miracle' (Kramer 1991, p. 1). Credit for this transformation was generally attributed to the reforms of 1948: 'This currency reform is generally recognized as the generating impulse of Germany's economic recovery and growth' (Landes 1969, p. 494; also Kramer 1991, p. 138). This unqualified association of reform and 'miracle' entered into the political mythology of the Federal Republic. In the early years, it was an important source of legitimation for the market economy: it thus contributed to political consensus and stability and, hence, to the foundations of West German economic prosperity. In 1990, however, this mythology of 1948 proved a misleading guide to the economics of unification.

In 1990, initial optimism arose from the expectation that monetary and economic union would do for the East what the currency and economic reform of June 1948 had done for the West. The immediate outcome of the two reform processes, however, belied their apparent similarity: in the first six months of the 1948 reform industrial production rose by more than 50 per cent, whereas following the 1990 reforms industrial production fell by more than 50 per cent. Faced with opposite rather than similar outcomes, the conflation of 1948 and the expected outcome of GEMSU was acknowledged as erroneous. For example, Otto Schlecht, state secretary at the economics ministry, admitted that 'we deceived ourselves about the size and depth of the restructuring crisis' and conceded that the government's much broadcast comparison between the hoped for recovery in east Germany and the positive aftermath of the currency reform in 1948 had been 'wrong from top to bottom' (FT, 29 April 1991).

The rest of this chapter explains why the apparent similarity of the reforms in 1948 and the terms of GEMSU in 1990 was misleading. They were implemented under entirely different circumstances and, hence, should not have been expected to yield similar results.

3.2 SIMILARITIES AND DIFFERENCES

3.2.1 The Reform Measures

In 1948, as in 1990, the existing currency (the Reichsmark or RM) was replaced by the Deutsche Mark (DM). In both cases, the consequence was a transformation of the relationship between 'financial stocks on the one hand and real assets and income flows on the other' (Tober 1997, p. 227). Moreover, in both cases the introduction of a new currency anticipated the dismantling of central direction of the economy in favour of market relations. (Table 3.1 sets out these measures for comparison.)

However, there are two obvious differences. First, the 1948 reforms were less radical in that they did not encompass a transformation of property rights. The Nazi system of resource allocation distorted but did not supplant the market economy (Landes 1969, p. 410). Above all, the economy that emerged from the débâcle of 1945 'was essentially one of private enterprise based on profit and material gain' (Landes 1969, p. 417; see also Borchardt 1991, p. 100). In 1990, however, a counter-revolution had to be implemented in eastern Germany to restore private property and the corresponding incentive of self-interest as the ultimate source of economic efficiency. Second, in 1948 there was no 'social' dimension to the reform process. In 1990, however, 'German Economic, Monetary *and* Social Union' was the reform programme of a mature *social* market economy. Accordingly, potential inequalities and social tensions were countered by restructuring the welfare system along West German lines and the provision of finance for raising pensions and paying unemployment benefit. In 1948, not only was there no such social dimension but the reforms tended to enlarge inequalities of wealth. The 10:1 conversion rate (see Table 3.1) meant that financial assets were, in effect, expropriated (to the cost of small savers, in particular) while material and productive assets were left untouched (to the benefit of their owners) (Kramer 1991, p. 138).

A third difference illustrates the adverse effect of the myth of 1948 on policy-making in 1990: namely, the implications of the 1948 and 1990 reforms for public finance. In 1948, the Allies secured the value of the DM in two ways. First, by making the new central bank – the Bank Deutscher Länder (the forerunner of the Bundesbank) – independent of government. Second, excessive budget deficits were forbidden in order to preclude the temptation to finance public debt by money creation. Indeed, in the mid-1950s budget surpluses 'contributed to the restraint on domestic demand' and, hence, to export-led growth (Carlin 1989, p. 60). In 1990, the value of the DM was still safeguarded by the independence of the Bundesbank. However, the impact of Unification was largely responsible for transforming a virtually balanced public sector budget in 1989 into a borrowing requirement equal to about 5.5 per cent of German GNP (see 1.9). In part this was the consequence of allowing policy to be guided by a mythologized version of 1948. Belief in the efficacy of reform without regard to the circumstances in which reform measures are implemented contributed to a drastic underestimation of the costs of Unification. In turn, this informed the belief that the costs of Unification could be covered without significant sacrifice. This made it difficult either to develop a coherent financial strategy or to persuade workers in either east or west of the need for, respectively, wage restraint and tax increases without compensating wage increases (see 1.9). Lack of wage restraint and public sector borrowing as a substitute for increased taxation both contributed to the Bundesbank's imposition of higher short-term interest rates, which had adverse consequences not only in Germany but throughout the European Union (see 8.1.5).

3.2.2 Reasons for Reform

The State Treaty signed by the governments of the BRD and DDR in May 1990 comprised measures that simultaneously abolished 'socialism' and reconstituted the DDR as a 'social market economy' (Treaty of 18 May

*Table 3.1   Comparison of monetary and economic reforms, 1948 and
1990*

1948: Currency and Economic Reforms	1990: GEMSU
Currency Reform: The Reichsmark was exchanged into the new DM on a 1:1 basis only for 40 marks per person plus another 20 marks two months later. Employers were allowed DM 60 per employee and public authorities the equivalent of one month's revenue. Recurrent payments – e.g., wages, rents, and pensions – continued at 1:1, while all financial assets and liabilities converted at DM 1 per RM 10. The net effect of the conversion was a rate of exchange of 100 RM to 6.5 DM – hence, a reduction of the money stock by 93.5 per cent. In March 1948, to protect the value of the new currency, the Allies had established the Bank Deutscher Länder to control the money supply and made it independent of government.	*Monetary Union*: The DM became the only legal means of payment in the DDR. The conversion rate between the DDR's Mark (OM – for Ost or East Mark) and the DM was 1:1 for wages and pensions, as well as for some savings, while the rate for financial assets and liabilities was 2:1. Accordingly, the Bundesbank became the central bank for the whole of Germany.

Economic Reform: On 18 June 1948, 'laws were passed to give Erhard powers to decide which goods, materials and services would be decontrolled after the currency reform, with the broad intention of giving preference to the free price mechanism rather than official planning' (Kramer 1991, p. 143). There were two fundamental steps.
1. On 21 June came the end of rationing on most consumer goods as well as the lifting of price controls on most manufactured goods and some foodstuffs.
2. The central allocation of resources likewise expired at the end of June.
'The Bizonal economy started into the second half of 1948 with genuinely free markets in almost all goods for which price controls had been removed' (Giersch et al. 1992, pp. 37–38). Deregulation was supported by other measures designed to improve incentives, stimulate investment, and generate growth.
1. Simultaneously with currency reform, the Allies enacted tax reform. This reduced personal and corporation tax
	Economic Union: This meant the opening and liberalization of the East German economy together with its structural assimilation into the West German social market economy. There were two fundamental elements (see Treaty of 18 May 1990, 1990).
	1. *Private ownership* of the means of production – but in the context of labour market law (including codetermination at board level, wage determination through collective bargaining, and the right to strike) and competition policy.
	2. *Free competition* – secured by
	  i. creating independent firms – by breaking up into separate firms and, hence, demonopolizing the existing state-owned *Kombinate* (or industrial groupings) and then privatizing them;
	  ii. freedom of economic activity – i.e., free movement of labour, capital, goods and services – thereby allowing market entry as a source of competitive pressure;
	  iii. free prices – requiring the abrogation of both price controls and the heavy subsidies applied generally to basic

(set in 1946 at levels of up to, respectively, 95 and 65 per cent), offered tax exemptions for saving and investment as well as allowing businesses to write off depreciation of capital at a high rate, and made overtime earnings free of tax.

2. On 3 November 1948 the wages freeze was lifted.

3. Foreign trade was controlled by the Occupation authorities. After three years in which 'foreign trade on commercial terms had played hardly any role at all', a sound currency together with bilateral trade agreements put West German foreign trade on a similar basis to that of 'most other West European countries' (Giersch et al. 1992, pp. 91–2).

goods under the command economy – thereby allowing markets and the price mechanism to operate without massive distortion and, hence, as a mechanism of resource allocation;

iv. creating an open economy – an end to currency inconvertibility and the state monopoly of foreign trade and, consequently, the liberalization of trade and capital movements – thereby exposing the economy of the DDR to competition from 'foreign' (i.e., Western) producers;

v. reform of the East German banking system along West German lines – thereby creating a capital market and subjecting the allocation of capital to the competitive process; and

vi. reform of the East German tax system along West German lines.

1990, 1990, pp. 65 and 68; see Table 3.1). Comprehensive reform in June 1948 also removed obstacles to a functioning market economy.

Monetary reform

In the years immediately following the war, the macroeconomic situation was one of sharply declining output and a huge monetary overhang (largely accumulated savings). Inflation, however, had largely been repressed by price controls, in place since 1936, and rationing.

- Between 1944 and 1946, GDP in the western occupied zones of Germany fell by 60 per cent (Maddison 1982, p. 174). By mid-1948, industrial production still stood at only 30 per cent of the level reached in the first half of 1944 (Schmieding 1991, p. 2).

- German rearmament and the war had been financed through monetary expansion and government borrowing. From 1932 to 1945 the stock of money – calculated on a broad basis – increased by almost 800 per cent, and Reich debt by more than 3,000 per cent, while national output (GDP) increased by less than 50 per cent (Maddison 1991, p. 213). The consequences are explained by Kramer (1991, pp. 124–5):

> [There was] *a loss of confidence in the currency*. If the Allies had not taken over the Third Reich's pay and prices freeze and had not continued the rationing of goods, the result would have been massive inflation ... The inflationary danger was obvious ... and the solution was simple: a reduction in liquidity and the issue of a new currency. (emphasis added)

Output, therefore, had shrunk in the context of a massively expanded money supply. The widening gap between the value of goods available for purchase and nominal purchasing power generated inflationary pressure. Price controls repressed inflation but left demand increasingly unsatisfied. This had severely adverse effects on the German economy.

- A considerable part of economic activity – above all, household expenditure – was displaced on to the black market where prices reflected the extent of excess demand.
- A large part of industrial output was displaced onto the 'grey market' of barter deals: 'Between one-third and one-half of all business transactions in the Bizone ... in September 1947 were through compensation trade' (Kramer 1991, p. 126).
- In June 1948, a sixth of industrial output in the Bizone was bartered by firms to (illegally) obtain food for their employees (Kramer 1991, p. 125) and so reduce absenteeism (Carlin 1989, p. 51). Commonly, workers were paid in kind to have goods to barter for food. These non-monetary exchanges reduced the average weekly hours worked below 40 as well as the work effort, thereby depressing productivity and output (Kramer 1991, p. 146). First, the time spent by workers in journeys to the countryside to barter for food or work on allotments could not be spent at work. Second, there was a lack of incentive to work for money wages: the food ration could be purchased with a fraction of money earnings, black market prices were too high in relation to money wages, and savings were already high (Carlin 1989, p. 51).

Repressed inflation precipitated breakdown of monetary exchange and widespread regression to barter. In this manner, the Reichsmark lost its function as money. Essentially, money is means of exchange – that is, a way of saving transactions costs. The lack of a valid currency, therefore, imposed huge additional costs on exchange and constituted a major obstacle to the continued recovery of output. Moreover, money prices enable firms to quantify and compare revenues and costs and, hence to calculate profit. In turn, profitability guides investment decisions. Monetary reform and the restoration of the price mechanism were preconditions not only for the continued recovery of output but also for the renewal of investment and thus for the growth and structural change of the German economy.[1]

Economic reform
The US occupation authorities used their influence to prevent widespread support for socialization being carried into law (Huster et al. 1973, pp. 46–9; Abelshauser 1983, p. 45; and Kramer 1991, pp. 41 and 115).

However, this political precondition for capitalism in western Germany was not sufficient to ensure a functioning market economy. It was also necessary to abandon centralized management of the economy.

After victory in May 1945, the allies took over the Nazi war economy more or less intact. Centralized management and allocation of resources continued together with direct control over the quantity produced of basic goods, the legal restriction of wages and prices to the levels of August 1936, the rationing of food and consumer goods, and the administrative allocation of raw materials, intermediate and final products, and – to a great extent – labour (Kramer 1991, p. 122). Even after reforms in 1947 under the US–UK Bizone, firm and household consumption remained subject to administrative allocation while wages and prices continued to be frozen (Kramer 1991, p. 123). There were no free markets in either goods or factors: fixed prices, of course, precluded relative price movements from guiding resource allocation. In mid-1948, therefore, the economy in occupied Germany had some of the characteristics later displayed by Eastern European command economies at the onset of economic reform. This system of planning and control had a certain success in concentrating resources on restoring the energy and transport infrastructure, which was the precondition for the recovery of industrial output towards pre-war levels (Abelshauser 1983, pp. 42–3 and Kramer 1991, pp. 99–101 and 122–3). However, the military principle of 'full forces at the point of attack' meant diversion of resources and shortages elsewhere (in particular, of consumer goods) and, hence, had limited capacity to promote recovery and growth more broadly. Moreover, the correspondingly severe constraints on market incentives and exchange – including control of foreign trade by the occupation authorities (much the same as the state monopoly of foreign trade under state socialism) – were an obstacle to efficiency and balanced growth. This was similar to later experience in the DDR (Abelshauser 1983, pp. 29–32 and 43).

3.2.3 Conditions and Consequences of Reform

In 1948
Currency and economic reform had their intended effect. The DM secured monetary stability and thus restored the monetary foundation of a functioning market economy, while liberalization – supported by tax incentives to save and invest – restored the possibility of producing and investing according to the price and profit signals of the market. The consequences were dramatic. In the second half of 1948, industrial production rose by more than 50 per cent and the capital stock by 5.6 per cent. At the same time, the economy underwent more rapid structural change than at any other time in the post-war period: the loss of 370,000

jobs in declining sectors was more than compensated by 600,000 new jobs in expanding sectors (Siebert 1991a, pp. 5–6).

In spite of appearances, however, it was misleading to conclude that currency and economic reform 'caused' the economic miracle of the 1950s in a way that could be replicated in the 1990s for east Germany. Although apparently similar, the circumstances under which reforms proceeded in 1948 were essentially different from those of 1990.

The 1948 reforms helped to realize a potential for recovery that was already present. In the aftermath of 1945, Germany possessed a world class productive apparatus. In 1938 German labour productivity – measured as GDP per man hour – was 80 per cent that of the UK (then the highest in Europe) (Maddison 1982, p. 212). In 1935, industrial sector productivity – measured as physical output per worker – was slightly higher in Germany than in the UK (Broadberry and Fremdling 1990, p. 404). This productive apparatus, moreover, had been expanded and modernized during the war (rather than, as commonly assumed, in large part destroyed).

1. Wartime production requirements forced an expansion of the capital stock. It was 11 per cent higher in 1948 than in 1936 in the western occupation zones (even allowing for war damage, depreciation and reparations) (Altvater et al. 1980, pp. 76–80; see also Kramer 1991, p. 18 and Carlin 1989, pp. 39–40). Moreover, the quality of the capital stock – as proxied by its age composition – improved: in 1935, 25 per cent of plant and equipment was less than 10 years old; in 1945, 64 per cent (Kramer 1991, p. 23).
2. The war made new demands on the technological prowess and capacity for innovation that had characterized German industry since the mid-nineteenth century (Landes 1969, p. 352). The result had been widespread introduction of new technologies (particularly those relating to mass production) (Landes 1969, pp. 411–12). Borchardt cites econometric evidence in support of the thesis that 'technical progress (together with changes in the qualification structure of employees) – a crucial determinant of growth – continued despite the devastation' (1991, pp. 114–15).
3. Between 1939 and 1946, the proportion of men aged 20–35 in the population fell from 12.1 to 7.4 per cent. However, quantitatively this was more than compensated by the inflow of migrants. Compared to 1939, the potential labour force (men between 14 and 65 and women between 14 and 50) in the UK and US zones was 7 per cent larger in 1946 and 14 per cent larger in 1948 (Kramer 1991, p. 11). Moreover, the quality of labour had been enhanced by improved training since the 1930s, enforced learning during the war, and upward mobility of German workers as slave labour was deployed for unskilled work (Kramer 1991, p. 11).

Both historical experience and growth theory suggest that a country with an adequate capital stock, a labour force adequate with respect to numbers and skills, capacity to innovate and an entrepreneurial tradition has the potential for growth. However, it is useful to distinguish between growth in 'normal' periods and growth in 'recovery' periods.

- In normal periods, more or less full utilization of resources keeps actual and potential output growing more or less in step with capital accumulation and technical progress (typically at rates between 2 and 4 per cent over long periods). (Potential or capacity output is the level of output with all factors of production fully utilized.)
- Recovery periods occur when actual output has fallen far below potential output. In this situation, so long as productive resources are not in the main destroyed or subject to atrophy, actual output can recover at a very high rate by bringing existing resources back into use.

The two can proceed together. In the years immediately following the war, normal growth was overshadowed by huge potential for recovery (which was clear not just in retrospect but also to some contemporary observers; Kramer 1991, p. 25). In western Germany after the 1948 reforms investment (hence, the 'normal' growth of capacity) rose sharply. Accordingly, until the early- or even mid-1950s, 'recovery' (increasing utilization of capacity) continued within the limits of a growing productive capacity.[2] In the remainder of this section, we argue that reform contributed to completion of *recovery* but also that a prior process of recovery was a precondition for successful reform. Once implemented, reform both facilitated the completion of recovery and enabled transition to a period of rapid but none the less *normal* capitalist development (that is, one powered by capital accumulation).

In the first half of 1948, the factories produced only 30 per cent of what they produced four years earlier with more or less the same capital, technology and labour. This was because 'constraint acted upon constraint to hinder growth beyond elementary levels' (Kramer 1991, p. 29). In the aftermath of defeat and occupation, Germany's productive potential could not be realized because of the breakdown of exchange and distribution. There were physical, administrative, political and monetary dimensions to the dislocation and collapse of exchange and distribution:

- devastation of the physical infrastructure – above all, of transport and communications – rather than the destruction of productive capacity caused the collapse of output in 1944–45 and was the main constraint on recovery in 1946–47 (Abelshauser 1983, pp. 21 and 36–7; Carlin 1989, p. 40);

- collapse of the German civil administration;
- the zonal division of Germany and the corresponding dislocation of interregional trade (see Abelshauser 1983, p. 19 and Kramer 1991, pp. 103–4);
- political uncertainty about Allied policy on the future form of economic organization (that is, planned or market economy) (Carlin 1989, p. 44);
- political restrictions on output to prevent the reconstruction of military potential (in the event, a minor problem; Kramer 1991, p. 101) and, worse, uncertainty about Allied intentions on the permitted level of industrial output;
- until 1948 the occupation authorities controlled foreign trade and severely restricted its scope (Abelshauser 1983, p. 29 and Kramer 1989, p. 105); and
- lack of means of exchange.

The task confronting policy-makers, therefore, was to remove these obstacles so as to inaugurate rapid recovery by mobilizing existing but underutilized capacity.

By early 1947, the transport infrastructure had been largely repaired. By 1948 civil administration had been restored, the western zones had been merged, and uncertainties about the future form of economic organization and attitude towards economic recovery had been resolved in favour of a market economy and full industrial recovery (Carlin 1989, p. 53). With the removal of physical barriers to exchange, together with the easing of the administrative and political obstacles to production, industrial output began to recover _before_ the reforms of 1948. The 'breakthrough to continuous and high growth rates of production' came in Autumn 1947, according to Abelshauser (1983, p. 44).[3] Figure 3.1 supports this view.[4]

The restoration of monetary exchange coupled with an end to the administrative allocation of resources removed monetary and policy-induced obstacles to free exchange. The immediate impact of currency reform was dramatic. In the first half of 1948 production had continued to grow (see Figure 3.1). However, in anticipation of currency reform, firms had been hoarding stock rather than selling goods for worthless RM. Accordingly, on the first day of the DM, previously hoarded goods were suddenly made available. This speculative stock building paid off as 'consumers spent their cash allocations on goods which had once more become available' (Carlin 1989, p. 55). Moreover, with goods to buy the incentive to work for money wages was restored, thereby reducing absenteeism and boosting productivity and output (Carlin 1989, p. 56).

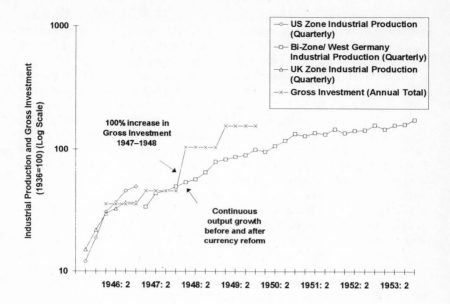

Source: Abelshauser (1983, pp. 34 and 64) for industrial production and Krengel (cited in Carlin 1989, p. 54) for gross investment.

Figure 3.1   Post-war recovery and growth of industrial production and gross investment in Western Germany (1936 = 100), 1945 Q3– 1953 Q4

These events were the *origin of the myth in which currency reform had a miraculous effect independently of the real economy context in which it was implemented* (Kramer 1991, p. 139; see also Abelshauser 1983, p. 51). Rather than seeing reform as enabling economic potential to be realized, this myth obscured the underlying potential of the real economy, which was the precondition for the success of reform. More than 40 years later, this myth of the 1948 reforms exerted a seriously misleading influence on the approach to Unification.

None the less, reform was a necessary condition for subsequent growth of a normal kind. Initially faltering and then continuous recovery beginning in 1947 was achieved on the basis of – hence, within the limits of – *existing* resources. However, by the early 1950s, to sustain growth – and the structural change associated with growth – investment was necessary to create *additional* and more productive resources. By reconstituting market exchange and coherent incentives, the reforms of 1948 created conditions under which production could, at first, continue to *recover* within the bounds of existing supply-side potential and then, increasingly, undergo sustained *normal* growth as potential output was itself increased by positive net investment and productivity growth. (Figure 3.1 shows that, unlike output, the recovery of investment clearly began in 1948.)

In the five years following the second half of 1948, investment was between half and two-thirds financed from retained earnings (Abelshauser 1983, pp. 72–3). In part, this was possible because of taxation policies designed to promote investment – for example, capital goods with a value up to DM 100,000 were subject to accelerated depreciation allowances of up to 50 per cent of their value within the first two years. By way of contrast, industrial collapse in the aftermath of GEMSU meant an almost complete absence of retained earnings as a source of investment finance. Since 1990, investment has been financed almost entirely from the west. A similarity, however, is that western investment in eastern Germany has been promoted by a system of incentives, which allow up to 50 per cent of the cost of investment to be refunded in the first year (JG 1992, pp. 72–4).

Exceptionally high profitability reflected exceptionally low wages (Carlin 1989, p. 62 and Kramer 1991, p. 130). Currency reform and the end of price control allowed prices to rise rapidly (Kramer 1991, p. 146). Wages, however, remained frozen until 3 November 1948 and, thereafter, were kept low by rapidly rising unemployment, the hostility of the occupying powers to trade unions (Altvater et al. 1980, p. 83), the mass inflow of refugees, and a renewed assertiveness on the part of management (Kramer 1991, p. 146).[5] Perhaps just as important, the organizations of the once-powerful German labour movement had been destroyed by 12 years of Nazi rule and had been unable to play a significant role in the overthrow of the regime. Because of this, German workers lacked both the confidence and the collective organization that might have restricted profitability or even challenged the revival of the western economy on a capitalist basis (Altvater et al. 1980, pp. 76–80). Finally, it is likely that defeat in war and the sheer hardship of daily life diminished expectations (food rations were often at or not much above a starvation level; Kramer 1991, pp. 71–80).

In 1948, real wages (weekly earnings relative to the cost of living) were 75 per cent of their 1938 level and regained their 1938 level only in 1950 (Carlin 1989, p. 56). Of particular importance for current profitability was that product wages (weekly earnings relative to output prices) were only 64 per cent of their 1938 level in 1948 and still only 85 per cent in 1952. Moreover, with the restoration of incentive to work for money wages and a rapid growth of output, productivity (industrial output per employee) rose very rapidly.[6] Currency reform had depreciated firms' debts by 90 per cent. Together with rising output prices, depressed wages and rising productivity generated high and rising profitability which, in turn, financed the investment boom. This was one of the fundamental elements of the economic miracle.[7]

In 1990

From a macroeconomic perspective, the economic problems of the DDR were not acute (Tober, 1997, p. 231). In contrast with western Germany in 1948, the economic problems of the DDR lay on the supply side.

The DDR had a command economy. Its producers were not firms in the Western sense, but state-owned monopolies producing according to a central plan. Foreign trade was conducted mainly with other Soviet bloc economies and was planned according to the 'residual principle'; that is, to secure products that could not be produced domestically. Eastern producers, therefore, were monopolies by virtue both of being sole producers in the GDR and of the state monopoly of foreign trade that protected them from western competition. Because of this systematic exclusion of competition, producers lacked experience of doing business in a market economy and entrepreneurial habits had undergone some degree of atrophy. Moreover, in large part the outcome of lack of competition and its associated incentives, the DDR's producers were not equipped for competition. In comparison with the BRD, productive capacity was obsolete and characterized by low productivity (no more than one-third of the west German level), low-quality products and – most fundamentally – the lack of any kind of dynamic with which to close the gap (see Chapter 2).

GEMSU integrated eastern producers into a single market with western firms and, hence, subjected the east German economy to free trade and competition as a *sudden and immense shock*. In essential respects these changes differed from the earlier reform process; either in ways that prevented the offsetting of supply-side deficiencies or, worse, in ways that actually compounded the competitive disadvantages of eastern producers.

Economic union constituted a sudden competitive shock that exposed supply-side weakness. In contrast, after the 1948 reforms, Germany's foreign trade developed in an environment 'in which tariffs were only gradually lifted and arranged in such a way as to favour both the import and export of capital goods relative to consumer goods' (Tober 1997, p. 240). Moreover, irrevocable *monetary union* precluded – by definition – devaluation as a means of rapid adjustment of price competitiveness (which was used not only in 1949 but has also been a feature of restructuring packages elsewhere in the old Soviet bloc). (And because of the relatively low quality of Eastern goods, non-price competition was precluded.) Worse, the terms of monetary union amplified this competitive shock by, in effect, imposing a currency appreciation of 300–400 per cent or more.[8] Ensuing wage rises and falling productivity (as output fell more rapidly than employment) – again, quite the opposite of developments following the 1948 reforms – completed the catastrophic impact of GEMSU on the eastern economy. Both demand-side and supply-side changes caused a collapse of output and employment.

Economic Union dictated free trade; and Monetary Union an overnight change from a non-convertible to a fully convertible currency. In their newly open economy, east German households and firms no longer had to buy from the old state suppliers – whose monopoly had been enforced by the non-convertibility of the currency – but, henceforth, could buy goods from the west. The consequence was quite the opposite of 1948: endowment of the population with DM and the consequent surge in demand was associated with falling demand for domestic (that is, eastern) output.

Simultaneously, conversion at 1:1 transformed eastern producers' costs and revenues into DM. The result was a catastrophic *price–cost squeeze*. GEMSU required east German producers to set prices as well as cover current costs – including wages – in DM. On the revenue side, competitive pressure exerted a severely downward pressure on output prices: by January 1991, average DM output prices in manufacturing industry were less than 60 per cent of their 1989 OM level (Statistisches Bundesamt, 1993b, p. 36). On the costs side, GEMSU exposed eastern producers to an increasing gap between low and falling productivity levels and rising real wages. In circumstances of falling output and employment, nominal wages rose by 42 per cent between the first quarter of 1990 and the following October. And by the end of 1991, negotiated wage rates in east Germany reached about 60 per cent of west German levels (Owen-Smith 1994, pp. 289–90).

This development of wages in eastern Germany was driven not by the economic fundamentals of supply and demand but by politics. Here the contrast with the aftermath of 1945 is absolute. It was the achievement of the East Germans to have made a successful democratic revolution. Expectations were enormously heightened and they were not in a mood to wait for the benefits. The following mechanisms ensured that wages would rise whatever the actual competitiveness of eastern producers.

1. *Parity between the OM and the DM*   This alone meant wages too high for competitiveness. None the less, wages did not subsequently fall under competitive pressure but continued to rise.
2. *The nature of wage bargaining in the aftermath of GEMSU*   Bargains were being struck with the help of experienced western unions on the one hand while, on the other, the existing managers – reckoning on either continued soft-budget constraints or their own demise – had little incentive to bargain for lower wages. (In the aftermath of 1948, assertive management confronted weak unions.) Moreover, because unemployment benefits are based on terminal wages, widespread expectation of unemployment and short-time working gave a positive incentive to increase wages.
3. *Government complicity*   Unions and government alike argued that high wages were necessary to prevent a more massive emigration.

GEMSU squeezed eastern producers between falling prices and rising wage costs. Eastern producers generally could not command a price capable of covering their variable costs of production (some products, indeed, scarcely being saleable at any price). GEMSU suddenly exposed eastern producers to competition but did so on terms that rendered them utterly unable to compete. By 1991, the consequence was clear: 'In the absence of massive productivity improvements or substantial subsidization, most Eastern industry will have to close down' (Akerloff et al. 1991, pp. 27–8).

The shock of competition, compounded by the effective currency appreciation, therefore, inaugurated a slump in output and employment sharper and deeper than even the slump of 1929–32 (the nearest peacetime comparison). Before stabilizing in 1991, eastern industrial output fell by almost two-thirds (see Figure 3.2) and national output by about one-third, while between GEMSU and the second half of 1991 about 45 per cent of the labour force lost their jobs (see 1.7). Living standards as well as much of the remaining employment have been maintained only by massive and continuing fiscal transfers from west Germany. This outcome could scarcely have differed more from the outcome of the 1948 reforms. Nor could there have been a more painful confounding of expectations and policies informed by the mythologized version of the 1948 reforms.

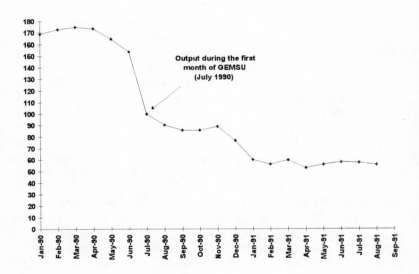

Source: Calculated from JG (1991, p. 63).

Figure 3.2   Industrial production in eastern Germany (monthly: January 1990–August 1991) (July 1990 = 100)

3.2.4 Main differences between 1948 and 1990

Some differences have been discussed in Section 3.2 or referred to else-where. Here, we comment on the essential contrasts.

1. Currency reform was not only necessary to sustain recovery and inaugurate 'normal' capital accumulation and growth but itself depended on strong prior recovery (Abelshauser 1983, p. 46). Substantial reconstruction and recovery of output, achieved under a planning regime, was the precondition for currency reform. For without this supply-side precondition, there would have been insufficient goods to buy after the currency reform (Kramer 1991, p. 143). Even a modest initial endowment of a valid currency was sure to boost aggregate demand. This could not be satisfied by imports because of a shortage of foreign exchange and continued Allied restriction of Germany's trade. The consequence of deficient aggregate supply would have been inflation – if not open then repressed – and rapid loss of confidence in the new currency. This, of course, was precisely the opposite of what occurred in 1990. Monetary union took place without regard for the productive potential of the DDR and so rapidly as to preclude any prior reconstruction. The consequent boost to aggregate demand took place as output collapsed. Excess demand was satisfied by imports.
2. In 1948, western Germany possessed productive capacity that was *underutilized* because of the lack of a functioning market economy: consequently, reform enabled existing supply-side potential to be realized and expanded. This enabled unprecedented growth. Before GEMSU, eastern Germany *utilized* its productive capacity in large part because it did not have a functioning market economy: the consequence of reform was to shrink potential output (although the capital stock continued to exist physically, the major part could not be used for profitable production – or even to cover variable costs – and thus had no economic viability). GEMSU, together with ensuing wage rises, ruthlessly exposed supply-side weakness. This triggered an un-precedented depression.
3. After the 1948 reforms, the liberalization of foreign trade was gradual. Moreover, devaluation in September 1949 – and, subsequently, not increasing the external value of the DM in line with relatively high productivity growth – reduced relative unit labour costs (which, for internationally traded goods, are calculated as the ratio of the wage rate to productivity multiplied by the exchange rate). This contributed to price competitiveness and growing demand. Together with the investment boom, the rapid growth of foreign trade was a fundamental element of the economic miracle (Carlin 1989, pp. 57–65). In contrast,

GEMSU not only imposed a 'shock therapy' introduction of free trade but combined this with an effective currency appreciation in excess of 300 per cent. This made a fundamental contribution to economic collapse.

4. Radically different political environments – the product of, respectively, military defeat and peaceful revolution – generated entirely different expectations and, hence, a contrasting evolution of wages. In the aftermath of 1948, wages grew at a rate lower than productivity. This reduced unit labour costs. As costs fell, output prices rose. Rising profitability provided both incentive and means for high investment and capital intensive growth (the 'actual "economic miracle"' according to Abelshauser 1983, p. 94). In 1990, the adverse competitive effect of currency appreciation was compounded by wages which rose as productivity and output prices fell. The resulting squeeze on profitability not only removed the means of financing investment but rendered continued output loss-making.

3.3 CONCLUSION

The currency and economic reforms of 1948 and economic, monetary and social union of 1990 included similar measures. Yet they were introduced in entirely different circumstances. In the aftermath of war enormous productive potential could not be realized, in large part because extreme macroeconomic disequilibrium precluded a functioning market economy. The aftermath of economic and monetary union combined minor macroeconomic problems with minimal productive potential. Accordingly, similar reform measures had contrasting outcomes. Currency and economic reform in 1948 enabled west Germany's productive potential to be realized in both continued recovery and a qualitatively higher rate of capital accumulation. Monetary and economic Unification in 1990 exposed the East's relative lack of productive potential, while imposing conditions unfavourable to competitiveness, and precipitated a collapse of output. This comparison demonstrates that, in 1990, a simple principle of policy formation was ignored: namely, the outcome of reform depends not only on the prescribed measures but also on the conditions under which they are implemented.

NOTES

1. 'Gross investment was less than depreciation in each year from 1945 to 1948 ... The inclusion of plant lost through reparations and dismantling (which amounted to much less

than originally proposed) meant a fall in the gross capital stock between 1945 and 1948 of just under 7 per cent.' However, gross investment doubled between 1947 and 1948 – with most of the 1948 investment occurring in the second half of the year – and increased by a further 50 per cent in 1949 (Carlin 1989, pp. 40–41, 53–4 and 57).

2. According to Dumke (1990, p. 467): 'Between 1950 and 1955 capital utilization rose much more sharply than capital stock'. Instead of defining recovery as a return to full capacity utilization it may be defined 'as the return to pre-war standards and levels of output' (Dumke 1990, p. 454). However, this does not make it possible to identify the end of the recovery phase with any greater precision. According to Maddison (1991, pp. 206–19) – whose estimates are corrected for territorial change – West German GDP recovered its 1938 level by 1951 and its 1944 level by 1953. Industrial output recovered its 1938 level by 1950–51 (see note 6 and Figure 3.1), but its highest wartime level only later. Industrial productivity series tell much the same story (see note 6).

3. Kramer supports 'Abelshauser's main argument that the economy was already growing before the currency reform' and defends this view against its critics (1991, p. 139; see Giersch et al. 1992, pp. 40–41 for a more critical view).

4. In Figure 3.1, Abelshauser's estimates of industrial output up to and including the second quarter of 1948 correct official statistics to take account of hoarding and, hence, non-reporting of output. His procedure is to use electricity consumption as a guide to output. The log scale means that whenever output – or any variable – alters by some percentage it rises or falls by the same vertical distance. This feature makes it easy to focus on changes in rates of growth: the steeper the curve, the faster the growth.

5. Unemployment rose from 3.2 per cent of the labour force in the second quarter of 1948 to 8.7 per cent and 10 per cent in the second quarters of, respectively, 1949 and 1950, peaking at 12.2 per cent in the first quarter of 1950 (Abelshauser 1983, p. 64).

6. With 1938 = 100, in the years 1948–52 industrial output was 61, 75, 94, 113 and 122 and industrial productivity was 59, 69, 82, 91 and 95 (Carlin 1989, p. 56).

7. Carlin (1989, pp. 57–65) locates the investment boom within a succinct analysis of the 'sources of growth, 1949–55'.

8. From the point of view of competitiveness, an appropriate conversion rate would have been in the region of 4:1. In 1989, for each OM 4.4 spent on producing goods for export to the BRD – and, hence, subject to competition – the planning authorities expected to earn DM 1 (Akerloff et al. 1991, p. 18).

4. Restructuring and Privatization

The first two years of GEMSU – the impact phase – were characterized by collapsed output and employment and only faint signs of recovery. This chapter examines first the preconditions and initial problems of reconstruction in eastern Germany and, second, the Treuhand as the agency of privatization and restructuring.

4.1 PREREQUISITES FOR REAL ADJUSTMENT

In line with the State Treaty, restructuring and transition to self-sustaining recovery were to be brought about by privatization and associated inward investment. Privatization was to change the behaviour of eastern producers – by removing 'soft-budget constraints' to enforce competitive behaviour – as well as to bring forth inward investment to rebuild the capital stock.

The construction of a competitive traded goods sector in eastern Germany depends upon inward investment. First, private sector investment is the means of restructuring at the level of the firm – as existing firms introduce new processes and products and new firms set up in response to market opportunities and pressures. Second, as competition guides the investment decisions of firms, so the economy as a whole is restructured – with respect to the sectoral distribution of output, the regional location of production and the trade pattern. Investment, then, is the key to restructuring and growth. Accordingly, Section 4.1.1 estimates the investment needs of eastern Germany in the immediate aftermath of GEMSU, and Section 4.1.2 discusses the initial obstacles to investment as well as the incentives that contributed to overcoming these obstacles. In the appendix to this chapter, we use a more formal analytic framework to discuss why investment was initially lower than expected as well as why it eventually picked up.

4.1.1 Required Scale of Investment

In mid-1991, more than 90 per cent of industrial employment was with firms that were not viable even in the short run. The capital stock and infrastructure inherited from the DDR continued to exist in physical terms.

Yet, in economic terms this industrial capacity was obsolete because, with current wage rates, profitable production was not possible. Economic revival, therefore, required renewal of the capital stock and infrastructure. In turn, in the absence of profitable production and the ability of eastern industry to generate savings, renewal of the capital stock depended on inward investment (see Siebert et al. 1991, p. 32; and JG 1992, p. 87).

Moving the eastern economy into the recovery and expansion phase of the output J-curve required huge inward investment to modernize the economy. Estimates of the investment requirement are subject to dispute (JG, 1991, p.88). However, the order of magnitude can be indicated.

Priewe and Hickel (1991, pp. 121–3) estimated the investment requirement of eastern Germany in public and private sector capital stock for the period 1991–2000. They assumed that (1) the east will achieve the *present* western standard of living – and, hence, productivity – by the end of the century, (2) the employed labour force will number 7.5 million, and (3) 5 million existing jobs will be maintained while 2.5 million will be newly created. In 1991, the average current capital requirement per job in the western industrial sector was DM 200,000. For the 5 million maintained jobs, they used Treuhand data to estimate an average capital requirement per job of DM 100,000. (By August 1991, western firms that had purchased eastern firms intended investment of about DM 117,000 per job: a similar figure can be calculated from data in JG 1992, p. 95.) Using a conservative figure of DM 100,000 per job, it will require investment of DM 500 bn to maintain 5 million existing jobs. In addition, 2.5 million new jobs will require the full average investment of DM 200,000 – in total, a further DM 500 bn. The total capital requirement, therefore, is DM 1,000 bn – that is, DM 100 bn per annum over the next decade.[1] Together with the investment requirements in infrastructure (DM 790 bn) and environmental renovation (DM 211 bn) (see below), the total investment needed in eastern Germany in the period 1991-2000 is about DM 2000 bn – or DM 200 bn per annum in constant 1991 prices. This total compares with gross public and private sector investment (including housing) in west Germany of about DM 530 bn in 1990 and about DM 290bn in the first half of 1991 (current prices) (JG 1991, p. 326). To bring eastern Germany up to the western standards of 1991 within a 10-year period requires, therefore, an annual investment equal to about 40 per cent of the west German boom-time level.

In the early years, investment did not approach this level. According to the report of the Council of Economic Experts published in November 1991, public and private sector investment 'quickened in the course of 1991' and was of 'decisive importance in stabilizing the economic situation in eastern Germany'. The report estimated a total for 1991 of DM 66 bn invested in the 'modernization and renewal of productive capacity, buildings, and infrastructure'. About 75 per cent of this was accounted for by business investments, 'above all in newly founded enterprises and in privatized firms' (JG 1991, p. 72). Nevertheless, these totals remained far short of the levels needed for the restructuring and recovery – as opposed to the 'stabilization' – of the east German economy.

Ultimately, willingness to invest is determined by expected profitability (Pugh 1997). For an investment to be initiated, the present value of future profits must exceed the cost of the investment (including – especially in the case of privatizing existing firms – associated adjustment costs). In this light, we consider the obstacles and incentives to investment in eastern Germany in the first two years or so of Unification.

4.1.2 Obstacles and Incentives to Investment

From the beginning, there was no unit labour cost incentive to locate low-tech, low-productivity production in eastern Germany. The initial east:west wage differential of less than 50 per cent was outweighed by a productivity differential of 300 percent.[2] Moreover, post-Unification wage growth continued to bear no relation to productivity. However, we argue at length in Chapter 6 that in the first phase of Unification rapid wage growth was part of a deliberate development strategy for eastern Germany. High wages were an instrument of 'creative destruction' that precluded a low-wage, low-tech development path in eastern Germany. Instead, the adverse locational effect of relatively high wages on eastern Germany was offset by subsidized investment which, in turn, was to create high-productivity jobs capable of sustaining a high-wage, high-tech development path in the medium to long run.

High wages may be considered part of an industrial strategy in which high-tech investment was to power eastern convergence to western productivity levels. However, in the immediate aftermath of Unification there was disappointment in government circles with the pace of investment (FT, 13 November 1990). At first, in spite of generous subsidy, there were a number of major obstacles to investment and privatization in the east. According to surveys of west German firms conducted in 1991 and 1992, these were – in order of importance – ownership uncertainty, deficiencies in public administration, infrastructural deficiencies, and ecological liability (JG 1991, pp. 75–6; 1992, pp. 94–5).

1. *Clarification of ownership rights* In West Germany, private property has been fundamental to the legal system since before 1848. East Germany had made a fundamental break with the rights of private property. With Unification, the five new Federal States adopted the legal system of the BRD. Consequently, there was no uncertainty over property rights *per se* (as there is, for example, in the former USSR). However, a general respect for property rights does not answer the

question of who owns what: 'property rights certainty does not yet guarantee ownership certainty' (Siebert 1991a, p. 19). Rather, there was the problem of *how* to bring eastern Germany back into line with Article 14 of the German Constitution that guarantees private property as a basic right which, only by way of exception, may be curtailed in the general interest.

In principle, restoring property to previous owners could have been dealt with either by restitution (which has to be dealt with *before* privatization and new investment) or by compensation (which can be dealt with *after* privatization and investment). In favour of compensation was the trade off between respect for private property rights and the necessity of the largest possible scale of inward investment (and, hence the general interest). Priority, however, was given to property rights: hence the policy of restitution to previous owners expropriated since 1949 (and prior to 1945). The problem was that, in practice, restitution was difficult to implement and impossible to implement quickly.

a. The sheer volume of claims made swift restitution impossible: by mid-1991, 1.5 million restitution claims had been made by previous owners (Siebert 1991a, p. 21) while, in the city of Dresden, for example, only 700 out of 40,000 claims had been decided. After three years of Unification, the situation was still hopeless: 'Officials at the Office for the Regulation of Property Questions admit it will take at least another ten years to close the files. That represents a lot of missed investment opportunities' (*The Economist*, 4 September 1993).
b. There was no clear rule for the assignment of property titles – for example, to distinguish between the ownership of a firm and the ownership of the land on which its buildings were situated.
c. The passage of time and the neglect of title records in the DDR led to conflicting claims.

All this benefited only lawyers. The consequences for privatization and inward investment were severe.[3] With a question mark over ownership, enterprises could neither persuade investors to commit finance nor provide collateral for bank loans. From March 1991, privatizations were suspended if the firm was subject to restitution claims (Siebert 1991a, p. 23). In 1992, relief was provided by the Property Law, which allowed compensation instead of restitution in cases where investment was threatened by ownership uncertainty. In the enterprise sector at least, the 1992 law helped to remove the major obstacle to investment. Thereafter, the Treuhandanstalt could reassure investors: 'No new investor need fear that a former owner can lay claim to a factory or plot of land after it has been sold' (THA, no date, p. 5).

2. *Efficient public administration* The five new Federal States of eastern Germany took over not only the political and legal system of the BRD but also its regulatory system. Yet, by the end of 1991, State and municipal government was 'still in the initial stages of organization' (JG 1991, p. 66). Moreover, there were shortages of personnel acquainted with modern management technique as well as modern office equipment. In a heavily regulated economy, deficient public administration is a serious obstacle to investment. Consequently, lack of efficient public administration in eastern Germany – with reference to, for example, 'the licensing procedures for firms (license to open a business, environmental licences etc.), land use planning, zoning and the procedures of land use for infrastructure' – hindered inward investment (Siebert 1991a, p. 54).

3. *Renovation of the physical infrastructure* Obsolete energy, transport and communications infrastructure imposes a serious constraint upon private sector activity.[4] Investment requirements to reach western standards in these three areas by the end of the period 1991–2000 have been estimated at DM 320 bn. If to this total is added the estimated investment requirement in housing (DM 470 bn), then the total infrastructural investment required by the end of the century rises to DM 790 bn (Priewe and Hickel 1991, p. 123 and Siebert 1991a, p. 67).

4. *Environmental renovation* Concern over environmental liability is a major obstacle to investment – particularly in sectors such as energy, mining and chemicals (JG 1991, pp. 66 and 75). Priewe and Hickel quote as authoritative an estimate of DM 211 bn for the cost of restoring acceptable environmental standards (1991, pp. 52–3).

In the first two years or so of Unification, the prerequisite for real economy adjustment was the removal of these obstacles to inward investment. Consequently, as these obstacles were reduced so the incentives to invest in eastern Germany began to act more powerfully, thereby inaugurating the investment boom documented in Chapters 1, 6 and 7.

By the end of 1992, the above-mentioned problems confronting investors had begun to ease: not only ownership rights as the result of the 1992 Property Law but also deficient state and local administration and deficient infrastructure (JG 1992, p. 88) as well as environmental problems and liability (for example, the Treuhand acted early to ameliorate this problem by assuming environmental liability in the form of 'risk limitation agreements' with respect to clean-up and compensation claims and so on; FT, 14 December 1990). Moreover, with a skilled labour force (see below) and the ability to train or import managerial talent, the capacity of the east to absorb inward investment increased. As these constraints on investment were relaxed, so the incentives to invest became more effective. First, public policy secured low-risk and investment subsidies. Second, these incentives were reinforced by market conditions on both the demand side (proximity to and links with markets together with public spending) and on the supply side (potential for rapid productivity growth). We complete this section by discussing these incentives to invest.

1. *Relatively low risk*   Compared to Eastern Europe and the former USSR, investment in eastern Germany is not hindered by uncertainty regarding exchange rates (caused by the normal instability of floating rates together with the possibility of devaluation), institutional conditions (the possibility of sudden changes in, for example, taxation), or the political environment. Consequently, to the extent that risk considerations are minimized, investment decisions can be taken on grounds of rate of return.

2. *Investment subsidies*   Since Unification, there has been a complex system of government-funded investment incentives (JG 1992, pp. 72–4). Similar incentives had been used to support peripheral regions in western Germany: 'large companies are typically attracted by regional subsidies to such peripheral areas' although control 'remains vested in the company's head office' (Owen-Smith 1994, p. 46). After Unification, investment incentives were used to reorder the balance of locational costs and benefits in favour of eastern Germany: 'The aim of financial support is to accelerate the construction of highly productive plant by offsetting the still remaining locational disadvantages' (JG 1992, p. 192). Even so, in 1991 and 1992, the simultaneous collapse of eastern manufacturing output and 'unification boom' in western Germany reinforced west German industry as the potential supplier of manufactured goods for the whole of Germany. Particularly in industries where increasing returns to scale 'implies that firms ... have an incentive to supply their goods from a single location', these initial conditions could have inaugurated a process of cumulative divergence between a western core and an eastern periphery. As industry expanded in the west and contracted in the east, so scale economies would continue to decrease unit costs in the west and increase costs in the east, thereby leading to additional expansion in the west and contraction in the east and so on (Brakeman and Garretsen 1993, p. 169; see also pp. 174–7).[5] Public policy intervention, especially through investment incentives, was necessary to offset a balance of locational costs and benefits that had the potential to be worsened through this process of cumulative causation.

Incentives – subsidies, tax relief, cheap credit and so on – are not mutually exclusive, but may be cumulated. This possibility is publicized by the Federal Ministry of Economics to attract inward investment:

There are capital gains and capital asset tax exemptions, a special depreciation allowance currently set at 50 percent, and tax credits of up to 10 percent of an investment. Outright grants can reach up to 50 percent of eligible investments and there are a variety of favourable credit and bank guarantee programmes. (*The Economist*, 'Survey on Germany', 9 November 1996, p. 18)[6]

The result of investment incentives is that 'roughly half of total investment has been financed by the public sector (through infrastructure spending and subsidies to firms), with private investment on average subsidized by one third' (Boltho et al. 1996, p. 13). When an enterprise is privatized, the scale of investment and restructuring required means, in effect, creating a new firm. By reducing the cost of capital, incentives enable a larger number of possible investments to become profitable and, hence, to be undertaken.

3. *Proximity to the market*   Proximity to large and growing markets is, in general, among the most important motives for direct investment. Survey evidence reveals that proximity to new markets in eastern Germany is the most commonly cited reason for intended investment by western firms (JG 1991, pp. 74–5). In so far as west German firms want to pre-empt entry by foreign firms into the German market, investment in the east can have a precautionary element.

4. *Trading links with Eastern Europe*   The collapse of export markets in Eastern Europe and the former USSR reduced the immediate appeal of eastern Germany in this respect. None the less, longer-term prospects made proximity and links to East European markets an additional incentive to investment (JG 1991, p. 75).

5. *Fiscal transfers and infrastructural spending*   An important addition to the east German market was public spending on infrastructure – estimated at DM 26 bn for 1991 (JG 1991, p. 75).

6. *Expected productivity growth*   Competitive pressure was expected to enforce productivity increase. Initially, even in the absence of substantial investment, there were several sources of rapid productivity growth.

   a. *The employment policies of a market economy*   Policy in the DDR was directed towards security of employment. Consequently, if an enterprise implemented labour-saving rationalization in one part of its operations, the normal procedure would to reemploy displaced labour elsewhere in the enterprise. Under market conditions, however, redundant labour ceases to be the responsibility of the rationalizing firm and becomes (in a *social* market economy) the responsibility of the social insurance system and active labour market policy. Freedom to rationalize – and the competitive incentive to do so – put an end to previous overemployment and increased productivity.

b. *More effective use of labour power*   First, quantitatively, empirical investigations under the old regime showed that, because of deficient organization, discontinuities in production commonly accounted for losses of 25–35 per cent of total working time. Better management practice – spurred by competitive pressure – enforced a rapid increase in productivity. Second, qualitatively, there were harder to quantify gains from better motivation and greater incentives for creativity. Once enterprises became independent of the central plan, there was more scope for taking responsibility, while a competitive rather than a monopolistic environment provided the incentive to do so.

c. *Reallocation of resources away from sectors with a comparative disadvantage towards sectors with a comparative advantage*   There was considerable scope for efficiency gains from reallocating resources from less to more productive sectors. This is because, previously, the state monopoly of foreign trade prevented the DDR from being integrated into the global division of labour, and thus reaping the benefits of specialization in sectors of comparative advantage.

These factors represented important reserves of productivity growth. Their effect, however, was largely static: that is, giving a once and for all productivity increase by way of a more efficient utilization of existing resources. For sustained productivity growth, a necessary condition – increasingly stressed by theoretical and empirical work alike – is a well-educated and highly trained workforce capable of adapting flexibly to investment and innovation.

d. *Skilled workforce*   Although lagging in economic performance, the DDR had an industrial tradition shared with West Germany and was possessed of an educated and skilled workforce. Some Eastern know-how became obsolete with Unification but schooling was generally very good (and, in mathematics and science, perhaps ahead of western Germany). In particular, eastern Germany is well endowed with skilled workers of the sort widely regarded as a major source of west Germany's industrial strength. East German engineering was technically relatively backward, but the basics of machine building were excellent.[7] (We consider further evidence on the quality of the eastern labour force in Chapter 5.) There are, of course, comparability problems. None the less, the east German workforce is generally recognized as high quality.[8] Even harder to judge are questions surrounding the 'mentality' of easterners and the conformability of their attitudes to a competitive environment. Yet comparisons with westerners are likewise by no means uniformly to the detriment of easterners. On the one hand there might be evidence of 'resignation' in response to the upheavals occasioned by

Unification but, on the other hand, there is also evidence of intense motivation to make up for lost time (apparent, for example, in a study of east German entrepreneurs and managers in Saxony-Anhalt conducted in 1993/94).[9] Finally, survey evidence shows skilled labour to be a major reason for investment in the east (JG 1991, p. 75; and *Treuhand Informationen*, September 1991, p. 1).

Taken together, there were powerful incentives to invest in eastern Germany. However, because virtually all the land and capital stock had been state property in the DDR, investment was inextricably linked with privatization. Accordingly, the rest of this chapter focuses on the work of the privatization agency, the Treuhandanstalt.

4.2 THE TREUHANDANSTALT: ORIGINS, OBJECTIVES AND ACHIEVEMENTS

The essence of eastern Germany's impending transition from planned economy to capitalism was specified in the State Treaty: 'Economic activity should primarily occur in the private sector and on the basis of competition' (Treaty of 18 May 1990, 1990, p. 93). This aim was to be secured by appropriate conditions for founding and expanding businesses. But first came the immediate precondition of selling state-owned enterprises to private owners. This chapter outlines the achievements of the Treuhand – the privatization agency – together with some of the associated controversies.[10]

The Treuhandanstalt (THA) – generally known as the Treuhand – was established in March 1990 as one of the final acts of the old regime. A belated attempt at reform, the THA was a trust agency for the management of state property, charged not with privatizing but with decentralizing the economy by allowing enterprises greater independence. However, in June 1990 the DDR's elected Christian Democratic government enacted the Treuhand Act that redefined the objectives of the THA as privatizing and restructuring the economy. This Act was incorporated into the Union Treaty with the Federal Republic and, hence, upon Unification, into Federal law. The Management Board of the THA was appointed by the Federal government and subject to the supervision of the Federal Ministry of Finance. In relation to the enterprises under its authority, the THA had the power of a Supervisory Board and thus had operational independence with respect to reorganizing enterprises according to market principles and their transfer to private ownership.[11]

The THA's wide-ranging objectives and autonomy made it the central institution in the transformation process. Its subsequent achievements are remarkable in three ways:

1. the speed with which the THA was built up and run down – a transitional institution of a new kind, which fulfilled the objective of rapid privatization and dissolved itself within five years (the THA was wound up on 31 December 1994);
2. the scale and complexity of its operations – the privatization and restructuring of an entire economy; and,
3. creating the institution and carrying out these tasks when previous privatization offered little guidance – with respect either to institution building or to the unique conditions of privatization in eastern Germany.

The scale and scope of privatization were enormous. State-owned enterprises accounted for 88 per cent of net output in 1988 (with cooperatives accounting for a further 8.4 percent) (Hofmann and Stingl 1990, pp. 43–4). The THA gained charge of almost 90 per cent of the DDR's productive capacity – including 126 centrally and 95 municipally directed *Kombinate* (industrial groupings) and 57 per cent of the land area – and employed up to half of its labour force. In comparison, privatization by the governments of Mrs Thatcher amounted to marginal adjustment: two terms of office (1979–87) reduced the proportion of GDP accounted for by state-owned enterprises from 11.5 per cent to 7.5 per cent and transferred, in the process, about 500,000 employees to the private sector (Vickers and Yarrow 1988, p. 1). Moreover, in the DDR there were no firms in the sense of autonomous producers operating in free markets: 'There were only administrative units in a hierarchically organized and centrally planned production system' (Hax 1991, p. 3). Accordingly, the task of the Treuhand was not just to transfer existing firms into private ownership – as in the West – but to bring firms into existence.

Table 4.1 gives a summary of THA activity together with its employment and financial outcomes. (Some of the data refers to 30 September and some to 31 December 1994, so components may not sum to totals.)

Prior to the THA, the Modrow government privatized about 30,000 small – mainly retail – businesses. Under the THA, the first and easiest stage of its work had been mainly completed by the end of 1990: lucrative sectors sheltered from international competition – including savings banks, insurance, energy and hotels – were taken over by west German firms. Here, the THA was not required to undertake significant reorganization of enterprises (Hickel and Priewe 1994, pp. 58–9). Indeed, the minimal THA role in these early large-scale privatizations was criticized for not having ensured a competitive bidding process. Other THA responsibilities included

- agricultural land – but this 'will need another decade for resolution, partly because of the complexity of restitution claims' (Kaser 1995, p.1); and

Table 4.1   Impact of the Treuhand, 1990–1994

		June 1990	By the end of 1994
1.	Number of enterprises (initial portfolio of 8,000 + enterprises newly created by THA)	8,000 (13,781 by 1992)	
2.	Number of establishments	40,000	
3.	Enterprises dissolved through merger or break-up; or otherwise excluded from the initial portfolio		1,418
4.	Contracts completed by THA and successor institutions		c. 50,000
5.	Outcome for 12,363 enterprises in THA portfolio[*]		
	a. privatization		6,464
	b. reprivatization (restitution)		1,571
	c. in liquidation		3,661
	d. remaining with THA (transferred to successor institutions after 31/12/94)		354 (192)
6.	Number of workers employed in Treuhand/ former-Treuhand companies (and employment promises by new owners)	4.1 million	930,000 (1.5 million, including employment promises)
7.	Proportion of total east German workforce (with and without employment promises by new owners)	45 per cent	Assuming a one-third decline in the size of the workforce: 15 per cent; 25 per cent (including employment promises)
8.	Investment undertakings by new owners (carried out mainly 1994–99)		DM 211 bn (including DM 130 bn contractually enforceable[*])
9.	Privatization revenue		DM 65 bn[*]
10.	Cumulative debt of THA, including		
	a. enterprise debts (initial debts + interest payments of DM 26 bn)	Initial debts: DM 75 billion	DM 101 bn
	b. enterprise restructuring		DM 154 bn
	c. environmental clean-up		DM 44 bn
	Total debt (allowing for privatization revenue)		DM 230 bn
11.	Anticipated borrowing of successor institutions		DM 45 bn (anticipated by 2000)
12.	Total debt by 2000		DM 275 bn

Note: * Data as of 30 September 1994.

Sources: Härtel (1994, p. 600); JG (1994, pp. 84–5; 1995, p. 88); and Zwölfte Bericht (1995, p. 80).

- 'communalization' – the transfer to municipal authorities of utilities and infrastructural facilities (for example, harbours, airports, water and sewage) as well as assets previously controlled by enterprises but now needed to fulfil municipal responsibilities (for example, sports and child-care facilities) (THA 1993, p. 15).

In this chapter, however, we are concerned with the hardest task of the THA: namely, restructuring and privatizing larger state-owned manufacturing and mining enterprises exposed to international competition.

The DDR's *Kombinate* were inefficient state monopolies and most could not be privatized directly. First, they were split up into legally independent enterprises with scope and structure congruent with west German enterprises (see Table 4.1, Rows 1, 2 and 3). This reduced horizontal and vertical integration and created smaller firms designed to 'make sense' to western investors. To decentralize decision-making and assist in the assimilation to German business culture of east German enterprises, the THA created Supervisory Boards for all enterprises with more than 500 employees and, generally, had them chaired by and including one or two other members from the west German business community (see Table 4.5) (Carlin 1993, p. 14). These were then helped to prepare business plans and 'opening balance sheets' in DM that were used to assess enterprises according to a scale ranging from profitable (hence suitable for rapid privatization) through potentially profitable (hence requiring restructuring before privatization) to no prospect of becoming profitable (hence requiring liquidation). Initial assessments suggested that up to 70 per cent of enterprises were at least potentially viable – some as a whole but many only in part and with a fraction of existing employment – and up to 30 per cent would have to be closed (Owen-Smith 1994, pp. 479–80 and Carlin and Mayer 1992, pp. 329–30).[12]

The main method of privatization was sale not to the highest bidder but to investors competent to make THA firms internationally competitive at relatively high wage rates. Overwhelmingly, this meant sale to west German firms with the necessary managerial and technological capability, marketing expertise and access to finance. As the most attractive firms were sold, the THA maintained the momentum of privatization by continuing the process of splitting up and hiving off so that, increasingly, it was able to attract buyers for particular establishments rather than complete enterprises (Härtel et al. 1995, pp. 150–51). Initial restructuring, and a continuous process thereafter of splitting up and hiving off, created a rising number of THA enterprises (see Table 4.1, Row 1 and Table 1.3) that could be sold either as legal entities or in 'asset deals' (Carlin 1993, p. 7). Indeed, Bischof et al. (1993, p. 143) concluded from case study evidence that the THA offered for sale not established firms – as in western privatizations – but 'combinations of physical assets, human capital and cash in exchange for management/organizational capabilities, technology and markets'. More than half of all THA sales did not concern complete enterprises (Härtel et al. 1995, p. 119): it is this which accounts for the large number of privatizations and, in part, privatization contracts (see Table 4.1, Rows 4 and 5).

4.3 PRIVATIZATION AND EMPLOYMENT

Privatization in eastern Germany could not proceed according to the experience of developed market economies. Owen-Smith (1994, p. 482) observed that in a market economy without distortions, 'the Treuhand would maximize social welfare by maximizing the proceeds from privatization'. Yet, compared to even the mixed economies of western Europe, the post-socialist economy was distorted in almost every conceivable way. Above all, 'wages were far above market clearing rates' (Owen-Smith 1994, p. 482). Wages were so far out of line with productivity that, within a year of GEMSU, 90 per cent of the industrial workforce were employed in enterprises whose revenue was unable to cover variable (that is, operating) costs (Akerloff et al. 1991, p. 27). Consequently, and different from privatization programmes in developed market economies, the major objective of the THA was not to maximize revenue but to promote employment. According to Dickertmann and Gelbhaar, as early as 1990 the Federal Ministry of Finance was inclined to maximize privatization revenue but was opposed by the THA, which also stressed structural and employment aims (1994, p. 317).

The THA's emphasis on employment was legally anchored in the Preamble to the Treuhand Act, which specified not only the aim of 'privatization as rapidly and widespread as possible' but also the aim of 'creating the maximum number of competitive enterprises, thereby securing jobs and creating new ones' (quoted in Härtel et al. 1995, p. 139). Accordingly, the THA promoted employment in two ways: by subsidy and by conditions of sale.

1. Most enterprises, even those judged potentially viable, required subsidy: first to secure liquidity and, second, to restructure and prepare firms for privatization.[13] Included in more than DM 150 bn of expenditure on enterprise restructuring (see Table 4.1, Row 10) were contributions to capital resources (enabling firms to maintain liquidity), the offsetting of losses, loans and loan guarantees, investment subsidies, payments to cover the costs of 'social plans' (required by law in the case of closure and/or redundancies), and the costs of privatization or closure (for

example, assuming responsibility for the liabilities of enterprises, payment of employment subsidies to purchasers, and so on) (JG 1995, p. 88). Together with DM 44 bn of expenditure on environmental clean-up, these huge subsidies enabled firms that otherwise would have been bankrupted to survive, to be restructured and, eventually, privatized.[14]

2. Privatization contracts typically traded off sales revenue for undertakings on employment and investment (which, in the long run, secures increased productivity and high-wage jobs).[15] These provisions secured 1.5 million jobs and over DM 200 bn of investment (see Table 4.1, Rows 6, 7 and 8). So far, less than one-tenth of these obligations have not been honoured. However, such shortfalls have been more than compensated by over-fulfilment elsewhere: in 1994, in line with previous years, promised investment was exceeded by 40 per cent and employment by one-sixth (JG 1995, p. 88).[16]

With 90 per cent or so of industrial workers in loss-making enterprises, continued employment on any significant scale depended on subsidy. The initial THA valuation of its portfolio was DM 1365 bn. Shortly before GEMSU, this was reduced to DM 600 bn (Carlin 1993, p. 5). Yet this still proved utterly unrealistic: with DM balance sheets, prevailing levels of productivity and wages dictated that in aggregate the productive apparatus of the DDR had a *negative* value from the point of view of profit-orientated production in an open market economy. Consequently, privatization revenues were little more than one-tenth of the sum initially anticipated and constituted only a partial offset to subsidies of about DM 350 bn (see Table 4.1, Rows 9–12). Without THA employment subsidies, the haemorrhage of jobs would have been even greater. Carlin explained THA policy as follows:

> Employment subsidies have been a key component of the sales strategy. Investors have been given a discount on the sales price of the enterprise according to the number of jobs guaranteed by the investor. In some cases, the price becomes negative (that is, the investor receives the enterprise plus a grant). The basic rule of thumb is: ensure that the investment per head will be sufficient to make the enterprise competitive (assuming West German wages within 3–5 years), then give a discount on the current asset value based on the number of jobs guaranteed. There was no centrally determined scale of subsidies used in negotiations, but subsidies varied according to the availability of alternative job opportunities in the area and the external effects of employment in the firm in supporting employment elsewhere. For example, in the sales associated with one Kombinat, discounts per job guaranteed varied from DM 10,000 for an enterprise on the outskirts of Berlin to DM 80,000 for one near the Polish border ... in industries identified as of strategic importance ... or subject to particular political pressure ... larger subsidies were provided (over DM 250,000 per job guaranteed in microelectronics ...). (1993, p. 18)

By securing investment undertakings and providing employment subsidies the THA secured high-wage, high-productivity jobs. Ironically, to do so it had to eliminate the high-wage, low-productivity jobs that GEMSU and its aftermath had inflicted on the THA. Restructuring had to be undertaken by the THA before privatization, because for the private sector the risks were too great. In particular, western firms were unwilling to undertake the full burden of mass redundancies. For west German firms, the risk of conflict with works councils and unions made likely adverse reputational effects and a consequent threat to implicit contracts and consensual relations with their western employees.

4.4 RESTRUCTURING ENTERPRISES AND STRUCTURAL POLICY

The scale of subsidy meant that the role of the THA went far beyond the search for appropriate buyers and the negotiation of the most favourable terms of sale. Ironically, to secure future high-wage employment and investment (hence, the security of employment in the long run), the THA had to begin the process of shedding labour and restructuring in order to prepare enterprises for privatization (JG 1995, p. 88). This exposed the THA to simultaneous and opposing criticism: namely, for too much and too little subsidy and restructuring activity.

From the outset, the THA was active in restructuring the enterprises in its portfolio:

- by creating independent firms with supervisory boards according to the west German model;
- by the financial restructuring through which subsidies brought asset and liability structures into line with similar west German firms (Carlin and Mayer 1992, p. 329); and
- by negotiating investment and employment guarantees with buyers.

Controversy centred on the THA role in 'strategic restructuring':

- 'the reorientation of an enterprise toward new markets requiring major investment in fixed capital and the development of new products' (Carlin 1993, p. 19).

At issue was the extent to which the THA should undertake strategic restructuring in preparation for privatization.

Collapsed competitiveness and loss of markets did not occur evenly across sectors but varied inversely with their degree of openness: the more goods were subject to interregional or international trade, the greater the loss of output and employment (Klodt 1994, pp. 323 and 329–30). The shrinking of the traded goods sector was at its most severe in the first year of GEMSU when the value of manufacturing output fell by 70 per cent (Klodt 1994, p. 323). This was reflected in the pattern of privatization. Privatization was most rapid in construction, services and trade while, by October 1991, manufacturing accounted for nearly two-thirds of jobs remaining in THA firms (with machine building alone accounting for over 15 percent) (Carlin and Mayer 1992, p. 333). Moreover, the more open a sector to international trade, the less interested were buyers in taking over the whole rather than particular parts of THA firms (Härtel et al. 1995, p. 119).

Machine building gives an example of THA restructuring and employment reduction in a sector where goods are traded internationally under competitive conditions.[17] Before GEMSU, machine building was a traditional and distinctive competence of both East and West Germany. Even at the beginning of 1991, in eastern Germany 20 per cent of all manufacturing workers were employed in machine building compared to 15 per cent in western Germany. However, major restructuring was necessary before eastern enterprises could be sold to western firms. First, because the structure of the eastern and western industries were different: the former concentrated on mass production of standardized products in large plants whereas, typically, the latter consisted of medium-size firms specializing in highly developed, often customized, special-purpose machines. Consequently, eastern enterprises were typically several times larger and thus too large for western firms to absorb. Second, because western machines were sold in demanding and intensely competitive western markets, whereas eastern machines had occupied an unchallenged position in COMECON countries. GEMSU revealed the competitive weaknesses of the eastern industry: obsolete, hence low-quality products (especially the lagging introduction of microelectronic components); obsolete process technology, hence low productivity, high costs and low quality; lack of experience and knowledge of western markets; and lack of experience and knowledge of east German machines by western customers. In addition, because investment goods require long-term service arrangements, customers assumed additional risk by purchasing from a THA firm that might not survive. Table 4.2 shows the result of THA activity in privatizing firms, returning firms to previous owners (restitution) and liquidation together with the impact of restructuring on employment.

The reduction of employment – in excess of 70 per cent – took place not only through liquidation but also through the restructuring of enterprises that were eventually privatized. Table 4.3 uses three examples of machine-

Table 4.2   Result of Treuhand activity in the machine-building industry, at 30 September 1994

Maximum number of enterprises in THA portfolio	Privatized	Reprivatized (restitution)	In liquidation	Remaining with THA *		Employment (number of workers in enterprises with more than 20 workers)	
				Total	Under offer	Beginning 1991	End 1992
1114	621	128	316	47	34	350,000	100,000

Note: * Transferred to successor institutions after 31 December 1994.

Sources: JG (1994, p. 84) and Härtel and Krüger (1995, p. 304).

Table 4.3   Examples of restructuring for privatization

	Employees	Turnover (DM bn)	Original number of establishments in *Kombinat*	Total subsidy (by Sept. 1993)	New firms created by initial splitting up of *Kombinat* holdings	
					From core activities	From periph-eral activities
SKET	1990: 17,000	1990: 0.6		DM 1 bn		
	1993: 5,000	1993: 0.27	29		2	4
TAKRAF	1990: 31,000	1990: 2.8		na		
	1992: 3,000	1992: 0.42	27		6	5
BAUKEMA	1990: 16,000 (including 4,000 in non-business-related activities; e.g., housing, childcare, and medical centres) 1992: 2,500				19 (number of firms privatized by mid-1992)	

Sources: JG (1993, p. 91); Härtel et al. (1995, pp. 308–11); and Bischof et al. (1993, pp. 129–36).

building *Kombinate* to show how privatization entailed restructured by splitting up enterprises into core and peripheral firms that could be sold separately as well as through mass redundancy. The first two examples – SKET (*Schwermaschinenbaukombinat* Ernst Thälmann producing cranes, cable and a variety of heavy machinery) and the TAKRAF *Kombinat* (also producing cranes and a variety of heavy machinery) detail changes before privatization took place. The third – the BAUKEMA *Kombinat* (encompassing multiple enterprises, some of which produced heavy machinery) – shows the situation after privatization.

In the absence of buyers for THA firms in the traded goods sector, there was intense political pressure on the THA to undertake the complete strategic restructuring of enterprises. The collapse of manufacturing threatened to deindustrialize and deprive eastern Germany of an export base altogether. Moreover, because of the industrial monoculture and overdevelopment of manufacturing under the old regime, deindustrialization threatened to remove the employment of whole regions and, thereby, generate enormous social costs.[18] Table 4.4 illustrates this point with data on the concentration of employment in two eastern *Länder* in manufacturing and particular manufacturing industries.

Table 4.4   Examples of employment concentration in eastern Länder (thousands employed)

	Year	Saxony-Anhalt	Saxony
Manufacturing industry	1991	328	569
	1992	188	291
Chemical industry	1991	75	16
	1992	42	10
Machine building	1991	77	126
	1992	38	67

Source: Härtel et al. (1995, p. 144).

Consequently, *complete strategic restructuring of manufacturing enterprises would have amounted to a THA-led regional or industrial policy for eastern Germany.*[19] The THA was to move only part of the way towards complete strategic restructuring.

The THA began strategic restructuring. The splitting up of *Kombinate* into enterprises with supervisory boards led by members seconded from west German banks and industrial firms provided business contacts and expertise (see Table 4.5). Together with several thousand western managers in functional roles (Härtel et al. 1995, p. 176), this helped reorientation towards western markets by giving advice on access and developing more acceptable products. Moreover, even in manufacturing the THA secured more than DM 50 bn of contractually enforceable investment guarantees (nearly 40 per cent of total legally enforceable investment; seeTable 4.1, Row 8) (Zwölfte Bericht, 1995, p. 80).

There were economic arguments for active restructuring. First, as we have noted in relation to the employment consequences of restructuring, because for the private sector the risks were too great. Second, there were social costs of closure – and, hence, benefits of restructuring and maintaining THA firms – which would not be taken into account by private investors. In particular, in regions of concentrated industrial activity, these included the costs of unemployment, retraining, and mobility and the loss of agglomeration benefits (Härtel et al. 1995, pp. 141–2 and 148). However, it was political pressure that tended to push the THA from a policy of using subsidy as the incentive for private investors to maintain a socially optimal level of activity in privatized firms towards a regional or industrial policy conducted through the active restructuring of firms still under THA control.

The THA at first resisted pressure to increase the level of active restructuring. For several reasons, the THA was reluctant either to subsidize indefinitely employment in its own enterprises (as had been the case in many declining west German industries) or *itself* to undertake the scale of investment needed to transform both process technology and products to the extent necessary to secure high-wage, high-productivity jobs (Carlin 1993, pp. 19–29 and Zwölfte Bericht, 1995, p. 77–8).

1. The THA privatization strategy was predicated on sale to entrepreneurs who had the experience and knowledge of markets to be able to develop a business plan and take the risk of investing to realize the plan. In the restructuring of THA enterprises, the binding constraint was 'special expertise or, more precisely, suitable experts who as far as possible also commit capital' (Schenk 1994, p. 175). For the THA to have substituted itself for experienced entrepreneurs would have been to exceed its limited entrepreneurial and managerial capacity as well as to divorce investment decisions from risk-taking. This would have established an inefficient system for allocating investment finance similar to that of the planned economy it was the task of the THA to dismantle.

2. As a holding company, for the THA to have undertaken the complete strategic restructuring of its enterprises would have been to rediscover many of the problems of a planned economy. In particular, the THA management would have been dependent on enterprise management for information. Consequently, it would have been difficult for THA management to assess restructuring plans or monitor their implementation. For decades, a similar 'information asymmetry' had been an intractable problem for the DDR's planning authorities. In particular, it proved a continual source of inefficiency in the allocation of investment finance.

3. Structural or industrial policy is the task of federal and state governments and not that of a transitional institution with a specific mission.

Pressure to enlarge the active economic role of the THA arose, in part, because the 'restructuring' part of the THA mission had not been tightly defined. Even in the Treuhand Law, there was an ambivalence between the THA role 'to privatize' and its role 'to promote the structural adjustment of the economy' (Siebert 1991a, p. 26). Soon, the fundamental issue of the appropriate balance of market forces and structural policy in the privatization process became the subject of academic and political dispute. Initially, even the BRD's Council of Economic Experts accepted that the process of privatization would be of long duration and that, therefore, it could be necessary 'in some sectors for the state to remain active as entrepreneur' (JG 1990, p. 279). In April 1991, however, the Council published a special study dedicated to 'holding the market-economy line' (JG 1991, p. 251). According to this, enterprises were to be judged by market criteria. Those judged by the market as viable would be privatized. Conversely, those which could not be privatized were to be judged as 'not worth continuing with' (JG 1991, p. 258). The tension between a totally free market policy (restructuring through privatization) and an active structural policy (supporting and restructuring enterprises before privatizing) was evident in debate over the role of the Treuhand.

The THA assumed the role of entrepreneur and participated in structural policy – in the sense of industrial or regional policy – in an *ad hoc* manner in response to mounting unemployment and political pressure.[20] By mid-1991, almost three million east Germans were unemployed or on short-time working. This was the context for the *Gemeinschaftswerk Aufschwung Ost* (common undertaking for recovery in the east) supported by Federal and State government, employers' associations and unions. This increased public funds for rebuilding eastern infrastructure and committed the THA to greater coordination with Federal and *Land* governments (Hickel and Priewe 1994, pp. 60–61). In particular, this increased the influence of eastern *Land* governments in THA decision making which, in turn, obliged the THA 'to take account of the employment and regional development consequences of its privatization activities' (Carlin, 1993, p. 25). The THA continued with passive restructuring – that is, subsidies to keep firms from bankruptcy, assistance with management functions such as marketing, but only minimal investment – and employment subsidies to new owners. But now, in addition, it responded to political pressure with more active restructuring. 'Policies for industries (and given the structure of GDR economic development) often also for regions... The chemical industry was the first to be openly identified as needing a "plan" in order to ensure its survival' (Carlin 1993, p. 25). However, the THA was still reluctant to undertake the restructuring of entire industries: for example, even though microelectronics had been identified by the Federal government as a 'sector which would be retained', the THA was not willing to manage the restructuring of an industry located in at least three of the *Länder*: this was viewed a matter for the Federal and *Land* governments (Carlin 1993, p. 25 and Bischof et al. 1993, pp. 136–41).

None the less, from mid-1992, amid growing fear of deindustrialization in the east, the Federal government supported a role for the THA, with financial support from *Land* governments, in maintaining 'industrial cores'. Although these were never precisely defined, this new policy meant that, finally, the THA had to function as entrepreneur for hard-to-privatize firms rather than schedule them for closure. In particular, this more active approach to restructuring meant agreeing investment plans for 500 firms (Hickel and Priewe 1994, pp. 60–61). Essentially, the policy was to create cooperative ventures in which *Land* governments and the THA identified THA firms that had too great a regional and – given regional concentration – industrial significance to close. For these, therefore, the THA undertook strategic restructuring with financial support from the *Land* governments (Carlin 1993, p. 26 and Hickel and Priewe 1994, pp. 60–66). Accordingly, investment per employee in THA firms rose from DM 4,640 in 1991 and DM 7,104 in 1992 to DM 15,200 in 1993 (although this remained well below the level per employee in privatized firms) (Hickel and Priewe 1994, p. 62).

4.5 A 'SOLD ECONOMY'?

This angry phrase sums up one line of criticism of the THA. It corresponds to the feeling that eastern Germany has virtually been colonized. Aspects of the THA's strategy fed this feeling.

First, Table 4.5 demonstrates the dominance of west Germans in the Supervisory Boards established for THA firms. This secured a channel for the transfer of 'know-how' but at the price of eastern self-determination. The recruitment of west Germans to senior management amplified the sense of exclusion.

Table 4.5   Composition of THA-enterprise supervisory boards (origin of members in per cent)

	Western firms (mainly West German)	West German banks	State institutions
Autumn 1991	60–70 (including 80% of chairmen)	20–25	10–15
	West Germany	East Germany	Non-German
Early 1992	90	9	2

Source: Härtel et al. (1995, p. 175).

Second, a downside of the THA's 'top-down' method of privatization was that it created mainly subsidiaries of west German companies. THA sales criteria tended to exclude east Germans, because they lacked appropriate management expertise, access to western markets and technology and, above all, finance (Carlin 1993, p. 21). Moreover, in spite of THA efforts to attract foreign investors, only 855 enterprises in whole or in part were sold to non-German firms, generating sales revenue of DM 6.2 bn and accounting for 150,000 job guarantees together with investment guarantees of DM 22 bn (JG 1994, p. 85). By comparing these figures with Table 4.1, Rows 9, 6 and 8, we can conclude that non-German firms – mainly from the European Union – accounted for around 10 per cent of privatization activity.

Finally, we should mention the creation of an east German *Mittelstand* as another aim of the THA. Although restitution made some contribution to this aim (see Table 4.1, Row 5), THA sales to east German buyers were largely limited to the early, small-scale privatizations and management buy-outs (MBOs) (Carlin 1993, p. 22; and Carlin and Mayer 1992, pp. 330 and 332). At the early stage of Unification, MBOs were regarded as a promising method for developing a new entrepreneurial culture in eastern Germany. At first sight, data on MBOs look appealing. By 1995, nearly 88 per cent of all MBOs established in 1990 were still in existence (Barjek et al. 1996). However, recent survey evidence indicates that a number of MBO features in eastern Germany did not meet firms' expectations. For example, in spite of the initial potential attributed to a transfer of know-how from western to eastern managers, only a minority of MBOs had been reassured with regard to sales and employment security (Barjak and Skopp 1996).

East Germany has thus been assimilated to German capitalism but lacks a substantial capitalist class. On the other hand, east Germans have been compensated for deindustrialization and high levels of unemployment by annual subsidies of about DM 200 bn. These permit levels of consumption – even for the unemployed, prematurely retired, and so on – and investment far in excess of what could have been achieved in an independent state.[21]

4.6 CONCLUDING COMMENTS

The THA was a transitional institution in two senses. As the temporary owner of former state-owned firms its success in rapid privatization of its holdings enabled first its own dissolution and, second, the completion of eastern Germany's transition from socialism to capitalism. Eastern Germany's economic problems are now those not of transition but more those of a relatively backward region in a developed market economy.

Scapegoating the THA misses the point that extensive deindustrialization and job losses were the result of 40 years of command economy and the terms of GEMSU. These constituted the ultimate and proximate causes of economic collapse rather than four-and-a-half years of the THA. In hindsight, better terms of privatization (especially in the first wave in 1990), more rigorous employment and investment guarantees, and more active restructuring might have improved the employment and investment outcome. However, it is hard to believe that the difference would have been fundamental. Hickel and Priewe – consistent critics of the THA – complain that 'nobody wanted ... to take over full entrepreneurial responsibility' (1994, p. 65). Yet Hickel and Priewe – who also criticize the extent of THA debt – do not explain why the THA could have had entrepreneurial success where it was not anticipated by risk-taking investors. Indeed, orthodox economists warned that active restructuring and industrial policy was a scenario for indefinite subsidies to firms for which lack of buyers provided a market-based proof of their unsuitability for restructuring.

The appendix analyses investment under conditions of uncertainty in order to extend the discussion of policy design, and concludes by identifying policy priorities for promoting investment and convergence.

NOTES

1. This calculation allows for neither depreciation nor reinvestment by eastern subsidiaries of western firms. The latter counts as inward investment and became increasingly important as privatization transformed eastern producers into subsidiaries of, in the main, west German firms. In so far as reinvestment outweighs depreciation – a minimal criterion for self-sustaining development – an increasing proportion of private sector investment will be generated from retained earnings.
2. Unit labour costs are calculated as the ratio of money wages per unit of time to output per unit of time (that is, labour productivity).
3. 'Probably the largest problem facing the Treuhand concerns property rights' (Treuhandanstalt 1991, p. 9).
4. Anecdotal illustrations of obsolete infrastructure abound: for example, parts of the Potsdam telephone system had not been renewed since 1922, while in parts of East Berlin the last major refit was for the 1936 Olympic games. After GEMSU, it took two years to renew telephone communications between east and west Berlin.
5. Scale economies internal to the individual firm may be less important than external economies. If only the former mattered, then relatively small factor price advantages might persuade west German firms to relocate. However, there are also agglomeration advantages – for example, availability of appropriately skilled labour, transfers of knowledge and know-how arising from personal contacts, and so on – which are external to the individual firm. These advantages arise from the concentration of similar firms in specialized industrial districts. The more important these external economies, the larger the factor price incentives necessary to persuade firms to invest in other locations.
6. No further attempt is made to describe the system of investment incentives. This is a specialist task. By the mid-1990s, there were more than 700 sources of investment subsidy: the Economics Ministry has issued a 400-page book describing the *main* funds, while the Treuhandanstalt has a software package to optimize incentives packages for investors. Personal communication by Mark Herzog at the Institute for German Studies Conference on 'The new *Länder* in locational competition' (June 1996).
7. These comments draw upon remarks of Dr Wolfram Fischer in his talk on 'Economic success factors in East Germany' at the Institute for German Studies Conference on 'The new *Länder* in locational competition' (June 1996).

8. According to Priewe and Hickel (1991, pp. 70–71), the proportion of the workforce without any vocational qualification is lower in the east (5.4 per cent) than in the west (16.1 per cent), while the proportions with qualifications at either the basic vocational level or coveted master craftsman level (or, equivalently, technical school graduation) in the east (61 per cent and 23.3 per cent) are higher than in the west (53.6 per cent and 16.7 per cent). Owen-Smith cites evidence that 'east Germans who migrated or commuted to western Germany ... appeared to earn a comparable return to their education as native west Germans' (1994, p. 265; see also pp. 267 and 272).

9. Personal communication by Mark Herzog about his own survey work, at the Institute for German Studies Conference on 'The new *Länder* in locational competition' (June 1996).

10. For further English-language sources on the THA, see Owen-Smith (1994, pp. 475–90); Carlin (1993); Carlin and Mayer (1992); and Bischof et al. (1993). This section draws on all of these. The most detailed and authoritative English-language source is Fischer et al. (1996).

11. Supervisory Boards are senior in German corporate governance and thus decide strategy.

12. Compare the earlier estimates reported in Chapter 1, note 4.

13. Losses of THA enterprises typically averaged up to one-fifth of turnover (Carlin 1993, p. 3 and JG 1994, p. 85).

14. From the beginning, the THA used liquidity credits to protect firms from the West German bankruptcy code which, with only minor amendments, was applied to eastern Germany: 'A total of DM 20 bn in liquidity credit was handed out in the first three months after currency union merely to ensure that the companies could pay their wages' (THA, no date, p. 9). In this way, the full rigour of hard-budget constraints was ameliorated. Consequently, as Carlin and Mayer argue (1995, p. 445): 'Just 11 percent of Treuhand closures can be accounted for by formal bankruptcies. The reason for this is clear. Liquidations allow the Treuhand to retain control of the closure process while formal bankruptcies transfer control to the courts ... The Treuhand was thereby able to impose its employment and investment criteria which would have been subsumed under creditor considerations in a formal bankruptcy.'

15. Typically, sales took place at less than asset value in return for guarantees on the number of jobs to be maintained and the value of future investment. In some cases, particularly when investors assumed current debts or environmental burdens, the THA accepted symbolic payment of DM 1 or handed over the enterprise with a subsidy.

16. Monitoring the implementation of privatization contracts with respect to undertakings on jobs and investment is now undertaken by one of the THA's successor institutions.

17. The main source of the following on machine building is Härtel et al. 1995, pp. 300–312.

18. In the DDR, the planning authorities attempted to increase productivity by concentration and specialization (that is, each item was to be produced by one enterprise).

19. According to Begg and Mayes (1994, p. 4) 'industrial policy' includes 'direct intervention to support emergent or declining sectors; help for innovation, diffusion of new technology or R&D; capital subsidies; sector strategies; and direct public production'. Because of the regional concentration of industry in eastern Germany, industrial policy and regional policy substantially overlap.

20. 'The new *Länder* governments predictably became the most vocal advocates of an eastern *Industriepolitik* – a term which meant preserving firms with a regional significance ... Because of the rising unemployment in east Germany the discussion became increasingly political' (Owen-Smith 1994, pp. 482–3).

21. Although, in terms of assets, east Germans are much poorer than west Germans. In comparison with east German incomes and consumption of 70 per cent or more of western levels, the average value of assets owned by eastern households is typically estimated at only 20 per cent of the western level.

APPENDIX 4A THEORETICAL NOTES ON INVESTMENT IN THE TRANSFORMATION PROCESS: POLICIES TO INCREASE INVESTMENT UNDER CONDITIONS OF IRREVERSIBILITY AND UNCERTAINTY

The purpose of this appendix is to apply the insights of the new investment theory associated with Avinash Dixit to investment problems in transitional economies.[1] A particular feature of this work is the analysis of investment decisions in situations that combine irreversibility and ongoing uncertainty. Accordingly, Dixit's work constitutes a particularly appropriate framework for policy-orientated analysis of investment in the transformation process.

The main insight is that when investments are irreversible and taken under conditions of uncertainty the optimum strategy can be for firms to 'wait and see': that is, to delay investment. The following explains the principles involved in the theory and then pursues the argument by means of a numerical example.

4A.1 Investment under Uncertainty: Explicit and Shadow Sunk Costs

There are two essential features of the analysis.

1. Investment is irreversible and there is no scrap value: that is, investment entails *sunk costs*. To the extent that labour market regulations or union power make employment decisions irreversible, Dixit's approach can be applied not only to capital investment but also to employment decisions.
2. The outcome of investment depends on the *future* business environment. Accordingly, the outcome of current investment decisions is *uncertain*.

With sunk costs and conditions of uncertainty, firms' investment decisions are prone to inertia: that is, firms will adopt a 'wait-and-see' strategy. By adopting a wait-and-see strategy, firms can avoid an investment should business conditions turn out to be adverse, while maintaining the possibility of investing should conditions turn out to be favourable. By waiting, firms can gather more information and thus increase the net present value of irreversible investments. This means that a wait-and-see strategy has an option value: in effect, the firm owns an option to invest in the future. An 'invest now' strategy entails the cost of exercising this option. Consequently, *uncertainty in the investment environment attaches an option value to the possibility of waiting and thus adds to the sunk costs of investment.* Moreover, the greater the degree of uncertainty over future business conditions, the greater the losses that can be avoided by a wait-and-see strategy: hence, the greater the degree of uncertainty the greater the value of the option. Accordingly, the cost of investment to a firm under conditions of uncertainty can be thought of as having two components: (1) explicit fixed costs, and (2) the shadow fixed cost of exercising its option to invest.

The net present value of a mooted investment will be positive – and thus the project will proceed – only if the present value of anticipated profits exceeds the total cost of *both* the explicit *and* the shadow costs of the investment. Consequently, because this shadow fixed cost increases with uncertainty, the greater the uncertainty the greater the cost of 'investing now' and the greater the benefit of a wait-and-see strategy. The firm will 'invest now' only when the cost of earnings forgone by not investing exceeds the benefit of waiting for favourable conditions.

4A.2 A Hypothetical Numerical Example

A representative firm has DM 1,000 to invest. It has an investment horizon of 10 years. It must choose one of two investment strategies: *either* to *invest now* in eastern Germany *or* to *wait* for one year until the business environment is known with certainty.[2] If it chooses the wait-and-see strategy then, at the beginning of Year 2, the firm must make another choice: in the case of a favourable environment in eastern Germany the firm invests there, but in the case of an unfavourable environment in eastern Germany the firm undertakes a marginal investment in western Germany (that is, one with a net present value of zero). We are interested only in the *relatively* greater uncertainty of investment in eastern Germany: hence we assume that investment in western Germany occurs under conditions of certainty.

The firm is risk neutral (and hence maximizes the expected present value of profit), and discounts future earnings at an annual rate of 10 per cent. To guide its investment decisions, the firm calculates the net present value of anticipated cash flows for each of the two investment strategies (1) *invest now*, or (2) *wait and see* until the beginning of Year 2 (when the business environment will be known with certainty), and for each of two equi-probable scenarios (that is, the probability (p) = 0.5 in both cases): (1) the business environment proves to be *favourable* (F); and (2) the business environment proves to be *unfavourable* (U).

In the '*invest now*' strategy, the firm invests immediately and receives profit at the end of each year.

- In the event of the business environment in eastern Germany turning out to be *favourable*, the firm will earn DM 400 in each of the 10 years of the project's life. (The high rate of return on invested capital reflects the policy of investment subsidies that, in effect, multiply private commitments into larger investments.)

- In the event of the business environment in eastern Germany turning out to be *unfavourable*, the firm still makes DM 100 per annum profit but this is not sufficient to secure a positive net present value from the investment.

In the '*wait-and-see*' strategy, at the end of Year 1/start of Year 2, the firm simultaneously receives DM 100 interest (10 per cent on the uninvested DM 1,000) and invests DM 1,000 (giving a net cash flow of –DM 900 for Year 1).

- If the investment environment has turned out *favourable*, the firm invests in eastern Germany and in each of the years 2–10 earns DM 400.
- If the investment environment has turned out *unfavourable*, the firm invests in western Germany where the net present value of the project within the 10-year horizon is zero for sure.

Table 4A.1 shows the payoffs for each investment strategy.

*Table 4A.1 Payoffs from investment strategies subject to equi-probable favourable and unfavourable outcomes**

Strategy 1: invest now			Strategy 2: wait and see		
	F (p=0.5)	U (p=0.5)		F (p=0.5)	U (p=0.5)
Investment at start of Year 1	–1,000	–1000	Investment at end of Year 1	–900	–900
Years 1–10 Profit	400	100	Years 2–10 Profit	400	156
Net Present Value (NPV)	1,458	–386	Net Present Value (NPV)	1276	0 (NPV in the West)
Expected NPV	536		Expected NPV	638	

Note: * All entries rounded to the nearest whole number.

When decisions have to be made about irreversible investments, uncertainty 'affects such choices by putting a premium on flexibility, and attaching an option value to the possibility of waiting for better information' (Dixit 1993, pp. 56–7). In this example, the cost of exercising the option to invest now is DM 102: that is, the difference between the expected net present value of investing DM 1,000 now (DM 536) and waiting for one year to invest DM 1000 (DM 638).[3] The premium on flexibility, or the option value of waiting for better information, outweighs profit forgone by delaying the investment decision.

This theory helps to explain why investment in the aftermath of Unification was unexpectedly low. Together, uncertainties with respect to ownership, public administration, infrastructure and ecological liability added a shadow sunk cost to the tangible or explicit sunk costs of investment in eastern Germany. This tended to make 'wait and see' the optimum strategy. Accordingly, firms were inclined to delay commitment.

4A.3 Policy Implications

The overriding priority in eastern Germany was to boost investment. In terms of our theoretical framework, significantly increased investment in eastern Germany could be secured only by convincing corporate decision-makers that a favourable outcome was appreciably more likely than an unfavourable outcome. If, instead of these two states being equi-probable in the minds of decision-makers, measures were implemented that changed their subjective probabilities to a 70 per cent chance of a favourable outcome ($p = 0.7$) and a 30 per cent chance of an unfavourable outcome ($p = 0.3$), then the optimum strategy changes to 'invest now'. Table 4A.2 shows how the payoffs are changed when firms have a greater degree of certainty – but not complete certainty – that the future business environment will be favourable.

Table 4A.2 Payoffs from investment strategies when a favourable outcome is more probable than an unfavourable outcome*

Strategy 1: invest now			Strategy 2: wait and see		
	F ($p=0.7$)	U ($p=0.3$)		F ($p=0.7$)	U ($p=0.3$)
Investment at start of Year 1	−1000	−1000	Investment at end of Year 1	−900	−900
Years 1–10 Profit	400	100	Years 2–10 Profit	400	156
Net Present Value (NPV)	1458	−386	Net Present Value (NPV)	1276	0 (NPV in the West)
Expected NPV	905		Expected NPV	893	

Note: * All entries rounded to the nearest whole number.

The only difference between Tables 4A.1 and 4A.2 is the subjective probabilities attached to favourable and unfavourable investment environments in eastern Germany. An increase in confidence about the future balance of obstacles and incentives discussed in Section 4.1.2 means less uncertainty about the future investment environment. Consequently, the expected net present value of investing now (DM 905) exceeds that of delay

(DM 893). Hence, it is no longer optimal for firms to forgo profit in Year 1 in order to wait for better information, in which case they are inclined to 'invest now'.

Securing a greater volume of investment is the key to successful transformation. Yet investors' expectations about the success of the transformation process are the key to investment. At the aggregate level, the outcome of the transformation process – with respect to a favourable or unfavourable environment for investment – is not exogenous to investment decisions. The uncertainties of the transformation process cause investors to delay. Ironically, the more uncertain the transformation process, the greater the incentive for investors to 'wait and see'. In turn, the lower the volume of investment, the more uncertain becomes the process of transformation, and the greater the incentive for investors to wait and see ... and so on. Consequently, *it is not just the timing but also the eventual volume of investment that is affected by uncertainty*. Uncertainty causes investors to delay, which – in turn – reduces the chance of a favourable outcome to the transformation process.

The above analysis supports two types of policy to break this vicious circle and to inaugurate a virtuous circle of more investment and a process of successful transformation.

1. Policies designed to reduce uncertainties in the investment environment. In the immediate aftermath of Unification, this included first and foremost the elimination of uncertainties with respect to ownership rights. In Chapter 6, we argue that by the mid-1990s the priority is to reduce uncertainty with respect to the future evolution of wage rates.
2. Policies designed to make investment decisions reversible: for example, relaxing employment protection laws; enabling employers to recoup training costs.

Either less uncertainty or greater reversibility of investments reduces the incentive to 'wait and see'.

NOTES

1. The most important references are Dixit (1993) and Dixit and Pindyck (1994).
2. In principle, this numerical illustration applies generally to investment under uncertainty.
3. This result is robust with respect to the investment horizon. For example, in the limiting case of investment returns in perpetuity, the cost of exercising the option to invest now is DM 103.

5. The Labour Market in Post-Unification Eastern Germany

5.1 INTRODUCTION

East Germany still struggles with high levels of unemployment, even six years after Unification. The transition from a planned to a market-led economy had dramatic effects on employment and labour utilization. Within two years of GEMSU the artificial full employment of the DDR days had given way to unprecedented levels of joblessness and job insecurity. By the end of 1991, the east German industrial sector alone had experienced a 50 per cent cut in jobs, equivalent to 27 per cent of all jobs available at the time (Deutscher Gewerkschaftsbund 1992). A number of key manu- facturing and associated metal products saw their industries contract by more than 30 per cent. By 1993 the number of all people employed had declined by about 50 per cent (Kühl 1993). At the beginning of 1996 registered unemployment is still more than 1.2 million, approaching 17 per cent, and significant reduction seems unlikely in the immediate future. The task ahead is to take account of past developments and to examine potentially promising policy instruments to paint a picture of east Germany's medium- and long-term future in the competitive European labour market.

In simple terms our aim is to explore the main features of the east German labour market since Unification. The emergence and persistence of unemployment are discussed, together with the policy response – especially the initial reliance on 'active labour market policies' (government training and job creation). Attention is drawn to the rapid change for the worse in women's labour market position. Possible scenarios for future development are sketched. Particular attention is devoted to future wage restraint – in line with or possibly even below productivity adjustments – as the key to economic success and gaining competitiveness in east Germany. As we will argue later, marked post-Unification wage increase has provided a platform for rather modest pay adjustments in the foreseeable future – a lesson that other economies in transition may want to take on board (see Chapter 6). Moreover, if correctly analysed, and provided that proper action is taken, the experiences in east Germany as a whole could prove to be an important and constructive phase in the evolution of policy design for other countries during their periods of economic, social and political transformation.

5.2 LABOUR IN THE GERMAN DEMOCRATIC REPUBLIC

The east German labour market post-Unification experienced unprecedented pressures. Before we begin to take account of developments since 1990, however, we need to remind ourselves of the divergence in conditions between the DDR and the Federal Republic in the previous four decades. Some obvious features, such as the differences in pay and labour productivity are well known: pre-Unification wages and productivity in the DDR were a third or less of those in west Germany (Blien 1994; Fitzroy and Funke 1994; OECD 1995: Owen-Smith 1994). But what lies behind these differentials is more interesting.

Table 5.1   Employment by sector, 1987 (as percentage of total employment)

	East Germany		West Germany	
	Men	Women	Men	Women
Industry	58.5	36.6	51.5	26.1
Agriculture	13.1	8.5	3.4	2.9
Commerce, transport, media	14.9	20.7	15.7	20.9
Services	13.5	34.2	29.4	50.1

Source: Owen-Smith (1994, p. 257).

For one thing, the pre-Unification pattern of employment in East Germany differed markedly from that in western regions, as Table 5.1 indicates. Grunert and Lutz (1995, p. 27) observe that the DDR 'had retained an industrial structure of employment that resembled that of West Germany in the mid-1960s'. Rapid integration with the Federal Republic was to lead to sudden dramatic shifts from agriculture and industry to services (OECD 1995).

Another way in which the DDR differed from the Federal Republic was the concentration of employment in large enterprises (for a discussion of the suppression of small and medium enterprises in East Germany, see Nicolai 1997). For example, in 1988 75.7 per cent of DDR mining and manufacturing workers were in enterprises employing more than 1000 employees, as against only 39.3 per cent in West Germany (Fritsch and Werker 1994).

These large enterprises, like those in the Soviet Union and its satellites or dependencies in Eastern Europe, were the locus of a range of welfare and social entitlements such as housing, childcare, medical services and support for retirement. All citizens had a constitutional right to work and, once engaged by an enterprise, could not normally be dismissed. The nature of the system, rather than the failings of particular enterprises and their managements, thus determined the low level of productivity and the heavy burden of non-wage costs. The corollary of these arrangements was the non-existence of institutions taken for granted in West Germany. These included a national system of social insurance, employment exchanges, external training and retraining providers, standard skills credentials and 'social partner' groupings such as national trade unions, employers' associations and chambers of industry and commerce (Grunert and Lutz 1995). The absence of these institutions in the DDR meant that integration with the West would inevitably mean a wholesale adoption of the Federal Republic model, a source of considerable resentment in some quarters.

This set-up also meant that the DDR was characterized by an extreme form of internal labour market. There was little mobility between enterprises. New labour market entrants were channelled by educational institutions into first jobs (there was only very limited choice), and afterwards workers were normally expected to stay with their enterprise unless they were required elsewhere by the demands of state plans. Exceptions could be made for husbands or, more commonly, for wives who needed to move with their spouse. Of course, there existed informal arrangements whereby people could move – but the system did not generally support labour mobility; indeed it tended to frown on it.

The existence of internal labour markets is typically associated with rigid pay scales and hierarchical structures: the DDR was certainly not an exception. However its pay scales were much more highly compressed than in capitalist economies (such as Japan) where internal labour markets are important. Internal markets also tend to be associated with an emphasis on specific rather than general training. This certainly seems to have been the case in East Germany. Although on paper the East German labour force was very well qualified, formal qualifications seem to have been concentrated on initial preparation for work, while the skills acquired on the job in employment were by and large not certificated. As a consequence, one problem faced by workers following Unification was their inability to demonstrate to new potential employers that they possessed the skills they claimed, reinforced by the fact that a large number of existing East German qualifications were not accredited by West German authorities.

5.3 EAST GERMAN UNEMPLOYMENT: CAUSES, CONSEQUENCES AND POLICIES

It is against this background that we need to understand the economic and social difficulties facing east Germany after Unification. Its enterprises and, arguably more importantly, its workforces were pitchforked into a market environment of which they had little experience or understanding. Becoming unemployed in east Germany in the early 1990s was a much more bewildering and traumatic experience than becoming unemployed in, say, the UK – where labour market institutions and social security entitlements are familiar and widely understood, where the status of being unemployed is becoming less stigmatized and where the rise in unemployment in the 1980s was rather more gradual. It is not surprising that adjustments in east Germany have been slow and painful and that economic and social unease will be with east Germans for years to come.

In the first year following Unification, the east German regions accounted for 20 per cent of Germany's total population, but for only 8 per cent of its gross domestic product (GDP). Per capita GDP was reported to be only one-third of west Germany's (Dobischat and Neumann 1992). The litany of problems facing east Germany on Unification was formidable. Old-fashioned goods of poor quality (thus lacking non-price competitiveness) and inappropriate industrial equipment; collapsing trade patterns as a result of breaking the links with the Soviet bloc and other communist countries; monetary Unification at a parity which, according to one estimate (Akerloff et al. 1991, p. 2), meant that only 8 per cent of workers were employed in economically viable jobs. Add to these factors the unpopular handling of privatization under political pressure by the Treuhand, and deindustrialization and mass unemployment, 'a depression ... virtually without historic precedent' (Akerloff et al. 1991) were predictable results.[1] Unemployment soon reached the 15 per cent mark and, after falling back a little, rose even further as the recession (exacerbated by the imperatives of the Maastricht convergence criteria) hit Germany as a whole (see Figure 5.1).

As a consequence of these unprecedented levels of unemployment (western) German authorities introduced large-scale training and work creation measures. Although after 1993 public spending for these schemes was reduced significantly,[2] as late as 1994 there were on average still more people counted as programme participants than were officially registered with an employment office (Gladisch and Trabert 1995). The total of 2.4 million may have been closer to the 'real' level of joblessness than the official unemployment figure. Against this background, the impact of labour market relief as a result of government schemes became considerable. In fact, taking both the large number of east German commuters and

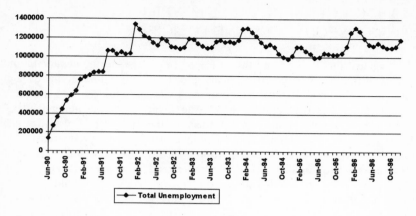

Source: Bundesanstalt für Arbeit (1997).

*Figure 5.1   Total unemployment in east Germany, June 1990–December
          1996*

government scheme participants into account, by January 1993 effective
unemployment would have come close to 30 per cent (Lange 1993). To give
credit where it is due, this rate was reduced by nearly 8 per cent between
1992 and 1994. However, this was not so much a result of increasing
employment opportunities or better-trained workers matching firms'
requirements, but largely a consequence of a reduced supply of labour.
Some analysts estimate the effective reduction in labour supply since
GEMSU to have been as much as 500,000 people by the end of 1994
(Gladisch and Trabert 1995).

Training, further education and work creation schemes were initially
seen as useful tools to ease the labour market crisis in east Germany and to
prevent the build-up of severe economic and social unrest. What appeared
first to be an east German problem, as the region struggled to keep open
unemployment at socially acceptable levels and to prevent a mass exodus of
discontented citizens from the former GDR to the West,[3] soon became a
financial burden for unified Germany. Since Unification, more than 4
million east Germans have participated in schemes and millions of
Deutschmarks have been spent to finance these measures. Yet east German
unemployment remains stubbornly high, a situation which has been
described as one major obstacle to improved economic performance in the
unified Germany (OECD 1995).

5.3.1 Training

In recent years, government training schemes have grown in popularity, in east Germany and elsewhere. It is usually assumed that on completion of training participants are more likely to find jobs, or find better-paid jobs, than would otherwise be the case. It is also assumed that they are less likely to reenter unemployment. However, the empirical evidence on the success of such programmes in many countries is weak (OECD 1993b). These schemes typically involve substantial displacement effects; the apparent success of programme participants is achieved at the expense of others. For example, if training schemes target the long-term unemployed, they may get back into employment at the expense of the short-term unemployed and overall unemployment may be little affected (Shackleton et al. 1995, Chapters 4 and 11; Robinson 1995; and Lange 1996). The arguments on wage increases are also far from being clear-cut. The effectiveness of training as a pay-enhancing mechanism continues to be a subject of debate among academics and policy-makers throughout the industrialized world. A recent study on training and wage growth in west Germany, for example, comes to the conclusion that although further training seems to positively affect wage growth, significant differences regarding the effectiveness of further training exist between male and female workers (Georgellis and Lange 1997). The positive effect seemed to be strongest for males. For females, on the other hand, the effect of further training on wage growth appeared to be insignificant.

It is further claimed that unless the east German workforce participates in western-style training schemes the development of a secondary labour market – a low-pay/low-skill equilibrium area with few connections to job ladders of any sort and poor working conditions – cannot be avoided. Certainly, this argument has some appeal and coincides with the recent revival of segmented and dual labour market theories.[4] It is argued that employment stability – the major characteristic distinguishing jobs in the primary sector from those in the secondary sector – is virtually impossible to test. Consequently, the selection process of east as well as west German employers seems very likely to rely on 'superficial' characteristics, including educational and vocational attainments, as approximations of potential job stability.

However, some of the evidence cited does not support the idea that east German workers face particular problems that only retraining schemes can tackle. For example, it is true that temporary part-time jobs have grown considerably, mainly in the service sector (Lange 1993). This, however, is a situation not unlike that in many other industrialized societies. In Britain, for example, more than a quarter of jobs are now carried out on a part-time basis.[5] Many of those east Germans who now work in part-time service sector employment experienced spells of unemployment before reentering the labour market, again a problem frequently observed elsewhere. In other words, the causes of east German unemployment may have been different, but the consequences are rather similar to those in other European economies. In contrast to largely unsubstantiated accusations of inferior east German workers and their alleged skills deficits, a recent study reports that most of those east Germans who remained employed are still in the same occupational class and the same occupation (Diewald and Solga 1995).

The heavy involvement in training and re-training is rather ironic for those who see formal qualifications as crucial to economic success: on paper the east German workforce was better qualified than that of the West before Unification (Shackleton and Lange 1993). In the late 1980s, only 13 per cent of east German workers possessed no vocational qualifications, compared with about 26 per cent in western regions (Knoll and Sommer 1992). This *ad hoc* observation is confirmed by a recent paper in which data drawn from the German Life History Study (conducted at the Max Planck Institute for Human Development and Education in Berlin) are used to examine the different educational levels in east and west Germany (Konietzka and Solga, 1995). The data in question belong to four birth cohorts (1929–31, 1939–41, 1949–51/1951–53 and 1959–61) and show, among other things, the distribution of occupational credentials upon entrance into the first job (see Table 5.2).

The first observation we can make is that the proportion of persons entering the labour market without an occupational credential strongly declined over the cohorts. This applies to east as well as west Germany. However, the increase in participation in training was considerably higher in east Germany than in west Germany. Whereas in the west about 25 per cent of the youngest cohort did not hold any of the occupational credentials before entering the first job, this proportion was less than 10 per cent in the east.

There are also some interesting structural differences between the two countries. In east Germany, one can see a much higher proportion of persons participating and completing apprenticeships in manual occupations, especially in the younger cohorts. According to Konietzka and Solga, this finding reflects the common knowledge that West Germany was and still is in transition to a 'service society', whereas East Germany was in the process of developing into a 'modern industrial society', but collapsed before ever reaching this stage. This point can be further emphasized by reference to Table 5.3.

It shows the distribution of occupational classes held in the first job and demonstrates – corresponding to the distribution of occupational credentials in the four cohorts – an increase of skilled working-class positions in East Germany, but a quite stable proportion of men and women entering this class in West Germany. In contrast to East Germany, the West German

Table 5.2   Distribution of occupational credentials when entering the labour market

A: West Germany (in percentages, only persons who had a first job)

Occupational credentials	Sex	All cohorts	1929–31	1939–41	1949–51	1959–61	N
No/below	m	27	39	25	19	27	422
apprenticeship	f	44	71	53	33	25	652
Apprenticeship in	m	51	46	57	52	50	791
craft or trade occupation	f	12	10	11	12	15	184
Apprenticeship in	m	11	10	10	14	10	167
commercial occupation	f	28	12	26	39	33	417
Vocational/	m	1	[0]	2	[1]	3	22
technical college	f	10	5	6	8	16	141
University	m	9	6	7	14	10	142
	f	6	2	4	8	10	95
Total N	m	1,544	348	375	350	471	
	f	1,489	336	343	354	456	

B: East Germany (only persons who had a first job before December 1989)

Occupational credentials	Sex	All cohorts	1929–31	1939–41	1949–51	1959–61	N
No/below	m	15	33	14	6	7	169
apprenticeship	f	30	77	24	7	9	348
Apprenticeship in	m	69	55	73	74	76	776
craft or trade occupation	f	29	13	30	36	37	343
Apprenticeship in	m	3	7	2	[0]	3	33
commercial occupation	f	20	7	30	22	20	231
Vocational/	m	5	2	6	6	4	51
technical college	f	15	2	10	22	24	171
University	m	9	4	6	14	11	96
	f	7	[1]	6	13	10	87
Total N	m	1,125	288	288	288	261	
	f	1,180	300	291	284	305	

Note: Sex: m = male, f = female; [ ] = cell counts fewer than 5 persons.

Source: Konietzka and Solga (1995).

Table 5.3   Distribution of occupational class held in first job

A: West Germany (in percentages, only persons who had a first job)

Occupational class	Sex	All cohorts	1929–31	1939–41	1949–51	1959–61	N
Upper service	m	5	3	5	8	5	80
class	f	5	2	2	5	9	71
Middle service	m	19	11	13	24	25	282
class	f	30	10	18	34	49	431
Lower service	m	10	7	8	12	13	156
class	f	28	23	38	33	20	411
Skilled workers	m	45	43	53	45	42	688
	f	7	6	8	10	5	106
Un- or semi-	m	17	31	15	8	14	252
skilled workers	f	25	45	28	15	15	362
Others*	m	4	7	5	3	2	59
	f	6	14	7	3	1	82
Total N	m	1,517	347	368	344	458	
	f	1,463	330	340	347	446	

B: East Germany (only persons who had a first job before December 1989)

Occupational class	Sex	All cohorts	1929–31	1939–41	1949–51	1959–61	N
Upper service	m	10	5	7	16	12	108
class	f	7	[1]	6	13	9	85
Middle service	m	10	9	10	10	9	108
class	f	37	12	35	47	54	436
Lower service	m	3	5	4	[1]	2	38
class	f	16	24	20	9	10	183
Skilled workers	m	58	45	60	62	67	655
	f	18	10	20	23	20	215
Un- or semi-	m	15	28	13	9	8	164
skilled workers	f	16	37	13	7	6	182
Others*	m	5	8	6	2	3	56
	f	6	16	6	[1]	2	76
Total N	m	1,129	287	293	288	261	
	f	1,177	293	292	286	306	

Notes:
Sex: m=male, f=female; [ ] =cell counts fewer than 5 persons.
* Others = self-employed, farmers, family workers.

Source: Konietzka and Solga (1995).

labour market appears to have experienced an occupational structure that became increasingly characterized by service class occupations. Although Germany usually praises the flexibility of its skilled workforce, these observations may at least in part explain why a large number of vocationally qualified east German workers post-Unification found it hard to remain in and/or return to work in a 'service society'. However, one still needs to emphasize that also in West Germany the skilled working class remained the most important class category.

Where critics may be on slightly firmer ground is when the point is made that the institutional arrangements and conditioning of the workforce in the former GDR may have inculcated a passivity and lack of enterprise, which discourage active and effective job search (Grünert and Lutz 1995). However many east Germans have shown considerable enterprise and been prepared to move long distances, so the problem cannot be universal.

Whatever merits one may be tempted to attribute to training activities, it has to be understood that skilling the workforce is a complementary measure which does not create jobs and thus needs to be looked at with a reasonable degree of caution when it comes to combating mass unemployment. It has become abundantly clear that the vocational qualification record of the east German workforce has little bearing on the high and persistent rates of unemployment.

5.3.2 Subsidized Employment

Publicly financed work creation has become one of the most popular policy options in east Germany. In 1992 on average 388,000 east Germans were participating in subsidized work creation schemes (*Arbeitsbeschaffungs-maßnahmen*) and, therefore, avoided featuring on the German unemployment register. As a result of financial pressures in subsequent years the number of participants was reduced considerably. In 1994, however, there were still 280,000 east Germans counted as work creation participants, more than 20 per cent of currently registered jobless.

Work creation schemes are usually targeted at the hard-to-place unemployed, although in the east German case some exceptions were made to accommodate the large number of jobless overall. Still, the long-term unemployed form the largest group of the participants. Subsidized employment means that the willingness of employers – both in the private and public sector – to take on the unemployed is compensated for by a direct wage subsidy, in the east German case of between 80 and 100 per cent (Brinkmann and Gottsleben 1994). This then creates a second and publicly financed labour market designed to provide work experience for the most disadvantaged in the labour market and, as a result, to make them more employable. Work creation schemes are thus meant to be only a gap-bridging exercise leading to stable and regular employment. The alleged stability of this employment, however, is open to question. It may be argued that public employment subsidies are used by employers as a means of acquiring a pool of cheap, temporary labour that will be replaced by other subsidized workers as soon as the subsidy period has come to an end. Furthermore, not unlike government training, work creation schemes suffer from substitution, deadweight loss and displacement effects. Suppose a scheme is instituted to give 100,000 otherwise unemployed individuals a one-year subsidized job with an employer. Of the 100,000 scheme participants, however, a proportion would have been recruited anyway; firms now simply get their costs subsidized. This is known in the literature as *deadweight loss*. Another proportion will take the place of other people who would have been employed in the absence of the subsidy. This is know as the *substitution effect*. Finally, the effect of publicly financed employment may actually lead employers to shed labour if those employers who do not qualify for the subsidy seek means of retaining competitiveness: *the displacement effect*. The net success of subsidized work is therefore rather limited.

There is no doubt that substitution, deadweight loss and displacement effects of employment subsidies are very considerable. The OECD has reviewed a number of studies, which include one of Ireland's 'Employment Incentive' schemes, showing a cumulative deadweight and substitution effect of 95 per cent; Australian 'Jobstart' schemes with deadweight losses alone of between 67 and 79 per cent; and Dutch recruitment subsidies with the sum of deadweight and substitution effects of between 76 and 89 per cent (OECD 1993b). Subsidies to self-employment suffer from similar, if not greater effects to those associated with other work creation schemes. Deadweight loss alone from such schemes has been estimated at more than 70 per cent in the UK, about 60 per cent in Ireland and 40 per cent in Australia (OECD 1989).

The OECD's conclusion (1993b) is that job subsidies with broad targeting (for example, all jobless) are difficult to defend, but that schemes focused on particular problem groups may be acceptable if the policy objective is to redistribute opportunities. One has to observe, however, that few if any schemes have ever been presented to the public as a means of spreading misery around more equitably. Moreover, even if it could be regarded as equitable to benefit the long-term unemployed at the expense of the short-term unemployed, because both groups are very heterogeneous it remains unclear whether welfare transfers between such broad groups are necessarily optimal.

In spite of this criticism, however, several commentators have advocated an expansion of the second labour market in east Germany until most workers are re-integrated in the competitive labour market. However, the limited areas of work on offer (work creation schemes are designed only for jobs that would not exist in the absence of the subsidy[6]) creates a situation where the demand for job placements in industry and commerce[7] is difficult to meet. Recent suggestions indicate potential solutions for this problem. Klös (1993), for example, argues that instead of conserving obsolete jobs by providing wage subsidies, experiments with training vouchers may be potentially worthwhile. The unemployed could cash in these vouchers with companies and employers of their own choice, which may result in improved occupational and regional mobility and potentially higher probabilities of being kept on after schemes have been completed. In the UK, the economist Dennis Snower has recently attracted attention with a similar proposal to turn welfare benefits into vouchers that can be used to subsidize employers who take on the long-term unemployed and provide some training (Snower 1994a and b).[8] The idea of training vouchers is not new and already has a history in Britain (where they are referred to as 'training credits'), but many remain sceptical about the effectiveness of these initiatives (Youthaid and NATFHE 1993).[9] Nevertheless, the introduction of effective legislation and innovative monitoring of the use and abuse of subsidies is needed to turn the above 'intervention pessimism' into unjustified criticism.

5.4 GENDER INEQUALITIES IN THE EAST GERMAN LABOUR MARKET

An important point to emphasize is that gender inequalities in the east German labour market are considerable. Women were an important element of the workforce in the DDR. Their labour force participation was one of the highest in the world, approaching 90 per cent, at the time of the dismantling of the Wall (Engelbrecht 1994). Women have suffered most from redundancy and declining employment opportunities in east Germany. Female unemployment rates have in recent years been almost double those of males, and other indicators point in the same direction. In 1994, 64.9 per cent of all unemployed were female, as were 60.6 per cent of all participants in further education and training schemes and 52.5 per cent of all subsidized (work creation) workers. Men were only dominant in short-term work and early retirement schemes.

Table 5.4 gives an impression of some dimensions of gender inequality in the east German labour market. Particular emphasis should be placed on the gender distribution of new regular employment. Over the three years net employment grew by about 250,000 jobs. However, these jobs were mainly taken up by males: 224,000 jobs went to male workers, equivalent to a male marginal employment share of 89.6 per cent. Between 1992 and 1994, female employment rates remained fairly constant. However, the difference between male and female employment rates grew consistently. If this picture does not change, a further fall in women's participation (already down significantly from its pre-1989 level) can be anticipated. The causes of these gender disparities are several, including the changing structure of the

Table 5.4   Employment by gender in east Germany (in thousands*)
            (German nationals only)

	1992		1993		1994	
	Men	Women	Men	Women	Men	Women
Working-age population (1)	5.098	4.632	5.131	4.610	5.144	4.596
Active labour force (2)	4.794	4.338	4.704	4.164	4.582	4.042
	(94.0)	(93.6)	91.7)	(90.3)	(89.1)	(87.9)
Employment in first labour market**	3.269	2.697	3.400	2.680	3.493	2.723
	(64.1)	(58.2)	(66.3)	(58.1)	(67.9)	(59.2)
Underemployment***	1.525	1.641	1.304	1.484	1.089	1.319
	(29.9)	(35.4)	(25.4)	(32.2)	(21.2)	(28.7)
Row (1)–Row (2)	304	294	427	446	562	554
	(6.0)	(6.4)	(8.3)	(9.7)	(10.9)	(12.1)

Notes:
*   Numbers in brackets give percentage proportion of row (1).
**   Excludes participants in labour market policy measures.
*** Including registered unemployed, short-term workers and participants in labour market policy measures (including early retirement schemes).

Source: Gladisch and Trabert (1995).

economy and the relative geographical mobility of men and women. However, to the extent that discrimination plays a role (for example, in access to 'good quality' retraining) it suggests a problem that is not easy to tackle.

5.5 WAGES AND THE COST OF LABOUR: EAST GERMANY'S COMPETITIVE EDGE

According to the Federal Statistical Office, 1992 labour productivity in east Germany reached only 40 per cent of west German standards, whereas average wages and salaries were almost two-thirds. Within two years productivity passed the 50 per cent margin while wages and salaries reached 71 per cent of the level in the west (Brinkmann and Gottsleben 1994). The productivity–wage gap is narrowing gradually with wages still well below those of west German workers. It is here where east Germany's comparative advantage lies, provided that the unions are prepared to delay wage parity for a further few years.

From the early stages of Unification, discussions in east Germany centred on whether the productivity of labour is a guide for wage agreements. The attempts by employers to renege on the timetable for transition to western rates of pay first provoked large-scale strike action in early 1993. However, several compromise agreements were reached, which resulted in eastern pay rates being extremely attractive to domestic and foreign investors. However, this investment needs to be transformed into productivity gains if east Germany is ever to catch up with western regions. A long-run development process lies ahead. As Pugh (1993b, p. 141) puts it: 'If east Germany can continuously beat or equal the historical best both in west Germany and in other countries, then equalization is likely to take between 15 and 30 years'.

This is, however, a big 'if'. Different analysts' assumptions yield longer or shorter periods of transition to equal levels of productivity and the avoidance of a permanent 'Mezzogiorno' problem. Hughes Hallet and Ma (1993) estimate a period of 30–40 years. Barro, quoted in Blien (1994, p. 12) has written of 'a couple of generations rather than a couple of years or a couple of decades'. Priewe (1994, p. 7) has surveyed a range of estimates and concludes that 'it is unrealistic to count on an "optimistic" trend, leading to rapid full convergence with west Germany'. However, he takes a more upbeat view on the differential in unemployment rates. As a result of declining birth and female participation rates, together with outward migration and early retirement, he expects east and west German unemployment rates to converge much more quickly. Needless to say, this process will be aided by slow rates of growth of pay in the east.

Table 5.5 shows the levels of collectively agreed-upon wage incomes (*Jahrestarifeinkommen*) in east Germany as compared with their west German equivalents for selected industries.

Table 5.5   Levels of collective wage income in eastern Germany, 1995

East German industries and locations	Level of collective wage income (%)	Column (2) based on following west German industries and locations (=100)
Building and construction in East Germany	80.9	Building and construction in West Germany
Metal sector Sachsen-Anhalt	86.3	Metal sector in Niedersachsen
Paper industry in east Germany	67.0	Paper industry in Bavaria
Brewery industry Berlin–East	86.1	Brewery industry Berlin–West
Brewery industry Thüringen	67.5	Brewery industry Berlin–West

Source: Kolb (1995).

However, it is not just the relatively lower wages in the east that appeals to western investors. Other elements of labour costs also play a significant role when it comes to investment decisions. Local and Federal government subsidies towards employers' social security contributions, vacation agreements, low Christmas bonuses[10] and comparatively higher weekly working hours all make east Germany an attractive place for new or expanding businesses, certainly compared with west Germany. (There is of course the growing problem of the competitiveness of the German economy as a whole, although this is a wider issue that cannot be tackled here.) Table 5.6 contrasts the different working hours arrangements between selected eastern and west German industries, while Table 5.7 compares east/west hourly labour costs in 1995.

Table 5.6   Weekly working hours compared, 1995

Industry/location	East Germany	West Germany	East/west (%)
Building and construction	39	39	100
Metal sector	39	35	111.4
Paper industry	40	38	105.3
Brewery sector in Thüringen	40	38	105.3

Source: Kolb (1995).

Table 5.7   Hourly labour costs in east and west Germany, 1995

East German industries and locations	Level of labour costs (%)	Column (2) based on following west German industries and locations (=100)
Building and construction in East Germany	80.9	Building and construction in West Germany
Metal sector Sachsen-Anhalt	78.7	Metal sector in Niedersachsen
Paper industry in East Germany	63.7	Paper industry in Bavaria
Brewery industry Berlin–East	83.9	Brewery industry Berlin–West
Brewery industry Thüringen	64.1	Brewery industry Berlin–West

Source: Kolb (1995).

The evidence confirms our story of east Germany's comparative advantage in terms of both hours worked and labour costs. On average, the east German worker appears to work longer hours and costs less than his or her western German counterpart.

5.6 PRODUCTIVITY DIFFERENTIALS AND WAGE ADJUSTMENT

Having raised the issues of labour productivity and wage growth we must pursue them further. First, however, it is worth emphasizing that the significant wage increases post-Unification were by and large the result of political pressures rather than economic reasoning. Immediately after the breach of the Wall – and indeed for some time before then – the east German population began to vote with their feet, resulting in mass migration and commuting. As a consequence, the labour supply in west Germany increased considerably. A total of 34,000 east Germans moved westwards in 1990. By 1991, this figure had risen to more than 200,000. Assuming an approximately 50 per cent labour force participation rate of these immigrants, in these two years alone the west German labour force grew by approximately 280,000. Additionally, the Federal employment office estimated that by November 1991 200,000 east Germans were commuting to western regions. Allowing for the comparatively small number of immigrants from the west to the east (mainly east German returnees), immigration and commuting together increased the west German labour force by approximate 550,000 (all figures: Bundesanstalt für Arbeit 1992). It is against this background that marked wage increases were necessary to provide sufficient incentives for the east German workforce to stay and work in the East.

In economic modelling terms this scenario can be illustrated by reference to a highly stylized two-sector migration model (see Figure 5.2). The total German workforce is measured on the horizontal axis (OB = western workforce; O'B = eastern workforce)[11] and real wage rates for western and eastern regions are shown on the vertical axes with eastern pay rates (O'we) immediately after Unification being considerably lower than in the west (Oww). The marginal productivity of labour in east and west Germany is represented by the downward-sloping schedules, MPLw and MPLe, which illustrate the lower productivity level in the east compared with western regions. Given the low population/GDP ratio of the east, we assume a distribution of labour as indicated by BF where labour productivity in east Germany (point L) is estimated to be one-third of the west German labour productivity (point M). At the assumed wage rates, OA equals western employment and O'E equals eastern employment. Applying the basic rule of optimal allocation of resources, the distribution of labour in unified Germany should be such that the marginal productivity of labour in the East, MPLe, equals the western productivity level, MPLw. The vertical line DH indicates such a distribution.

At first sight, migration from eastern to western regions seems to be beneficial for the east German labour market. The east German labour of BD would move westwards (that is, BF would move to the right). This means more workers in the west and a net benefit in terms of additional GDP equal to the triangle LMJ; it also means that unemployment in the east can be reduced considerably from BE to DE. Using some features of the Harris–Todaro framework (1970), however, the distribution as indicated by

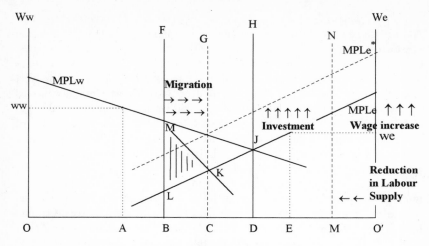

Figure 5.2 Migration, labour productivity and investment

DH is unlikely to happen. In the Harris–Todaro model, expected wage differentials are the main determinants for migration. In the German context, the probable wage differential in unified Germany is p(Ww − We), where p represents the likelihood of finding a job in west Germany. In Figure 5.2, the schedule MK illustrates the evolution of p(Ww − We), where p is assumed to fall with rising migration. Western marginal productivity falls as migration continues, that is, the potential wage differential falls with rising migration and, hence, increasing employment in the west. The shaded triangle can therefore be seen as the shrinking expected wage differential. Assuming these wage considerations, migration will come to an end at CG. Although such action would still reduce east German unemployment by BC, *ceteris paribus*, unemployment in the west, AB, would increase by the same amount. Although this may be an exaggeration as not all migrants to the west became or remained unemployed, it is not unreasonable to assume that due to massive migration and respective growth rates of the west German labour force, increasing unemployment in the west immediately after Unification was, at least to a certain extent, caused by east German migrants.

Since then, however, various developments in the east German labour market could be witnessed which incorporate dynamic elements into the model and thus increase its complexity.

Looking back over the years since Unification we have seen a considerable degree of investment in both physical and human capital. Conversely, there have also been counterproductive activities with respect to unemployment reductions, including marked wage increases (and thus a halt to mass migration) and a significant cut in the east German supply of labour. These developments are illustrated in Figure 5.2 by the new productivity schedule for east Germany, $MPLe^*$, an increased eastern wage level (see Table 5.5 for industry-specific breakdowns) and a shortened horizontal axis as indicated by the vertical line MN as a result of the previously mentioned reduction in the east German workforce.

In isolation, the shift from MPLe to $MPLe^*$ offers an alternative by which the negative side-effect of simple redistribution of unemployment can be avoided. Treating the marginal productivity of labour in the west as a constant, assuming low pay rates in the east and increasing MPLe, the labour productivity schedule of east Germany will shift to the left leading to reduced unemployment in eastern regions without burdening the west German labour market. In addition, instead of shifting BF, DH now moves closer to the actual distribution of labour as shifting the MPLe schedule to the left creates new distributive optima. However, the explicit assumption of low rates of pay cannot be justified. A short period of transition to west German pay rates was eventually agreed on, with foreseeable consequences in job losses. Furthermore, following a short period of reduced unemployment a considerable reduction in east German labour supply (MN) over time led to a proportion of unemployed workers which was once again well in excess of 15 per cent.

Ironically, this means that despite unprecedented levels of investment unemployment in east Germany remains stubbornly high. Assuming that the cutting of labour supply (through attractive benefit packages, early retirement allowances, and so on) has come to an end, and assuming furthermore that a reasonable degree of real capital investment can be sustained for the foreseeable future, it becomes abundantly clear that wage restrictions now play a vital role in the development of east Germany from a backward region into an economy blessed with continuous growth based on competitiveness.

5.7 CONCLUDING REMARKS

Since Unification, workers in east Germany have experienced a series of dramatic changes. The institutions to which they had grown accustomed have vanished; for the first time since the Weimar Republic a fully-fledged labour market operates. It has been, and continues to be, a bumpy ride. The economic inefficiencies of large-scale state enterprise were cruelly exposed with the collapse of trading links to the east, a rushed process of privatization, rapid wage increases and monetary union at an inappropriate parity. Unemployment rose sharply and, despite various forms of active labour market policy, remains at unacceptably high levels. An extra dimension was added to the problem by the emergence of much more marked gender inequality. One success of the DDR regime was its encouragement of high levels of female labour market activity (supported by provision of childcare). Women appear to have suffered most from the fall in job opportunities in east Germany.

The lot of the eastern worker may appear rather bleak. It certainly appears unlikely that there will be a full equalization of productivity and living standards between the old and new *Länder* for many years. However, providing that current differentials between pay and conditions in east and west Germany are not eroded too rapidly, it may be possible to narrow unemployment differentials between the two regions in the not too distant future. (However, since the unemployment rate in the west appears to be trending upwards, this may not be quite the achievement it appears.)

Progress towards lower levels of east German unemployment is likely to be more rapid if agreements on moderate pay increases can be reached. In 1996, for example, east German employers in the metal sector will face only 86.1 per cent of the equivalent labour costs experienced in western regions. It is now left to other trade unions to emulate this model and keep east Germany on the road to a successful and competitive economy.

NOTES

1. Nicolai claims that 'de-industrialization in east Germany has reached such proportions that the area has sunk to the level of Honduras when a number of parameters are applied' (Nicolai 1993).
2. The 1993 cuts in labour market policy spending have to be seen in the light of the financial year of 1992 when east German employment office revenues amounted to DM 5.3 bn compared with spending of DM 42 bn (Siebert 1992). As one result, the number of east German workers participating in work creation schemes was reduced from 388,000 to 280,000 in 1994.
3. Economic decline in the east also caused pressures on the west German labour market. In the first two years following Unification one could witness considerable numbers of migrants and commuters from eastern to western regions.
4. For a formal discussion of labour market segmentation and how education and training can be used to 'transform' employees from secondary to primary workers see Doeringer and Piore (1971) and Gordon (1972). For some German specifications, see Sengenberger (1987) and Freiburghauser and Schmid (1975).
5. Between 1971 and 1993, the number of British part-time employees increased by 2.8 million people. In contrast, the number of British full-time employees fell by about 3.2 million (Lange and Atkinson 1995).
6. Sometimes referred to as the *additionality clause*.
7. The two employment sectors with the largest growth rates in east Germany.
8. In the German context the training element would be of particular importance. So far, German work creation schemes do not usually contain formal training or re-training elements leading to vocational credentials.
9. What was particularly criticized was the only voluntary involvement of employers, subsequent evaluation and monitoring difficulties and insufficient support and funding.
10. A Christmas bonus is usually paid in most industrial sectors, except building and construction.
11. O'B > OB is of no significance; the diagram is stylized, not scaled.

6. Catching Up with the West: The Achievements and Limitations of Creative Destruction[*]

6.1 INTRODUCTION

Unification left eastern Germany with an acute imbalance between physical and human capital. A well-educated and trained workforce is a necessary condition for physical investment to generate sustained productivity growth. This is grounded in theory as well as the experience of South Korea and Taiwan where, since the 1960s, high investment promoted by public subsidy has powered growth and convergence with the developed market economies (Rodrik 1995, pp. 53, 96 and 100). Accordingly, in eastern Germany a fundamental feature of transition strategy has been government support for investment – both directly in infrastructure and indirectly through financial incentives for the private sector.

Contrary to historical precedent, however, and unique among the transitional economies, is a second feature of the transition strategy in eastern Germany: namely, initial support from government, unions and even business for high wages. While investment subsidies increased the *quantity* of investment, high wages were supported for their influence on the *quality* of investment. High wages were to ensure that the only profitable investment would be 'high-tech', thereby precluding 'low-tech' investment intended to profit from cheap labour.[1]

6.1.1 Strategies for the Upswing

Sinn and Sinn distinguish three possible 'strategies for the upswing' (1992, p. 143ff.). The second characterizes what actually happened while the third is what, in the opinion of Sinn and Sinn, should have happened.

---

[*] This chapter is largely reprinted from the authors' essay of the same title in J. Hölscher and A. Hochberg (eds), *East Germany's Economic Development – Domestic and Global Aspects* (Macmillan Press, London; St. Martin's Press, New York, 1997).

1. The 'maintenance strategy', in which wages would have been kept low enough to maintain eastern employment as it was at the time of GEMSU. This is the strategy that the other ex-Soviet bloc countries have had to adopt. In eastern Germany, however, it was not politically feasible. Moreover, it was not a credible strategy. First, it would have led to excessive migration (see 5.6 above). Second, it would have minimized structural change and, hence, slowed growth and delayed 'catch-up'.

2. The high-wage, high-tech strategy that was broadly supported by government, unions and business (Sinn and Sinn 1992, pp. 153 and 164–8). In its effect, this was to be a process of creative destruction. This strategy allowed rapid wage convergence with western Germany by imposing wage increases far in excess of productivity increase. The rationale is that production units unable to survive higher wages 'are weeded out immediately and that reorganization investments not worth making at these wage rates are not allowed to take place. Only the most modern factories meeting the highest Western standards are allowed' (Sinn and Sinn 1992, p. 152). This strategy presupposed, first, subsidies to stimulate the investment necessary to raise productivity so as to support wage growth and, second, social transfer payments to subsidize jobs or compensate workers made unemployed as wages grew in advance of productivity.

3. Between these extremes, Sinn and Sinn argued for a compromise that 'could well be optimal from an efficiency point of view' (1992, p. 145). Their strategy of 'organic system transformation' 'is a gradual change in the price structure that keeps pace with the gradual change in the pattern of production' (1992, p. 145). Although wages would be higher than in the maintenance strategy, at least during its initial stages Sinn and Sinn's restricted-wage strategy would have dictated lower wages than the prevailing high-wage, high-tech strategy. It is in this sense that we use the term 'low-wage' strategy.

The essential feature of Sinn and Sinn's strategy is that wage rates should have risen in accord with market forces – hence, as a *consequence of* capital accumulation and productivity growth rather than, as in the high-wage, high-tech strategy, *in advance of* capital accumulation and productivity growth. The principle of Sinn and Sinn's strategy is to maximize the role of the price mechanism in the transition process. We argue that a high-wage strategy in at least the initial stage of transformation was more favourable to rapid convergence. The principle of our counter-critique is that private decisions taken in response to current information provided by the price mechanism (for example, low wages) may lead to an outcome that is efficient in the short run but inconsistent with dynamic efficiency – that is, innovation and productivity growth – in the long run.

6.1.2 An Alternative, Two-phase Strategy

Our approach does not neglect adjustment through the price mechanism. Instead, we adopt an eclectic approach by considering not only the cost of a high-wage, high-tech strategy but also the benefits. Analysis of convergence strategy based only on relative prices is static: as wages rise relative to productivity, output and employment are lost. These effects lead to no further changes. Our intention is to broaden the analysis to take account of benefits arising from dynamic processes: in particular, the possibility that wages rising relative to productivity may, when combined with investment subsidy, contribute to cumulative causation effects that perpetuate growth. By definition, these are realized over time. Accordingly, at any one time, dynamic benefits are realized only in part: because cumulative causation perpetuates benefits, the other part exists as the present value of future benefits yet to be realized.

We argue, first, that there are conditions under which dynamic benefits may be promoted by a high-wage, high-tech policy but are blocked by a low-wage, low-tech strategy. Second, static costs and dynamic benefits coexist and the balance between them can change. This changing balance is associated with *two phases in the convergence process*.

- In the *first phase*, rising wages preclude development on a low-wage, low-tech basis and, when coupled with subsidized investment, promote a high-tech growth path. In this phase, the output and employment costs of high wages are offset by dynamic benefits; both *actual* benefits currently realized and *potential* future benefits from ongoing cumulative processes. This phase requires wages to rise sufficiently to function as an instrument of 'creative destruction' in relation to existing low-tech, low-wage production, especially in the traded goods sector. This phase is necessary but not sufficient to secure self-sustaining economic development on a high-wage, high-tech basis.

- If wages continue to rise beyond the level required to inaugurate this first phase, 'destruction' continues unabated but with diminishing 'creative' effects. First, the more wages continue to rise above average productivity, the more output and employment are choked off in low-tech sectors in the non-traded sector. Second, once a high-wage, high-tech convergence path has been established, continuing wage increases are unlikely to generate further dynamic benefits. Moreover, even in the high-tech sector, wage increases curtail profit growth, thereby reducing both incentive and means to invest which, in turn, reduces potential output and employment. Consequently, there is a point at which wage rises cease to be associated with actual and potential dynamic benefits in excess of static costs. Beyond this point, rising wages impose additional static costs that are increasingly greater than additional dynamic benefits. This defines a *second phase* in which wage moderation is necessary not only to secure a more favourable environment for low-tech firms in the non-traded-goods sector but also to maximize dynamic benefits from high-tech sectors producing traded goods.

This two-phase model structures our approach to convergence strategy for eastern Germany. In the first few years of Unification, rising wages together with investment subsidy precluded a low-wage, low-tech strategy while creating actual and potential dynamic benefits. These, we argue, offset static losses. However, by the mid-1990s, the costs of continued wage increases increasingly overwhelmed the dynamic benefits of the high-wage, high-tech strategy. We conclude that wage moderation is needed to realize fully the potential of a high-wage, high-tech strategy.

To analyse the first phase, we develop two models that, together, constitute a dynamic complement to the argument of Sinn and Sinn. They give first a demand-side and then a supply-side rationale for a convergence strategy in which high wages drove out of business the least efficient producers while investment subsidy secured the investment necessary to restructure the eastern economy towards high-wage, high-tech production for high-growth markets.

6.2 DEMAND-SIDE RATIONALE FOR A HIGH-WAGE, HIGH-TECH STRATEGY

6.2.1   An Application of Thirlwall's Growth Rule

A simple theory of growth can be derived from the principle of external balance: namely, that imports (M) into a country or region in excess of exports (X) must be paid for by borrowing or inward financial transfers (that is, by some form of capital inflow, F). We can write this as,

$$M = X + F. \tag{6.1}$$

In which case,

$$m = \lambda x + (1-\lambda)f \tag{6.2}$$

where

m, x, and f approximate the percentage rates of growth of, respectively, imports, exports, and capital inflow, and

λ is the share of export revenues in total foreign exchange receipts; $(1 - \lambda)$, accordingly, is the share of capital inflow in total foreign exchange receipts.[2] Equivalently, λ and $(1 - \lambda)$ are, respectively, the proportions of the import bill covered by export receipts and capital inflow.

Equation (6.2) can be transformed by dividing through by m and multiplying both sides by the percentage growth of GDP (y):

$$y = \left[\lambda x + (1 - \lambda)f\right]\frac{y}{m}. \tag{6.3}$$

We can give economic interpretation to the final term on the right-hand side (y/m). The income elasticity of imports (π) measures the responsiveness of imports to a change in national income. It is calculated as the percentage change in imports divided by the percentage change in income (which causes the change in imports). Accordingly, y/m is the inverse of the income elasticity of demand: that is, $1/\pi$. And equation (6.3) may be written

$$y = \frac{1}{\pi}\left[\lambda x + (1 - \lambda)f\right]. \tag{6.4}$$

Equation (6.4) suggests that the growth rate of national (or regional) income is positively related to

- the rate of growth of exports (x), and/or
- the rate of growth of capital inflow (f)

and inversely related to

- the income elasticity of demand for imports (π).

For eastern Germany, the overriding policy objective is self-sustaining growth: that is, a rate of growth of national output (y) that enables convergence at a politically acceptable rate while restricting the growth of capital inflow and, ultimately, reducing the major element accounted for by fiscal transfers. Indeed, within two or three years of GEMSU annual fiscal transfers of about DM 200 bn reached a politically acceptable ceiling. Moreover, current levels of private sector investment are already so large – up to 50 per cent or more of eastern GDP – that a substantial rate of growth of capital inflow is unlikely. The corollary of no significant growth in capital inflow ($f=0$) is that equation (6.4) reduces to

$$y = \frac{\lambda x}{\pi}. \tag{6.5}$$

Equation (6.5) reproduces Thirlwall's 'growth rule' (McCombie and Thirlwall 1994). This suggests that growth and, hence, convergence in eastern Germany depends positively on the rate of growth of exports (weighted by the share of export revenues in total foreign exchange receipts), and inversely on the income elasticity of demand for imports. Income elasticity of demand for imports tends to increase with income (increasing income generates increasing demand for product diversity and, hence, increasing demand for imports) (McCombie and Thirlwall 1994, pp. 372 and 416). Consequently, it is difficult to enhance growth by influencing consumer preferences against imports (thereby, reducing income elasticity of demand for imports). Instead, the engine of growth has to be exports.

With respect to both analysis and policy prescription, there is little distinction to be made between minimizing income elasticity of demand for imports and maximizing the rate of growth of exports. In any particular market, the rate of growth of east German exports can be calculated as the growth of income multiplied by the income elasticity of demand for east German exports in that market. Maximizing export growth, therefore, also depends on the relevant income elasticity. In turn, income elasticities depend on product quality: that is, on all those product characteristics apart from price that influence consumer preferences (reliability, durability, technical sophistication, design, after-sales service, and so on). As incomes rise, consumers substitute away from lower- towards higher-quality goods and services. In turn, the highest-quality, mass-produced products tend to be the product of investment in new product and process technologies. Hence, the high-tech, high-wage strategy exploits a causal link between high-tech investment, product quality, high-income elasticity of demand and high growth. Correspondingly, a low-wage, low-tech strategy would tend to lock east German industry into producing low-quality goods with a low-income elasticity of demand. This is one reason why such a strategy would restrict the rate of growth and delay convergence.

6.2.2　Evidence on the Link between Technological Level and Growth

Maurer (1994, pp. 310–11) provides empirical support for the positive link between technological level and growth rate. He classifies OECD industries in the manufacturing sector according to their technological and growth characteristics. Following the standard OECD classification, industries are allocated to 'high-' 'medium-' and 'low-technology' sectors according to research and development 'intensities' – that is, OECD average shares of research and development expenditure in sales revenue – of, respectively, more than 10 per cent, between 0.9 and 10 per cent, and less than 0.9 per cent. The growth dynamic of each industry is proxied by a weighted average of annual export growth of 12 OECD countries over the period 1970–90 and sectors characterized as 'high growth' (more than 5.8 per cent), 'medium growth' (3.5 to 5.8 per cent), and 'low growth' (less than 3.5 per cent). Table 6.1 shows a positive correlation between the technological intensity and growth of industries. A corollary is that the more an economy specializes in high- or medium-tech output the more it produces for high- or medium-growth markets (Maurer 1994, p. 313).

Table 6.1   *Technological level and growth in the OECD (by industry)*

	High growth	Medium growth	Low growth
'High-tech'	Computers and office machinery Aerospace Consumer electronics	Pharmaceuticals	
'Medium-tech'	Electro-mechanical * Automobile	Chemicals Plastics oil refining Precision engineering and optical * Quarrying and stone working (ceramics, glass and mineral products) Other processing industries	Machine construction Non-ferrous metal production Shipbuilding Other transport
'Low-tech'		Food processing Metal working Paper and printing Wood working and wood processing	Iron and steel Textiles

Note: * See note 3.

Source: Maurer (1994, p. 312).

The data in Table 6.2 show that since 1991 in eastern Germany the growth of manufacturing has continuously increased potentially exportable output. Moreover, Table 6.2 shows that this growth has been sufficient to increase steadily the share of manufacturing in eastern GDP. Comparison with Table 6.4 shows that while the contribution of manufacturing to GDP in east Germany is smaller than in west Germany, it is in line with the three other major economies of the European Union (EU).

Table 6.2 *East German manufacturing output and contribution to GDP (percentages)*

	Growth of real manufacturing output over the previous year	Share of east German GDP
1991	–	16.8
1992	5.2	16.4
1993	11.7	16.9
1994	15.5	17.9
1995	6.7	18.1
1996 *	5.25	18.6

Note: * Estimate.

Source: JG (1996, p. 72).

Table 6.3 *Contribution of high- and medium-tech sectors to total east German manufacturing output*

	Share of east German manufacturing output (%)			
	Output growth (1991 = 100)	1991	1995 (1st half)	Type (according to Table 6.1)
Computers and office machinery; electro-mechanical; precision engineering and optical	147.9	11.2	11.8	Medium–high-tech; medium–high growth
Automobile	172.4	10.7	13.2	Medium-tech; high growth
Chemicals (including pharmaceuticals)	106.9	8.5	6.5	Medium-tech; medium growth
Plastics	355.7	1.3	3.4	Medium-tech; medium growth
Quarrying and stone working (ceramics, glass and mineral products)	282.9	5.1	10.2	Medium-tech; medium growth
Coking plants and oil refining	117.4	3.0	2.5	Medium-tech; medium growth
Sub-total		39.8	47.6	
Machine construction	72.7	18.1	9.3	Medium-tech; low growth
Total		57.9	56.9	

Source: Calculated from JG (1995, p. 81).

Table 6.3 shows that within manufacturing restructuring has enabled high- and medium-tech industries with high or medium growth not only to increase output (Column 2) but also between 1991 and the first half of 1995 to increase their share in total output by about a fifth (Columns 3 and 4).[3] In comparison, machine construction – a medium-tech but low-growth industry – has undergone both reduced output and a greatly reduced share in total manufacturing output.

Since the early collapse of eastern manufacturing, restructuring to create competitive, high-wage firms has increased not only the share of manufacturing in total output but also the share of manufacturing accounted for by high- and medium-tech sectors with high or medium growth. Table 6.4 – also using the OECD classifications – shows that the total share of high- and medium-tech sectors in manufacturing output (56.9 per cent; from Table 6.3) is in line with west Germany and the other major industrialized economies. For reference, we list the shares of national output accounted for by manufacturing in each country. Here we have some evidence of success for the high-wage, high-tech strategy in restructuring east German industry towards knowledge-based manufacturing sectors with medium- to high-growth prospects.

Table 6.4   Share of medium- and high-tech sectors in manufacturing in selected industrialized countries, 1990 (percentages)

	West Germany	US	Japan	France	Italy	UK
High-tech	21	24	22	19	14	22
Medium-tech	34	27	33	28	26	22
Total	55	51	55	47	40	44

Share of national output – GDP – accounted for by manufacturing (current prices) (1992)

	West Germany	US	Japan	France	Italy	UK
	26.5 *	18.3[†]	27.9	20.5	20.5[‡]	19.3

Notes:
* Estimate for 1996 (JG 1996, p. 72).
[†] 1991 data.
[‡] Includes mining and quarrying.

Sources: *Economic Bulletin*, Vol. 32, No .9 (September 1995), p. 13; United Nations (1995, pp. 179–87).

6.3 SUPPLY-SIDE RATIONALE FOR A HIGH-WAGE, HIGH-TECH STRATEGY: THE ACCUMULATION OF CAPITAL AND 'LEARNING-BY-DOING'

This section explains why convergence depends on renewing the eastern *capital stock* at the highest technical level. Such investment increases the capital:labour ratio and embodies new technology. In addition, high-tech investment raises productivity by maximizing opportunities for learning-by-doing.

Increasing productivity and growth of output are generated by process innovation and product innovation. Innovation, or technical progress in the broad sense, may be seen as a series of problem-solving activities; that is, a learning-by-doing process (Ricoy 1991, p. 732). Learning-by-doing is the hypothesis that management and workers learn through experience and that experience is obtained during production. Accordingly, learning-by-doing generates dynamic economies of scale and increased productivity of labour.[4] Moreover, learning-by-doing benefits are not necessarily confined to the individual firms that expand output over time. Labour turnover is one way in which knowledge obtained within one firm can be communicated to other firms. In this case, learning-by-doing within firms entails a positive externality – that is, learning spillovers – by increasing the stock of knowledge available to all firms within the economy. Accordingly, economic growth is a learning process that enhances productivity: that is, learning and productivity increases are endogenous to growth.

Learning-by-doing effects are not just a once-and-for-all source of growth but are a potential link in a process of unbounded growth. This process of cumulative causation sustains a virtuous circle – that is, a self-expanding process – in which increased output induces productivity increase and thus further output increase (in principle, for ever).

Learning-by-doing and cumulative causation support the dominant strategy for eastern Germany in two ways: (1) by amplifying the productivity effect of investment; and (2) because these amplification effects are maximized by investment at the highest technical level. The rest of this section develops these arguments.

6.3.1 Promotion of Investment on the Largest Possible Scale: The Case for Investment Subsidy

In this section we explain how investment drives growth of output and employment.[5] We start with three supply-side effects whereby investment – particularly in machinery and equipment – raises productivity.

1. Net investment – that is, investment in excess of depreciation – increases the capital stock per worker. Increasing the *quantity* of equipment at the disposal of each worker enables output per worker to rise. However, raising productivity by investing in more of the same is limited by diminishing returns to capital. Initially, this constitutes an incentive for investment in eastern Germany. With diminishing returns, the east's relatively low capital:labour ratio means that the potential return from capital investment is relatively high. Hence, precisely because eastern Germany is relatively poorly endowed with capital, it has the potential to grow at a faster rate and converge with western Germany.

   Ultimately, diminishing returns dictate that productivity growth from accumulation of capital at the existing level of technology is limited. However, productivity growth generated by the accumulation of knowledge and its application to production is potentially unlimited. Positive interactions between investment and technological advance – for example, the possibility of inward investment embodying highest prevailing levels of technology as well as learning-by-doing effects – give further and more important reasons why eastern Germany has the potential to grow at a faster rate and converge with western Germany.

2. Investment is the vehicle of technical progress. In two ways, investment is the means whereby knowledge is introduced into production.

   b. Technical progress is not exogenous but is embodied in new equipment. Accordingly, investment usually improves the *quality* of the capital stock through the installation not just of more equipment but of better, more efficient equipment.

   c. 'The introduction of new capital may lead to better organization, management, and the like. This may be true even if no new technology is incorporated in the capital equipment' (Wolff 1991, p. 566).

   Accordingly, in eastern Germany the potential return from capital investment is relatively high not only because of its relatively low capital:labour ratio but also because investment offers the opportunity to modernize equipment and bring production towards the technological and managerial frontiers.

3. New processes and products bring uncertainties that are resolved through experience as well as further research and development (Ricoy, 1991, p. 732). Consequently, investment not only introduces knowledge into production but also requires the generation of *new* productive knowledge. Learning-by-doing means that 'technological advance should be correlated with the accumulation of capital stock' (Wolff, 1991, p. 566). Subsidizing and accelerating investment has the initial effect of raising the capital:labour ratio and so increasing productivity

and output. This initial increase, moreover, has the potential to be amplified and perpetuated by learning-by-doing effects.

In addition, there is the 'Verdoorn or Kaldor effect, whereby investment growth may lead to a growth in demand and thereby to the maintenance of a generally favourable economic climate for investment' (Wolff 1991, p. 566). Accordingly, inward investment may be seen as powering a process in which further increases in investment and productivity growth are endogenous (that is, part of a self-generating cumulative process).

Demand-side theory reinforces the three supply-side causal links between the rate of capital:labour growth and productivity growth (for empirical support for this link, see Wolff 1991). Together, they suggest that high-tech investment is the key to eastern catch-up. Moreover, these investment effects are to a large extent 'external' to individual firms. General learning effects and experiences with the handling of new technology (as opposed to specialized training programmes) benefit not only the firm in which they occur but also – via labour turnover – producers as a whole. Likewise, the firm increasing output benefits not only itself – say, through static scale economies – but also raises demand for other firms. In this case, investment subsidies for eastern Germany fulfil the public policy role of making good the inability of markets to stimulate private investment to a level reflecting its social return.

6.3.2   Promotion of Investment at the Highest Technical Level: The Case for a High-wage Strategy

In eastern Germany, rather than maintain the existing productive apparatus through low wages, a strategy of thoroughgoing reconstruction in the presence of a high level of human capital should constitute the most favourable environment for the process of learning.[6] In other words, the alleged need for publicly financed training as a way out of industrial decline fails to materialize. Investment in high-tech real (rather than human) capital provides a platform for skills, knowledge and experience to develop without an explicit intervention in the east German labour market. The more rapid is structural change and technological renewal the speedier the corresponding learning process. This enhances skills and generates higher productivity growth. In turn, the result is higher output growth, which eases the process of structural transformation.

From the point of view of firms, shock therapy, amplified by high wages but supported by investment subsidy, enforces increased efficiency of production but also enhances the learning process. From this perspective, there are three problems with a strategy based on relatively low wages and, hence, relatively low-quality output.

- The first, as explained above, is that such output will be subject to relatively slow demand growth and, hence, minimal learning-by-doing effects.
- Second, if we assume that learning-by-doing on the basis of essentially unchanged technology is subject to diminishing returns then, even if demand for the products of existing and slowly changing east German technology could be increased, the benefits of learning-by-doing would still be minimal.
- Third, and most important, a low-wage strategy would perpetuate existing eastern technologies so that learning-by-doing might tend to reinforce adherence to obsolete technology, thereby retarding radical restructuring and the renewal of learning-by-doing at a higher level and rate. At best, learning-by-doing in the context of an obsolete and, hence, well-understood technology yields minimal benefits. At worst, it reinforces adherence to existing technology and retards change.

  a. *Learning-by-doing with obsolete technology: the best case* A large part of learning-by-doing arises from the operation of existing plant and equipment. Even that part which arises from investment decisions can be a response to shortcomings in the operation of existing technology, giving rise to learning that is concerned with incremental supplement or modification of existing processes and products. The downside of such a learning process is the possibility that the value of such learning is constrained by obsolete technology. In this case, firms – or, as in the case of eastern Germany, whole industries – can devote themselves to gaining experience, knowledge and technological mastery of processes and products that are increasingly incapable of yielding competitive advantage. In the best case, therefore, the benefits of learning-by-doing with an obsolete technology are minimal. This conclusion is reinforced if we allow for diminishing returns as the existing technology becomes more familiar and the returns from learning effects diminish over time.

  b. *Learning-by-doing with obsolete technology: the worst case* Obsolete technology not only devalues the learning process but may also be an obstacle to fundamental restructuring. Because the trajectory of change and learning is defined by existing technology, producers operating with obsolete technology can become trapped into dedicating their resources – above all, their time and energy – to the incremental improvement of relatively high-cost and low-quality output. The alternative for the producer with lagging technology is to undertake fundamental restructuring to reduce costs and enhance product quality. However, while the possibility remains for further improvement of the old technology, there is a ready excuse for continuing the old ways as well as a powerful case against undertaking the cost of radical change. In eastern Germany, anecdotal evidence for this is provided by attempts as late as 1990 to modernize hopelessly obsolete products – the Trabant among them. Even when the arguments are compelling, it is enormously difficult to engineer radical change in place of adherence to existing technology. According to Michael Porter, corporate change is difficult and complacency more natural: consequently, 'pressure to change is more often environmental than internal' and 'outsiders' ... are often the innovators' (Porter 1990, pp. 51–2). In this worst-case scenario, Sinn and Sinn's 'organic' strategy, in which eastern firms survived because of low wages, would have reduced pressure for radical restructuring and encouraged micro-level inertia and resistance to change. Moreover, at the macro level, a low-wage strategy would have slowed the process of structural change, tending to restrict the eastern economy to low-wage, low-tech production and thus delaying convergence indefinitely. Conversely, allowing wage pressure as the 'environmental' agent of change and subsidizing investment by western 'outsiders' entailed lost output but accelerated the pace of transformation.

Producing on the basis of low wages and obsolete technology would have risked this 'worst case' in which learning-by-doing reinforces adherence to existing technology and counteracts the incentives to change. Instead, productivity growth has been secured by allowing high wages to force producers in eastern Germany to 'forget' existing technology and to adopt state-of-the-art western technology: new and high-tech investment was necessary not only for a once-and-for-all raising of productivity to prevailing western levels but also to ensure the benefits of learning-by-doing in relation to current rather than obsolete technology.[7]

6.4 CUMULATIVE CAUSATION: VICIOUS AND VIRTUOUS CIRCLES OF GROWTH

Table 6.5 sets out in schematic form how learning-by-doing effects compound the demand-side argument of Section 6.2 in a process of cumulative causation. Both models display mechanisms whereby investment and growth are mutually endogenous (hence, self-perpetuating).

Together, they show how a low-wage, low-tech strategy generates a *vicious circle* of (relatively) low quality, minimal learning effects, low productivity growth and low output growth, while a high-wage, high-tech strategy generates a *virtuous circle* of high quality, maximal learning effects, high productivity growth and high output growth.

Table 6.5 Vicious and virtuous circles of growth

'Low-wage, low-tech' strategy		'High-wage, high-tech' strategy	
Investment		Investment	
⇒ Increased capital/labour ratio		⇒ Increased capital/labour ratio	
⇒ Increased labour productivity		⇒ Increased labour productivity	
⇒ Increased output		⇒ Increased output	
But process technology still obsolete and output of relatively low quality		*Increasing proportion of technology at or approaching world's-best standard*	
Best Case			
Channel 1	*Channel 2*	*Channel 1*	*Channel 2*
⇒ Obsolete, hence familiar technology	⇒ Relatively low quality	⇒ Learning-by-doing at a higher technical level	⇒ Relatively high quality
	⇒ Relatively low export growth and high income elasticity of demand for imports		⇒ Relatively high export growth and low income elasticity of demand for imports
⇒ Relatively little learning possible	⇒ Relatively low growth of demand and output	⇒ Learning-by-doing effects maximized	⇒ Relatively high growth of demand and output
⇒ Relatively low productivity effect from 'learning-by-doing'		⇒ Relatively high productivity effect from 'learning-by-doing'	
⇒ Relatively low output growth		⇒ Relatively high output growth	
⇒ Relatively slow growth of (induced) investment		⇒ Relatively high growth of (induced) investment	
Worst Case			
'Learning-by-doing' reinforces adherence to obsolete technology			
⇒ Restructuring delayed			
⇒ Growth slowed still further			
⇒ (Induced) investment reduced still further			

Table 6.5 links investment, export performance, and economic growth into a single self-perpetuating process. Section 6.4.1 presents some informal evidence that in eastern Germany a joint process is under way of investment in medium- and high-tech manufacturing, improving export performance and high growth.

6.4.1   Empirical Evidence on Investment, Export Performance and Growth

Table 6.6 shows the sectoral composition of investment in eastern Germany for each year 1991–94. Although, in this period, manufacturing investment declined steadily from 30 per cent of total investment in the enterprise sector (excluding housing) to 24 per cent, in each year it was considerably in excess of the share of manufacturing output in GDP (see Table 6.2). Over time, this should increase manufacturing output and develop eastern Germany's export base.

Table 6.6   Investment by sector (DM million), 1991–1994

	1991	1992	1993	1994	Percentage increase (1991–1994)
Agriculture, forestry and fishing	950	1,090	1,300	1,500	58
Utilities	8,940	12,690	15,500	17,500	96
Mining	1,420	1,440	1,500	1,600	13
Manufacturing	18,510	22,500	23,700	24,600	33
Construction	3,610	4,440	4,500	5,500	53
Trade	4,360	5,330	5,700	6,000	38
Transport and communications	16,140	22,512	24,900	26,700	65
Banking and insurance	1,380	2,110	2,100	1,600	16
Housing	15,900	23,910	31,400	44,900	182
Other services	6,430	8,630	13,400	16,900	163
Total Enterprise sector	77,640	104,652	124,000	146,800	89
Other (state and private non-profit sector)	14,920	23,250	26,500	32,200	116
Total	92,560	127,902	150,500	179,000	93
Enterprise sector (excluding housing)	61,740	80,742	92,600	101,900	65

Source: Statistisches Bundesamt (1995), *Das Gesamtergebnis* (Table 28).

Table 6.7 shows that in 1994 nearly two-thirds of investment in manufacturing was in high- and medium-tech industries. (From 1991 to

1993 the proportion was consistently greater than 60 per cent.) Hence, given the correlation between the extent to which industries are information based and their growth (see Table 6.1), western investment is developing an export base mainly in high- and medium-growth industries.

Table 6.7   Manufacturing investment by technological category (DM million), 1994

	High-tech[*]	Medium-tech	Low-tech
Total investment	2,340	13,530	8,730
Share of manufacturing investment	10%	55%	35%

Note: * Includes electro-mechanical and precision engineering; see note 3.

Source: Calculated from Statistisches Bundesamt (1995), *Das Gesamtergebnis* (Table 28).

Table 6.9 shows that by Spring 1996, east German enterprises depended for somewhat more than half of their turnover on east German customers, about one quarter on west Germany and one-sixth on true exports.[8] In a number of respects, the export data is encouraging.

- While at the end of 1995 the volume index for export orders was still only at a little more than 80 per cent of the 1991 level, this comparison hides the reorientation of east German exports from undemanding COMECON markets to fiercely competitive markets in industrialized Western countries.
- The importance of western medium- and high-tech investment in rebuilding east Germany's export capacity is revealed by the commodity structure of the turnover of eastern enterprises. Table 6.8 shows that the more technologically intensive goods (especially investment goods) are showing signs of export capability distinct from lower-tech sectors dependent on regional markets.
- Table 6.9 shows a strong positive correlation between growth and export performance. In the five years 1991–95, Thuringia and Saxony had the highest growth of the five new *Länder* and by the beginning of 1996 sales on the west German market or exports accounted for more than half of enterprise turnover. In turn, this is related to the relatively high proportion of investment goods producers in these states. Moreover, with the exception of Berlin (East) – with an industrial structure in this period dominated by services and construction – there is a perfect rank correlation between 'export' performance (Column IV) and real GDP growth (Column V). Table 6.9 also shows the extent in Spring 1996 of export activity in the eastern *Länder*, the growth performance over 1991–95 of both

eastern and western *Länder*, and – as a rough guide to weighting – *Land* populations in 1990.

Table 6.8   Commodity composition of east German exports

	Spring 1996: percentage of business turnover arising from sales in east Germany, west Germany and other countries		
	East Germany	West Germany	Other countries
Construction	92	8	0
Raw materials and semi-manufactures (Produktionsgüter)	73	16	11
Services	65	27	8
Consumer goods	37	42	21
Investment goods	32	39	30
Total	56	27	17

Source: Survey of 498 east German enterprises conducted Spring 1996 by the Institut der Deutschen Wirtschaft, Köln.

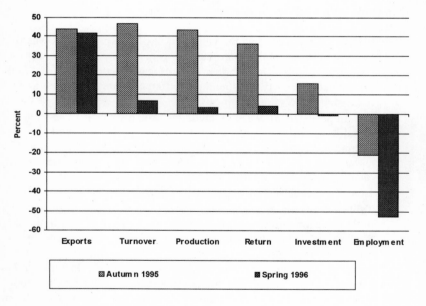

Source: iwd (16 May 1996, p. 8).

Figure 6.1   Balance (in per cent) of positive and negative expectations of east German enterprises

Table 6.9   Export and growth performance

	Spring 1996: percentage of business turnover arising from sales in east Germany, west Germany, and other countries [1]				Growth record (percentage change) [2]		Population (million) (1990) [3]
	(I) East Germany	(II) West Germany	(III) Other countries	(IV) 'Exports' (II+III)	Growth of real GDP (1991–1995)	Growth of real GDP (1994–1995)	
Thuringia	32	43	25	68	+ 40	+ 4.6	2.5
Saxony	42	33	26	59	+ 35	+ 7.4	4.9
Brandenburg	60	25	16	41	+ 31	+ 4.9	2.7
Saxony-Anhalt	61	23	16	39	+ 30	+ 4.3	3.0
Mecklenburg-West Pomerania	64	25	12	37	+ 24	+ 5.9	2.3
Berlin (East)	77	15	7	22	+ 32	+ 5.0	3.2 (Berlin)
East Germany	56	27	17	44			
Hessen					+ 8.0	+ 2.3	5.5
Schleswig-Holstein					+ 7.0	+ 2.2	2.6
Hamburg					+ 7.0	+ 2.1	1.6
Lower Saxony					+ 6.0	+ 2.1	7.2
Bavaria					+ 6.0	+ 1.6	10.9
Germany					+ 6.0		
North Rhine-Westphalia					+ 3.0	+ 1.6	16.7
Rhineland-Palatinate					+ 2.0	+ 1.1	3.6
Bremen					+ 2.0	+ 1.8	0.7
Baden-Würtemberg					+ 1.0	+ 1.3	9.3
Saarland					+ 1.0	+ 2.0	1.1
Berlin (West)					– 4.0	– 1.5	3.2 (Berlin)

Sources:
1. Survey of 498 east German enterprises conducted Spring 1996 by the Institut der deutschen Wirtschaft, Köln.
2. Volkswirtschaftliche Gesamtrechnung der Länder (compiled by the Institut der deutschen Wirtschaft, Köln).
3. Owen-Smith (1994, p. 40).

The robustness of this developing export capability is indicated by a survey of business confidence published in May 1996 by the Institut der deutschen Wirtschaft, Köln. The survey of 498 eastern enterprises confirmed the downturn in eastern Germany. Striking, however, is *continued optimism with respect to exports to industrialized western countries* (that is, excluding exports to former COMECON countries). Figure 6.1 summarizes the main results of this survey. It shows the balance of optimistic and pessimistic expectations with respect to the main indicators of economic health (a negative balance on, say, investment, means that more firms intend to reduce than to increase investment).

Amid this general anticipation of worsening business conditions, eastern enterprises expect to be able to maintain the dynamic of export growth to industrialized Western countries established during the years 1993–95 (in 1995, increasing by 15 per cent compared to west Germany's 6 per cent). This is a more sanguine view than that of the German Institute for Economic Research (DIW) supported by data indicating that eastern firms account for only 2 per cent of German exports and little more than one per cent to industrialized Western countries.

Table 6.10   East German exports as a share of German exports

Share of east German firms	1991	1992	1993	1994	1995
In total German exports	2.6	2.1	1.9	1.8	1.9
In exports to western industrial countries	0.8	0.8	0.8	1.0	1.2

Source: Vierzehnter Bericht (1996, p. 55, Table 23).

However, widely cited data of the kind reported in Table 6.10 gives a too pessimistic impression. The decline in eastern exports as a share of total German exports is explained by continued growth of west German exports to former COMECON members at the same time as exports from east German suppliers shrank. Meanwhile, the increased share of eastern firms in total German exports to western industrial markets reported in Table 6.10 is possibly a serious underestimate. As the DIW report notes, intra-firm deliveries are not taken account of in this data. Consequently, because a large part of the east German economy is made of branch plants of west German firms, an unquantifiable but certainly large part of eastern output is delivered to western parent firms. These deliveries from east to west can subsequently be exported directly – after minimal further value added (for example, packaging) – or indirectly – having entered as intermediate goods into products finally exported – but are not counted as eastern exports.

6.5   THE LIMITS OF A HIGH-WAGE STRATEGY

Barry and Bradley's comments on the strategic choices facing the EU's southern periphery are relevant to eastern Germany (1994, p. 23):

Do they permit the fairly rapid destruction of their indigenous, inefficient, labour-intensive, low-wage sector and facilitate its replacement by an efficient capital (or R&D) intensive, high-wage sector? As in the Irish and Spanish cases, this route appears likely to entail substantial structural unemployment and an associated high tax burden if social welfare systems are put in place.

In comparison with Greece and Portugal, eastern Germany is privileged with respect to the existing level and rate of accumulation of physical infrastructure and human capital and, above all, inward investment. This has enabled eastern Germany to avoid condemning a large part of its population to the status of working poor, occupying 'low-skill, low-productivity, low-pay' 'bad' jobs. The downside is a high long-term unemployment rate supported by the German system of social insurance.

In the first five years of Unification, the prevailing high-wage, high-tech strategy supported by publicly subsidized inward investment and fiscal transfers has enabled dramatic restructuring and productivity growth. However, as productivity rises, increasingly the problem in eastern Germany is *not the average productivity level but the proportion of the population employed at this level*. Again, comments of Barry and Bradley are relevant (1994, p. 22):

> Average productivity levels in Spain and Ireland are now not far behind the EU average, but there is still some leeway to make up. However, the greater part of the shortfall in average living standards in these countries is due to the fact that in both an exceptionally low proportion of the population is employed at these productivity levels.

Table 6.9 shows that in the five years 1991–95 growth in the five new *Länder* was both higher and more even (ranging from 24 to 40 per cent) than in the western Länder (ranging from 1 to 8 per cent after excluding West Berlin). However, during 1995 the pace of eastern Germany's catch-up slowed significantly. Construction output was stagnant, while manufacturing in general and investment goods in particular underwent declining growth rates. The pessimistic results of the Spring 1996 business survey evidence reported in Figure 6.1 indicated a downturn persisting into 1996. This has been confirmed by a sharp decline of annual GDP growth. In the convergence process, we can distinguish the period 1992–94 in which the annual rate of real GDP growth in east Germany was on average 8.2 per cent higher than in west Germany from 1995–97 in which the difference has shrunk to 1.3 per cent (JG 1996, p. 22). Indeed, the estimated difference for 1996 of 0.5 per cent and a forecast for 1997 of −0.25 per cent suggests that convergence has stalled.

The main *proximate* causes of stalled convergence were

1. slower growth in western Germany, and
2. the stabilization of inward fiscal transfers at about DM 200 bn per annum. This is probably the extreme upper limit of what is politically

feasible: 'Yet the most that a constant volume of government support can do is to help maintain the level of output achieved in the wake of the impulses originally induced. No additional expansionary effects are being generated by this support' (*Economic Bulletin*, January 1996, p. 11).

The *underlying* cause is that convergence is still not a self-sustaining process. Given that a declining proportion of inward fiscal transfers is devoted to investment, to increase or even maintain the level of investment requires investment-led growth independent of government incentives. This dynamic is precluded, however, by lack of profitability. Corporate investment in Germany is particularly sensitive to profitability as both incentive and means (most investment is financed from retained earnings) (Pugh 1997, pp. 89–92). In eastern Germany, the astounding fact is that 'firms as a whole are not realising any profits per working hour at all. There can consequently be no investment dynamic in the absence of government incentives' (*Economic Bulletin*, January 1996, p. 11). The Spring 1996 business survey evidence reported in Figure 6.1 demonstrates a sharp decline in the balance of firms with positive rather than negative expectations about profitability (returns), 'to which corresponds the clear decline in enterprise investment plans'. Indeed, comment the editors of the Report, 'for the first time since the survey began the balance of enterprises intend to reduce their investment' (iwd, 16 May 1996, p. 8).

Productivity has risen rapidly. In particular, between the beginning of 1991 and the end of 1994, manufacturing productivity (net output per working hour) more than tripled. Yet both at the level of the eastern economy as a whole and at the sectoral level of manufacturing labour costs have risen at least as fast (*Economic Bulletin*, September 1995, p. 7; January 1996, p. 13; and November 1996, p. 24). Consequently, *there is no gap between productivity and hourly labour costs to generate profit* and, hence, investment financed out of retained earnings.

Many of the benefits of high wages in combination with subsidized investment depend on unmeasured – and possibly unmeasurable – externalities and, hence, are difficult to compare with the costs of this strategy. However, it is likely that by the mid-1990s the benefits of further wage increase are exceeded by the costs. In this case, the *first phase of the convergence process* is at an end. In the early years of Unification, wage increases could be justified as an instrument of 'creative destruction' that precluded eastern Germany from becoming trapped in a vicious circle of low wages, low skills, low productivity and low growth. After five years these benefits have been secured: wages, skills, productivity and growth are all relatively high. Consequently, it is likely that the potential for further benefit from wage increase has been exhausted. Conversely, the costs of this strategy continue: unit labour costs remain at such a high level that eastern firms, especially new small- and medium-size firms, cannot earn sufficient profit to finance the investment necessary for self-sustaining recovery. Indeed, given that the growth of fiscal transfers and externally-financed inward investment have reached their limits, the costs of continued wage increase tend to intensify in terms of curtailed growth and prolonged convergence. Additional wage increase, therefore, is likely to generate increasingly more cost than benefit. This suggests a *second phase of the convergence process* characterized by strategic reorientation towards wage restraint. The initial high-wage strategy must give way to something like Sinn and Sinn's 'organic' or restricted wage growth strategy.

NOTES

1. 'Low- medium- and high-tech' refer both to the extent to which particular industries – especially in manufacturing – are knowledge based (that is, R&D intensive) and to the extent to which investment within any industry is in leading-edge technologies (that is, those embodying the latest technical and managerial 'know-how'). These concepts are clarified below, in Section 6.2.2.
2. Equation (6.2) applies the rule that *the growth of a sum is the weighted average of the rates of growth of the components.*
3. Table 6.3 does not account accurately for the separate shares of medium- and high-technology output in east German manufacturing. First, because definitional discrepancies prevent a complete and exact mapping of industrial sectors from the German data (for example, coking plants and oil refining) on to the indicative categories of Table 6.1 (for example, oil refining). Second, the technology-intensity categories group activities that can be very different: within, say, a generally medium-tech sector (for example, chemicals), there might be high-tech sub-sectors (for example, pharmaceuticals) which are over- or under-represented in a particular location. And, third, classification systems differ: for example, electro-mechanical and precision engineering are sometimes listed as high-tech (for example, *Economic Bulletin*, September 1995, p. 9) and sometimes as medium-tech (for example, Maurer 1994, p. 312).
4. See Vassilakis (1991, p. 151): 'Empirical studies of the production process in various industries have demonstrated a positive association between current labour productivity and measures of past activity like past cumulative output or investment'. On the economic logic of this empirical relationship, see Ricoy (1991, p. 732).
5. Section 6.3.1 focuses on the causal link between investment and productivity growth that, necessarily, generates output growth. Empirical evidence for a causal link between investment and *employment* growth is furnished by Dinenis and Funke who, in a study of UK and West German manufacturing, discover that the investment rate 'has a positive impact upon manufacturing employment in both countries' (1994, p. 418).
6. Wood (1995, p. 24) surveys recent evidence that the upgrading of skills occurs in the context of embodied technical progress: 'various studies have found rises in the skill intensity of employment in particular industries or firms to be correlated with rises in "technology indicators", meaning measures of capital stock, computer use, R&D expenditure, and so on ... There is a lot of econometric evidence that skill and capital are complementary'. Similarly, in a review of recent research on post-war European growth, Crafts (1997, p. 2) emphasizes that in assessing investment in human capital it is important 'to recognise that production strategies and skills accumulation are strongly interrelated'.

7. Balasubramanyam et al. (1994 and 1996) provide econometric evidence on the contribution to growth of learning-by-doing effects.
8. Collection of data on intra-German trade was suspended at the end of 1994. Consequently, only business survey evidence is available on eastern 'exports' to western Germany.

7. Convergence and Catch-up: Results and Prospects

7.1 DIVERGING ESTIMATES OF CONVERGENCE

Early estimates of the time it will take for eastern Germany to converge with and catch up western levels of productivity and living standards (measured by per capita output) shifted rapidly between extremes of optimism and pessimism. Some widely cited estimates are given in Table 7.1.

Table 7.1   Estimates of the period of convergence

Mayer [*]	Sinn and Sinn (1992, p. 142)	Hughes Hallet and Ma (1994, p. 1735)	Dornbusch and Wolf [†]	Barro and Sala-i-Martin [†]
10 years	> 20 years	30–40 years	50 years (80%)	84 years (80%)

Notes:

[*] *Borrowed Prosperity: Medium Term Outlook for the East German Economy* (Goldman-Sachs International: London, May 1992); cited in Kaser (1995, p. 7).

[†] To 80 per cent of western levels; cited in Burda and Funke (1993, pp. 6–7).

In Chapter 3 we suggested that misleading comparisons with 1948 gave rise to unfounded optimism about the speed of convergence. In Section 7.2 we criticize the more pessimistic predictions. Sections 7.3 and 7.4 argue that complete equalization of eastern productivity and per capita output with western Germany is not necessarily the most appropriate performance criterion, and that in terms of the development of per capita output comparison of eastern Germany and Italy's Mezzogiorno is misleading. Section 7.5 shows that a convergence period of 10–15 years can be supported by extrapolation of east Germany's growth rates in the first five years of Unification. This provides a lower bound for plausible estimates of the convergence period. Very high growth in the years 1992–95 depended on unprecedented rates of investment and productivity growth. Projecting the former is conditional upon a radical improvement of profitability, while an element of the latter came from sources that cannot be repeated. At best, therefore, these conditions for growth in the early years can be maintained only partially. Accordingly, simple extrapolation is likely to overpredict future growth and underpredict the convergence period. Finally, Section 7.6 uses historical and comparative data to argue that a convergence period of 20–30 years is plausible, conditional upon prolonged wage restraint allowing sustained profitability in the eastern enterprise sector.

7.2　WHY THE MORE PESSIMISTIC ESTIMATES MAY BE MISLEADING

The pessimistic predictions of Columns 4 and 5 of Table 7.1 stem from empirical work suggesting that the typical speed of regional convergence – that is, the amount by which the annual growth rate of poor regions exceeds that of the richest regions in the same country – is about 2 per cent (Barro and Sala-i-Martin 1995, p. 413). However, this 'two-per cent rule' for regional convergence may have little relevance to eastern Germany. Both data and theoretical framework are limited as a valid basis for assessing eastern Germany.

This empirical regularity of regional convergence at an annual rate of 2 per cent arises from studies of convergence among US states, Japanese prefectures and the regions of eight European countries. However, as Burda and Funke point out, projecting this on to eastern Germany neglects 'the special situation of the ex-GDR as a previously inefficient planned economy with a large potential for rapid productivity improvements' (1993, p. 3). Sources of rapid initial growth are discussed in Section 7.5.2, below. These had the potential to generate a 'jump' increase in productivity by using existing resources more efficiently. There was no such source of growth in the developed market economies from which was derived the 'two-per cent' convergence rule. Consequently, its application to eastern Germany overestimates the convergence period.

Equally serious objections to the application of the two-per cent rule to eastern Germany's convergence process arise from the limitations of the growth theory from which it is derived. First, it does not take account of either migration or inward investment (Burda and Funke 1993, p. 13). In Chapter 6 we argued that inward investment in particular is a prime mover of growth in eastern Germany. Second, the theory does not take account of the productivity and growth effects of equipment investment. These are emphasized by Burda and Funke (1993, pp. 16–17).

> recent results reported in Levine and Renelt ... find that a one percentage point increase in the overall investment share is associated with a 0.17 per cent increase in per capita growth rates in a sample of 101 countries over the period 1960–89. [Moreover,] De Long and Summers ... adduce evidence that the high correlation of investment and

growth is primarily due to the component business machinery in the former ... equipment investment is a catalyst for learning-by-doing and upgrading skills and its effect could be greater, ceteris paribus, than say residential construction ... they estimate that an extra point in the equipment investment share of GDP raises long-run growth by 0.3 percentage points compared with a mere 0.02 percentage points for other investment.

In the years 1990–92, in west Germany the gross investment share in GDP was about 20 per cent and the gross business equipment share in GDP about 10 per cent while in east Germany these ratios were about twice as high (Burda and Funke 1993, pp. 15 and 17). Section 7.5.1, below, shows that the gross investment share reached about three times as high in 1994 with the gross business equipment share likely to rise beyond its 20 per cent share. Applying the estimates cited by Burda and Funke to these investment share differentials yields a 'crude guess regarding the impact of such investment rates on per capital growth' (Burda and Funke 1993, p. 16). Together, they suggest that higher investment in east Germany should generate a higher annual per capita growth rate of at least 3.4 per cent.[1] A third link between investment and growth emphasized by Burda and Funke (1993, pp. 17–18), but neglected by the growth theory used to derive the two-per cent rule, is the role of public infrastructure.

Infrastructure refers to the cumulative investment spending of central, regional and local government agencies and public enterprises (postal service, telecommunications, hospitals, and railways) ... such spending has external effects on the productivity of private economic activity; for example, firms with access to a good telecommunications system are capable of operating more efficiently ... public investment is a policy measure which can spur both private capital formation as well as total factor productivity.

Table 7.3, below, shows that in east Germany per capita infrastructure investment has been up to 75 per cent higher than in west Germany. The rapid pace of infrastructure investment is thus a further reason to expect that the growth differential between east and west Germany will be substantially more rapid than suggested by the two-per cent rule. Finally, the same arguments relating to the growth effects of investment also qualify the pessimistic convergence estimate of Hughes Hallet and Ma whose key assumption in this respect is that 'investment does not take off as expected' (1994, p. 1746). Table 7.3 shows that this assumption is not justified. Evidence that investment has 'taken off' together with evidence that investment powers growth suggests that the higher estimates of the convergence period reported in Table 7.1 are too pessimistic. In this chapter, we discuss what might be plausible in the light of historical and comparative data. We adopt this approach because no model exists which takes into account all the growth factors discussed here and in Chapter 6.

7.3 WHAT IS THE CONVERGENCE TARGET?

Convergence may be interpreted literally, as equivalent per capita GDP in eastern and western Germany. Achieving convergence becomes less daunting if account is taken of the extent and speed of reduction of regional variations within western Germany. Figure 7.1 compares approximate percentage deviations of real per capita GDP from the West German mean in 1950 and 1990.

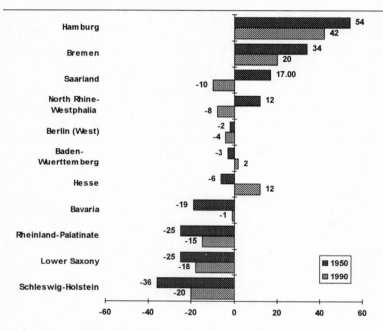

Source: Barro and Sala-i-Martin (1995, p. 372).

Figure 7.1   Proportionate deviation of real per capita GDP in West German Federal States from the country mean, 1950 and 1990

The apparent decrease in the range of divergence (the standard deviation declined by about one-third) took place mainly in the twenty years after 1950 (Barro and Sala-i-Martin 1995, p. 401). The best performing of the 1950 laggards closed or more than closed the gap with the national average by between five and 18 percentage points. In comparison, even allowing 20 years confronts eastern Germany with a far more daunting task: in 1994, eastern per capita GDP was still slightly less than half that in western Germany (JG 1995, p. 89).

A less daunting task can be set if we note that the three poorest of the western Federal States have a combined population similar to that of eastern Germany – about 13.5 compared to 16.5 million in 1990 – and per capita GDP between 15 and 20 per cent less than the western average.[2] Accordingly, should eastern Germany converge to 80 per cent of western per capita GDP it will be within the range of what was acceptable in the BRD before Unification.

7.4 EASTERN GERMANY'S CATCH-UP

Eastern Germany is often compared with Italy's Mezzogiorno. The value of this is open to doubt. The Mezzogiorno – the Italian South – is not a precisely defined area and in a number of other ways is not comparable with eastern Germany (for example, being predominantly agricultural and having a major problem with organized crime). It stands rather as a metaphor or warning of the consequences of non-convergence: a relatively backward region permanently dependent on fiscal transfers, which help to increase prosperity but are incapable of closing the gap with the national average.

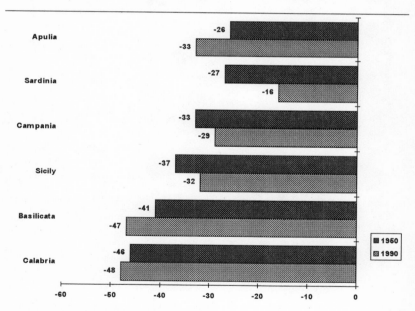

Source: Barro and Sala-i-Martin (1995, pp. 373–4).

Figure 7.2 Proportionate deviation of real per capita GDP in Italy's Mezzogiorno regions from the country mean, 1950 and 1990

Figure 7.2 compares approximate percentage deviations of real per capita GDP in the six poorest – also the six southernmost – Italian regions from the national mean in 1950 and 1990. With a combined population of about 19.5 million in 1990 – about one-third of the total – three of these regions actually diverged from the Italian average over the period and the

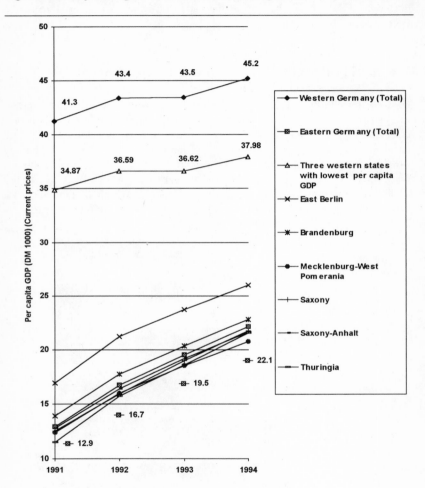

Source: JG (1995, p. 89) and own calculations.

Figure 7.3   East German catch-up: per capita GDP in western Germany, the three poorest western states, eastern Germany, and the five eastern states (plus East Berlin)

average catch-up (weighted by 1990 population) was less than three-quarters of one percentage point. The experience of Italy's backward South is thus quite different from west Germany's backward regions.

The experience of Italy's Mezzogiorno is also very different from the convergence dynamic across eastern Germany in the first four years of Unification. Figure 7.3 shows the extent of the catch-up of eastern per capita GDP with western Germany and the population-weighted mean for the three poorest western states (shown in Figure 7.1). Data for the eastern States separately shows a homogeneity in the catch-up process. (East Berlin is markedly higher, but the population is too small to exert undue influence on per capita GDP for eastern Germany, shown in other figures.)

Figure 7.4 depicts catch-up in terms of eastern per capita GDP as a share of per capita GDP in both west Germany as a whole (almost a half in 1994) and in the three poorest western states (almost 60 per cent in 1994).

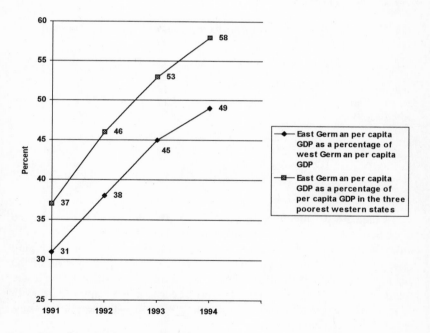

Source: JG (1995, p. 89) and own calculations.

Figure 7.4 East German catch-up: per capita GDP as a proportion of per capita income in west Germany and the three poorest western states

The first five years of Unification established a convergence dynamic very different from Italy's Mezzogiorno. However, this largely reflects the scale of inward fiscal transfers. In the long run, the comparison will prove completely misleading only if investment and growth become self-sustaining, thereby allowing the steady reduction of fiscal transfers. In turn, this is conditional on establishing the conditions for profitable production in eastern Germany.

7.5 GROWTH AND CONVERGENCE TRENDS AFTER FIVE YEARS OF UNIFICATION

Table 7.2 shows two phases of convergence: 1992–94 when growth in east Germany was 6 per cent or more higher than in west Germany; and from 1995, when convergence slowed and stopped (or even began to reverse, according to the pessimistic forecast for 1997).

Table 7.2   Real GDP growth rates in eastern and western Germany, 1992–1997

	1992	1993	1994	1995	1996 [*]	1997 [†]
Eastern Germany	7.8	8.9	9.9	5.3	2.0	2.25
Western Germany	1.8	−1.9	2.2	1.6	1.5	2.5
Difference (East–West)	6.0	10.8	7.7	3.7	0.5	−0.25

Notes
[*] Estimate.
[†] Forecast.

Source: JG (1996, p. 22).

In Chapter 6 we attempted to explain these two phases and discussed the policy reorientation needed to renew convergence. In this chapter, the more modest aim is to establish a plausible time scale for convergence. In Figure 7.5 we generate a best case scenario by using a linear extrapolation of the catch-up of per capita GDP displayed in Figure 7.4: if we exclude lower growth rates from 1995, complete convergence of per capita GDP with western Germany is projected for the year 2003 and with the three poorest western states by about 2000.

Convergence within 10 to 15 years may be regarded as a lower bound for plausible estimates. According to our argument in Chapter 6, Section 5, high growth in per capita output implies high productivity growth, which presupposes investment. On the one hand, investment in relation to GDP has reached an unparalleled level in eastern Germany. Yet maintaining this

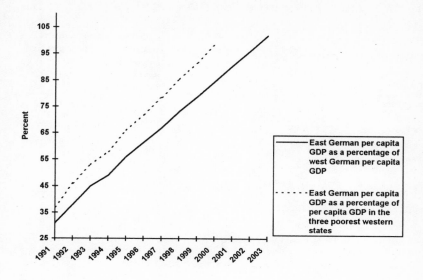

Figure 7.5 East German catch-up extrapolated from 1991–1994

kind of investment level is conditional upon an increase in profitability that is by no means guaranteed. On the other hand, a part of the early boost to productivity was generated by a once-and-for-all improvement in the use of existing capital stock rather than the renewal of the capital stock upon which growth depends in the long run. The two following Sections discuss investment and productivity.

7.5.1 Investment Trends after Five Years of Unification

Table 7.3 shows a uniformly high and increasing level of investment in private sector capital stock, housing and in public sector infrastructure.

Investment:GDP ratios of 60 per cent or more are historically unprecedented. Table 7.4 indicates the range of investment:GDP ratios achieved by the countries with the highest rates in previous periods. The only comparable example is Singapore, which for much of the 1980s achieved investment:GDP ratios in excess of 40 per cent.

At 19 per cent in 1994, the investment:GDP ratio in equipment alone was close to the typical Western European level for the total investment share. Moreover, the high rate of building investment – double the per capita value for west Germany – points to further investment in equipment. Equipment is decisive for productivity: hence, a continuing high rate of investment in equipment augurs well for future productivity growth.

Table 7.3   Investment in east Germany (DM bn at 1991 prices)*

	1991	1992	1993	1994	1995[†]	Per capita values as a percentage of west Germany 1994 [‡]	Investment: (eastern) GDP ratio 1994 (1995)[†]
Enterprise							
sector	61	75	85	94	101	140	36 (37)
• Equipment	39	42	46	50	53	110	19 (19)
• Building	22	33	39	44	48	202	17 (17)
Housing	17	23	28	38	47	89	15 (17)
Government	14	20	21	24	24	177	9 (9)
Whole economy	92	118	134	156	171	126	60 (62)

Notes
*   Gross fixed capital formation; values rounded.
†   All 1995 values based on forecasts.
‡   Investment per capita: east Germany as a percentage of west Germany.

Sources: *Economic Bulletin*, October 1995 and JG (1995, p. 79) (own calculation).

*Table 7.4   Rates of investment achieved by previous pace-setters
              (investment as a percentage of GDP)*

USA 1885–1910	West Germany post-1955	Italy post-1960	Japan post-1960	Taiwan post-1970	South Korea post-1980
20–25	20–25	20–25	30–35	25–35	30–35

Sources: *Socialist Economic Bulletin* (1991, pp. 8 and 12); Rodrik (1995, p. 59).

Investment in east Germany has enormously increased the capital stock in terms of both quantity and quality. Capital stock data does not reflect fully the quantitative increase because of depreciation – both of obsolescent stock being written off and of new capital stock rapidly depreciated for tax purposes. None the less, between 1991 and 1995 investment increased the gross capital stock in the east German enterprise sector (that is, excluding housing) from DM 604 bn to DM 835 bn or, in per capita terms, from 46 to 61 per cent of the capital stock per inhabitant in west Germany (JG 1996, p. 57; data in 1991 prices). More useful is data that shows the increasing quality of the capital stock, as measured by a steady increase in the proportion of total gross capital stock in the eastern enterprise sector (excluding housing) installed since Unification. This rose from less than 10 per cent in 1991 to more than 45 per cent in 1994 (Deutsche Bundesbank, 1995).

7.5.2 Productivity Trends after Five Years of Unification

Increase and renewal of capital stock is powering increased productivity (see Chapter 6). Table 7.5 shows the rate of increase of productivity – real GDP per employee – together with the increase in productivity as a percentage of western levels both in the economy as a whole and in industry. The total employment level is added to establish that rising productivity since at least 1992/93 is the result of supply-side transformation and not merely the reflection of reduced employment.

Table 7.5   East German productivity growth (percentages), 1991–1995*

	1991	1992	1993	1994	1995
Percentage increase (whole economy)	na	24	10	7	4.5
Percentage of west German productivity					
• whole economy	31.0	43.1	51.6	54.3	55.2
• industry [†]	28.8	43.1	52.8	58.1	59.3
Total employment (1000)	7,321	6,387	6,208	6,303	6,457
Percentage change in total employment		−12.76	−2.80	1.53	2.44

Notes
*   GDP per employee (current prices).
[†]   Manufacturing, mining, utilities – water and energy – and construction.

Sources: Percentage of western levels from JG (1996, p. 77); all other data from JG (1995, pp. 384, 386 and 103) (own calculations).

Very high initial productivity growth rates can be partly discounted. At the onset of Unification there were important reserves of productivity growth.

1. *Employment policies*   Policy in the DDR was directed towards security of employment. Consequently, if an enterprise implemented labour-saving rationalization in one part of its operations, the normal procedure would be to reemploy displaced labour elsewhere in the enterprise. Under market conditions, however, redundant labour ceases to be the responsibility of the rationalizing firm and becomes (in a *social* market economy) the responsibility of the social insurance and training systems and so on. Freedom to rationalize – and the competitive incentive to do so – put an end to previous over-employment and increased productivity.
2. *Use of labour power*   First, quantitatively, empirical investigations under the old regime showed that, because of deficient organization, discontinuities in production commonly accounted for losses of 25–35 per cent of total working time. Better management practice – spurred by competitive pressure – was a source of rapid increase in productivity.

Second, qualitatively, there were the harder to quantify gains to be made from better motivation and greater incentives for creativity: once enterprises were independent of the central plan, there was more scope for taking responsibility while a competitive rather than a monopolistic environment provided the incentive to do so.

3. *Reallocation of resources away from sectors with a comparative disadvantage towards sectors with a comparative advantage* Relative productivity differentials between east and west Germany varied widely (from as low as 10 to as high as 90 per cent; see above, Chapter 3 and Burda and Funke, 1993, pp. 9–10). Accordingly, there was considerable scope for efficiency gains from reallocating resources from less to more productive sectors. Unification made this possible because, previously, the state monopoly of foreign trade prevented the DDR from being integrated into the global division of labour, and thus reaping the benefits of specialization in sectors of comparative advantage.

The potential effect of these productivity reserves was partly *static*: that is, giving a once-and-for-all productivity increase by way of a more efficient utilization of existing resources. These static benefits help account for large productivity increases in 1992 and 1993 but, after five years of Unification, are likely to have largely been realized. To this extent, productivity in the early years grew at a rate that cannot be expected to persist. However, the early growth effects also reflect the potential of educated and skilled labour working in a newly competitive environment. Competitive pressure enforces maximum effort in production and innovation and is thus the source of *dynamic* benefits: that is, an ongoing increase in the rate of productivity growth.

Competitive pressure acting on a skilled workforce with increasing access to state-of-the-art equipment will generate productivity growth. To the extent that productivity in the early years grew at a rate conditioned by these factors, high growth rates can be expected to persist.

1. Competitive pressure is an established fact.
2. Eastern Germany has a well-educated and trained workforce capable of adapting flexibly to investment and innovation (see Chapter 4, Section 4.1.2 and Chapter 5). Moreover, high wages in the presence of both high unemployment and high investment in fixed capital and R&D may induce workers to invest in education and training (Redding 1996). The quality of human capital is thus high and rising.

None the less, even given competition and skilled labour as necessary conditions, rapid productivity growth depends on investment in fixed capital. In turn, a high rate of fixed investment requires improved conditions for profitable production.

A linear extrapolation from 1991–95 data in Table 7.5 of the increasing ratio of eastern to western productivity gives catch-up by the year 2015 in the economy as a whole and by 2002 in industry. Industry includes the preponderance of traded goods so that rapid catch-up is encouraging from the point of view of developing the export base in eastern Germany. However, to raise the performance of the economy as a whole towards the productivity growth rate of industry requires a high rate of productivity growth in services (including the financial sector): in 1994, productivity in this sector was still only 35 per cent of the west German level (JG 1995, p. 396).[3] In turn, this requires the rate of capital accumulation in services to be raised towards the rate in industrial sectors. In 1994, the per capita capital stock in the east German service sector (excluding housing) was only 12 per cent of the west German level while in the industrial sector it was 47 per cent (*Economic Bulletin*, October 1995, p. 5).

The final section offers a perspective on securing profitability throughout the eastern economy and, hence, the continued investment needed to secure high rates of productivity growth over the long run.

7.6 A HISTORICAL AND COMPARATIVE APPROACH TO CONVERGENCE

The rate of productivity growth in the long run will be decisive for convergence. To judge whether or not it will be achieved at all and, if so, how long it will take we need some perspective on profitability and investment.

For productivity in eastern Germany to become self-sustaining, rather than financed by subsidy, investment will have to be motivated and financed from retained earnings. Blocking this, however, is earnings growth in excess of productivity growth. Table 7.6 shows that in 1995 average gross earnings in eastern Germany were more than 70 per cent of the western level while average productivity was only 55 per cent (or, at best, 59 per cent in industry).

Table 7.6   East German gross earnings relative to west German, 1991–1995

	1991	1992	1993	1994	1995
Eastern real gross earnings relative to western	49	63	68	71	72

Sources: JG (1995, p. 384); 1995 figure calculated from JG (1996, pp. 351 and 363).

Figure 7.6 shows the contrasting gaps between the value of output and earnings per employee in west and east Germany (1991–94). This explains why in the aggregate eastern enterprises are not profitable. After paying wages, eastern firms do not have sufficient revenue to cover other costs including profit (considered as return on capital and risk-taking).

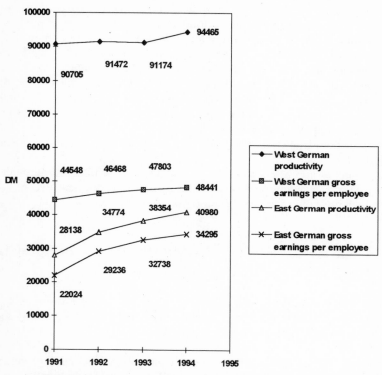

Note: * Productivity is GDP in 1991 prices per employee; gross earnings are nominal wages and salaries per resident employee deflated by the producer price index.

Source: JG (1995, pp. 384 and 455).

*Figure 7.6   Output and earnings per employee in west and east Germany, 1991–1994**

Table 7.7 shows that whereas in western Germany a fairly steady 50 per cent of the value of output produced per employee is accounted for by gross earnings, this proportion has been about 85 per cent in eastern Germany.

We have seen that even if the initially very high rates of productivity growth are not discounted, a mechanical extrapolation gives productivity

*Table 7.7   Gross earnings as a percentage of productivity in west
Germany, 1980–1994, and in east Germany, 1991–1994*

	1980	1981	1982	1983	1984	1985	1986	1987	1988	1989	1990	1991	1992	1993	1994
West Germany	50	49	48	47	46	45	48	50	50	48	49	49	51	52	51
East Germany	–	–	–	–	–	–	–	–	–	–	–	78	84	85	84

Source: JG (1995, pp. 384 and 455) (own calculations).

convergence within 12 to 25 years depending on whether we extrapolate
from the 1991–94 growth rates for industry or the whole economy. Whether
or not either extrapolation anticipates actual developments depends on
establishing the conditions for profitable production which, in turn, secures
the possibility of maintaining a high rate of investment and renewal of the
capital stock from domestic resources rather than from inward transfers.

In Spring 1995, a survey conducted by Germany's network of economic
research institutes found that while 40 per cent of industrial firms were
profitable 30 per cent were running at a loss (JG, 1995, p. 87). In order to
finance investment from retained earnings, profitability will have to be
increased (see 6.5, above). Figure 7.6 and Table 7.7 make it clear that this
can happen only if a prolonged period of wage restraint allows the gap
between output and earnings per employee in eastern Germany to widen to
at least the norm for western Germany. To the extent that this does not
happen, growth will slow and the period of convergence diverge upwards
from the lower bound of 10–15 years suggested by the most favourable
extrapolations for output and productivity.

There is mounting evidence that in eastern Germany formal tariff
agreements are being ignored with the tacit compliance of unions. If we take
an optimistic stance, then the social market ethos of consensus building in
the German labour market could make these informal arrangements into the
harbinger of a more formal agreement between unions and employers to
allow productivity to grow more rapidly than earnings in order to increase
profitability and, hence, investment and job security in the long run. West
Germany in the 1980s provides a partial precedent. Table 7.7 shows that in
the first half of the decade unions allowed the gap between gross earnings
and output per employee to widen by 10 per cent. In turn, this allowed the
rate of profit to rise and supported an investment boom. The precedent is
only partial, because while the process needed is similar it is on an
altogether different scale: instead of a 10 per cent widening of the gap, what
is needed in eastern Germany is a more than 300 per cent increase in the
percentage gap between out put and earnings per employee.

To conclude, we shall assume that wage restraint will increase
profitability thereby sustaining a high rate of capital accumulation. Granted

this condition of productivity growth, any estimate of the likely period of convergence depends on a judgement about the feasible rate of productivity growth in the medium to long run. One approach is to appeal to historical and comparative data for guidance as to the typical productivity growth rates of which market economies at their most dynamic are capable. Maddison's data tells us that for 16 industrial countries over the period 1870–1989, the most rapid average annual growth rate in labour productivity over a decade was that of Japan from 1960–70 (9.96 per cent). The next highest rates were that of Italy between 1960 and 1970 (6.69 per cent) and that of the BRD during the 1950s (6.64 per cent) (the decade of the economic miracle!) (1982, p. 212 and 1991, pp. 274–5). Moreover, 'the rapid development of ... the East Asian NICs [newly industrialized countries] since the 1960s produced productivity growth rates of 6–7 per cent *at most*' (Hughes Hallet and Ma 1992, p. 9 – original emphasis). (Comparison with Table 7.4 shows that these are the countries or regions with the successively highest investment:GDP ratios.)

We can use the arithmetic of compounding to calculate the rate of growth of productivity necessary for convergence over different periods and to different levels:

- for convergence to the 1991 level of productivity in western Germany;
- for convergence to the future level of west German productivity; and
- for convergence to 80 per cent of the future level of west German productivity under the assumption that labour productivity in west German manufacturing industry will increase at an average annual rate of 2 per cent.[4]

We take the initial level of eastern productivity to be 30 per cent of the western level. Under these assumptions, Table 7.8 shows the annual rates of productivity increase needed for convergence in different periods.[5]

Table 7.8   Scenarios for east Germany's productivity catch-up

Period of convergence (from 1991)	Necessary annual growth rate of productivity for convergence to the 1991 BRD level	Necessary annual rate of growth of productivity for equalization of productivity	Necessary annual rate of growth of productivity to achieve 80 per cent of the western level
10 years	12.8	14.0	11.8
15 years	8.4	10.0	8.5
20 years	6.2	8.0	6.9
25 years	4.9	6.8	5.9
30 years	4.1	6.0	5.3

In the light of historical and inter-country comparison, it would seem that equalization after 10–15 years of Unification requires a rate of growth of productivity that is unlikely to be accomplished. Only Japan has achieved protracted productivity growth in excess of 8 per cent per year. If eastern Germany can continuously beat or equal the historical best both in Germany and in other past and present productivity leaders (say, 6–7 per cent per year), then *equalization* is likely to take between 20 and 30 years depending on the benchmark. Even to catch up to the 1991 western level within this period requires productivity growth rates not far short of this.

NOTES

1. Calculated first as a differential of between 20 and 40 percentage points multiplied by 0.17 and, second, as a differential of 10 percentage points multiplied by 0.3 plus a differential of between 20 and 40 percentage points multiplied by 0.02.
2. For the populations of Schleswig-Holstein, Lower Saxony and the Rhineland-Palatinate, see Table 6.9 in Chapter 6. Using these population figures to weight the per capita GDP deviations in Figure 7.1 gives a weighted average deviation of minus 17.6 per cent.
3. The outstanding performer was the agriculture, forestry and fishing sector with productivity at 73 per cent of the western level in 1994.
4. The average annual growth of labour productivity – GDP per employee – from 1983 to 1993 (one complete business cycle) was 1.78 per cent.
5. The calculations were performed as follows. Column 2: if P is eastern productivity in 1991, A is western productivity in 1991, r the rate of growth of productivity, and t the catch-up time in years, then

$$P(1+r)^t = A, \text{ and } r = \left(\sqrt[t]{A/P}\right) - 1.$$

Columns 3 and 4: if α is the extent of catch-up, r the rate of productivity growth (with superscripts W and E denoting respectively, eastern and western Germany), t the catch-up time in years, e the exponential, and Π_{91}^E, Π_{91}^W the 1991 productivity level in, respectively, eastern and western Germany, then

$$\alpha \Pi_{91}^W e^{tr^W} = \Pi_{91}^E e^{tr^E}, \text{ and } r^W - r^E = \frac{\ln\left(\Pi_{91}^E / \Pi_{91}^W\right) - \ln \alpha}{t}.$$

8. International and Domestic Repercussions of German Unification

Section 8.1 is a case study in international economic linkages. It analyses trade and financial repercussions of German Unification on the domestic economies of Germany's EU partners as well as on monetary cooperation within the EU. In the case of the UK, we attempt to quantify the external repercussions of German Unification. Section 8.2 considers the impact of Unification on the external value of the DM and the consequences for German competitiveness. In considering these wider repercussions, we find that the monetary stance of the Bundesbank is a prime mover.

8.1 CONSEQUENCES FOR GERMANY'S EU PARTNERS AND FOR MONETARY COOPERATION IN THE EU

Fiscal expansion associated with Unification is the starting-point of the analysis. We then discuss the main channels through which Germany's EU partners have been subjected to spillover effects.

1. Unification generated increased exports for Germany's trade partners.
2. The Bundesbank responded to the inflationary consequences of Unification with higher short-term interest rates. The European Monetary System (EMS) transmitted higher German interest rates to the rest of the EU. The output and employment cost of higher interest rates offset the benefits of increased exports.

Finally, we examine the impact of German Unification on the EMS and suggest that a fixed exchange rate regime with no possibility of realignment cannot survive major economic shocks.[1]

8.1.1 The Domestic Impact of Unification

The starting point for analysing the economic spillover effects of German Unification is the enormous cost of west Germany's financial support for eastern Germany. This has been documented in Chapter 1 (see Table 1.2). This unprecedented *fiscal expansion* came when the West German economy was in its eighth year of growth with particularly strong real GNP growth in 1988 (3.53 per cent) and 1989 (3.86 per cent) together with substantial growth in employment. After eight years of economic upturn culminating in three years of rapid growth (1988–90), the West German economy did not have sufficient spare capacity to meet the demands of the east. The West German economy was operating close to – perhaps marginally in excess of – potential output (JG 1991, pp. 87 and 269). Consequently, western and eastern demand together exceeded potential German supply by more than 5 per cent of total output.

When demand exceeds supply in an open economy, the predictable consequences are *inflation and/or an import boom*. In a free market, excess demand causes prices to rise. In an open market economy, however, importing acts as an external source of additional supply and thus reduces upward pressure on the price level. These effects are recorded in Figure 8.1: between 1989 and 1991, Germany's current account surplus collapsed and inflation, after stabilizing in 1990, continued to rise towards an unacceptable level.

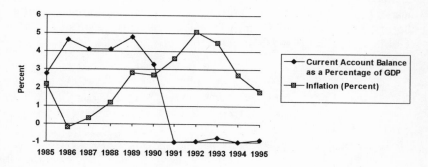

Sources: JG (1995, p. 21) and Datastream (own calculations).

Figure 8.1 Current account balance (percentage of GDP) and inflation, 1985–1995

8.1.2   External Spillover Effects

Increased imports and upward pressure on the price level were the two main channels through which German Unification affected the rest of the world and, in particular, the economies of EU partners.

- On the one hand, increased imports mean increased exports for Germany's trading partners and, hence, a significant boost to aggregate demand and national output.
- On the other hand, upward pressure on the price level forced the Bundesbank to raise interest rates. In turn, this exerted deflationary pressure throughout the EU.

These external effects of German Unification offset one another.

8.1.3   Trade Effects of German Unification

Under the pressure of Unification and fiscal expansion, the German current account balance with industrialized Western countries deteriorated by an amount equivalent to 5.5 per cent of GNP – from a surplus in 1989 of DM 107,190 million (equivalent to 4.77 per cent of GNP) to a deficit in 1991 of DM 23,207 million (equivalent to 0.83 per cent of GNP).[2] This sudden turnaround was caused by a step increase in imports associated with Unification. Figure 8.2 shows the value of exports and imports from first quarter (Q1) 1988 to Q4 1992.[3] There was a step increase in imports during the first two quarters of German Economic, Monetary and Social Union (GEMSU) (that is, Q3 and Q4 1990).

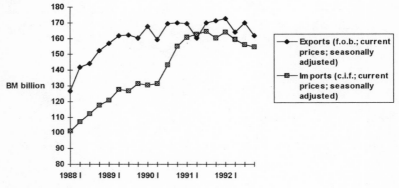

Source: Datastream.

Figure 8.2   German exports and imports before and after GEMSU, Q1 1988–Q4 1992 (current prices)

From the point of view of the German current account, GEMSU meant new citizens who imported but were unable to export like the existing population. This is illustrated in Figure 8.3, which measures exports and imports as a proportion of GDP. Until GEMSU in mid-1990, exports and imports moved together with an export surplus. GEMSU added the DDR's GDP, a new source of import demand, but very little in the way of exports. Accordingly, the import:GDP ratio was relatively little affected by GEMSU, while the export:GDP ratio plummeted. Exports and imports continued to track each other, but without the pre-GEMSU export surplus. Germany's imports, of course, are other countries' exports. All the main EU countries increased their exports to Germany more or less in step.

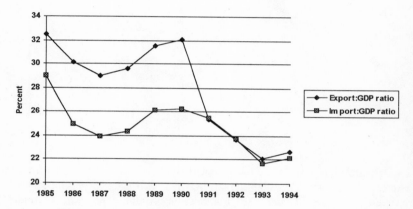

Source: JG (1995, pp. 347 and 353–4) (own calculations).

Figure 8.3   German Export:GDP and Import:GDP ratios, 1985–1994

Figure 8.4 shows UK, French and Italian exports to Germany indexed to 100 at the beginning of 1989 and displaying much the same pattern. The impact of GEMSU was sufficient to offset the typical Q3 fall in imports and to generate a sharp rise in the fourth quarter of 1990. Overall, by the end of 1991, Italian exports to Germany had increased by 42 per cent since the beginning of 1989, UK exports by 37 per cent and French exports by 56 per cent. Similar increases were shown by exports from Belgium and Luxembourg – 33 per cent – and the Netherlands – 31 per cent (all data from Datastream).

The step increase in the level of UK exports to Germany between Q390 and Q490 was 20.3 per cent – from £3,112 million to £3,744 million. Measured in terms of factor cost GDP – that is, in current prices net of indirect taxes and subsidies – this increased the proportion of UK output

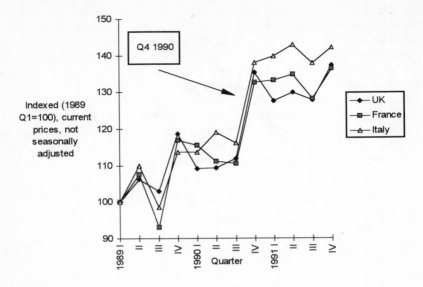

Source: Datastream.

Figure 8.4   German imports (f.o.b.) by source

exported to Germany by 0.51 per cent (from 2.57 per cent in Q390 to 3.09 per cent in Q490). This comparison between two successive quarters may be misleading. First, because this data is available only in seasonally unadjusted form. And, second, because there was a tendency for exports to Germany to increase as a proportion of GDP *before* Unification: in 1989, growth of UK exports to Germany (16.2 per cent) was more than 60 per cent higher than the growth of nominal GDP (9.98 per cent) (Datastream).[4] None the less, bearing in mind that GEMSU-generated imports offset a seasonal fall in imports, this simple comparison is indicative of a beneficial trade effect boosting UK GDP by as much as half a per cent.[5]

8.1.4   Unification and Inflationary Pressure in Germany

In spite of the safety valve of imports, Unification generated inflationary pressure within the German economy. The price level – defined as the cost of living for all households – actually declined by 0.1 per cent in 1986. However, as the economy grew strongly from 1986, inflation once again took hold – the price level stabilizing at a rate of increase of 2.8 per cent and 2.7 per cent in, respectively, 1989 and 1990 (see Figure 8.1). Inflation, therefore, did not begin with Unification. Rather, Unification – taking place in a booming economy – gave an upward twist to inflation.

From the German perspective, an inflation rate over the medium term of more than 2 per cent is unacceptable (JG 1991, p. 116). Moreover, Germany has powerful institutions designed to keep inflation within acceptable bounds. And among the instruments of monetary control at the disposal of the Bundesbank are two key interest rates: the discount rate and the Lombard rate.

- *The discount rate* is the interest rate used to determine the discount at which the Bundesbank buys short-term financial instruments (bills) from the commercial banks. In effect, it is the rate at which the banking system can borrow funds from the Bundesbank in order to maintain liquidity. Borrowing at the discount rate is the cheapest form of refinancing for banks but is subject to quotas. Consequently, bank lending and interest rates are influenced also by the higher Lombard rate.
- *The Lombard rate* is the normal rate of interest at which banks can be sure of borrowing Bundesbank funds – against security – to meet short-term liquidity needs. Since 1988, the Lombard rate has generally been set about 2 per cent higher than the discount rate.

Commercial rates of interest are particularly sensitive to the Lombard rate. Commercial banks frequently have to borrow from the Bundesbank in order to maintain liquidity. Consequently, by imposing restrictions on borrowing at the discount rate and other forms of short-term liquidity, the Lombard rate can be made to bite (JG 1991, p. 125). Increasing the Lombard rate, therefore, increases the cost of borrowing to banks and thus forces them to raise the cost of borrowing to their customers. Figure 8.5 demonstrates the major influence of the Lombard rate on the money market. It shows changes in the Lombard rate together with an important money market rate – the three-month Frankfurt interbank offered rate (an interbank rate is a rate at which banks can borrow from other banks in order to maintain short-term liquidity).

To suppress the inflationary tendency within the German economy (see Figure 8.1) the Bundesbank successively raised the Lombard and/or discount rates. Figure 8.5 charts the longest continuous rise in lending rates in German history. The Lombard rate more than doubled in steps from 4.5 per cent during the first half of 1988 to 9.75 per cent from December 1991. In turn, the interbank rate rose from 3.46 per cent at the beginning of 1988 to 9.75 per cent in June 1992. Finally, this meant a similar increase in base rates and the cost of borrowing throughout the economy. There are a number of channels through which higher short-term interest rates can suppress inflation.

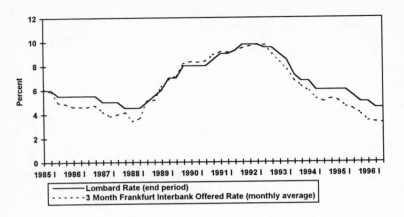

Source: Datastream.

Figure 8.5   German nominal interest rates, Q1 1985–Q3 1996

1. The purpose of ratcheting up interest rates is to raise the cost of credit. In turn, this reduces demand for loans from firms and individuals. In response to reduced demand, bank lending is reduced which reduces the rate of creation of new bank deposits and, hence, the rate of growth of DM M3 (a definition of money supply that includes bank deposits). Finally, reducing the rate of increase of the money supply reduces the rate of increase of the price level (in the medium to long run).

2. Figure 8.9 shows that the *real* short-term interest rate – calculated as the three-month Frankfurt Interbank Offered rate minus the rate of inflation – more than doubled from 2.66 per cent at the beginning of 1988 to 6.43 per cent in June 1992. The real interest rate is important, because it is the real cost of borrowing. Consequently, a rise in the real interest rate has a deflationary impact on consumption and, in particular, on investment. By reducing aggregate demand, upward pressure on the price level is reduced.

3. Rising short-term interest rates on the money market induce investors to substitute short-term for long-term assets, which tends to lower the price of long-term assets and raise long-term capital market rates. In turn, because most bank lending is in long-term funds, business investment is curtailed and aggregate demand is reduced (*Economic Bulletin*, Vol. 33, No. 1, January 1996, p. 16).

4. By raising short-term interest rates, the Bundesbank is also sending a signal to wage bargainers and public authorities that inflationary wage increases and fiscal policy will be countered – in the cause of price stability – by deflationary increases in interest rates (JG 1991, p. 122).

In the labour market, the intention is to create expectations of low inflation and, hence, reduced wage settlements.

The transmission mechanism between interest rate changes in Germany and the rest of the EU is the Exchange Rate Mechanism (ERM) of the European Monetary System (EMS).

The 'anchor' currency of the ERM is the DM – which means that the overriding monetary target for monetary authorities throughout the EMS is the DM exchange rate of their currency. In other words, the interest rates of participating countries are locked into German rates: higher interest rates in Germany mean higher interest rates throughout the EMS. Higher interest rates cause short-run capital inflow into Germany and a demand for deposits denominated in DM. In turn, increased demand for DM on the foreign exchange market causes an incipient appreciation of the DM against other ERM currencies. Conversely, this means an incipient depreciation of all other ERM currencies against the DM. However, because of the ERM commitment to keep currencies within prescribed bands around an agreed rate, this incipient depreciation has to be countered by increased interest rates throughout the EMS.

Figure 8.6 shows that between the beginning of 1989 and Summer 1992 the DM appreciated significantly – a little more than 15 per cent – against both the US dollar and the Japanese yen, but scarcely at all against the other currencies of the EMS.

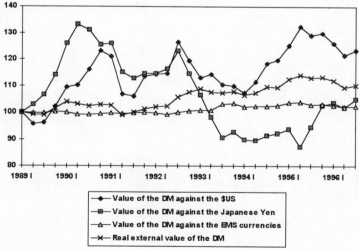

Source: Datastream.

Figure 8.6   The external value of the DM, Q1 1989–Q3 1996
(Q1 1989 = 100)

As rising German interest rates caused the DM to appreciate against the dollar and the yen, the US and Japanese governments were free to allow their currencies to depreciate against the DM. In contrast, EU governments had to keep their currencies in line with the strengthening DM. We can now see why – in spite of beneficial trade effects – German Unification exerted a deflationary effect throughout the EU: (1) because interest rates were higher than they otherwise would have been; and (2) because the EMS currencies as a group tended to appreciate against non-EU trading currencies.

8.1.5 Higher Interest Rates within the EU

Figure 8.7 shows the evolution of the Lombard rate (end period) together with the UK (end period) and French (period average) three-month Treasury bill rates (representing, respectively, UK and French money market rates) from the inception of the EMS in March 1979. From the early 1980s, French short-term interest rates show a clear convergence towards the level set by the German Lombard rate. The UK joined the ERM only in October 1990: from then on, until the exit of sterling in September 1992, there was likewise convergence of UK rates towards the Lombard rate.

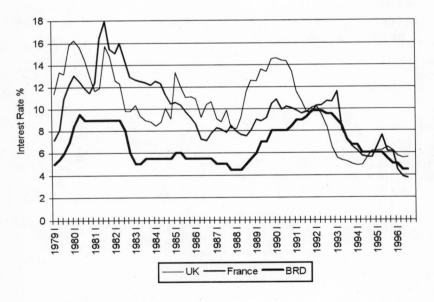

Source: Datastream.

Figure 8.7 Short-term nominal interest rates for France, Britain and Germany, Q1 1979–Q3 1996

Interest rate convergence was generated by inflation convergence. This is because most trade on the foreign exchange market is speculative: that is, funds are switched between currencies in search of the highest rate of return. The rate of return on a deposit in any particular currency is determined mainly by two factors: (1) the rate of interest paid in the particular currency; and (2) the expected rate of appreciation/depreciation of the currency. In turn, the main factor influencing expectations about the rate of currency appreciation/depreciation is the inflation differential. This accounts both for interest rate differentials and for eventual interest rate convergence within the EMS. The currencies of high inflation economies – until recently, including France and the UK – were likely to devalue against the low inflation DM. Consequently, investors in the foreign exchange market demanded a higher interest rate from high inflation currencies in order to offset expected depreciation (or the risk of devaluation within the ERM). However, because in the early 1990s German inflation rose while French and UK rates fell, inflation rates converged with the German level. Indeed, Figure 8.8 shows that the aftermath of GEMSU drove German inflation to the upper level of the major European economies and was not returned to an acceptable 2 per cent until 1995.

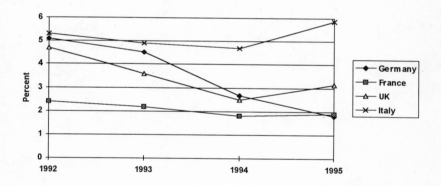

Source: Datastream.

Figure 8.8 Annual inflation rates in the main EC economies, 1992–1995

In the foreign exchange market, this meant that the franc and sterling were no longer expected to depreciate against the DM because of relatively higher inflation. Accordingly, a significant interest rate differential was no longer necessary to offset expected depreciation.

As the inflation differential dwindled so, therefore, did the interest rate differential between Germany and the UK and France. The problem is that *UK and French interest rates converged towards a German level that was rising.* Instead of converging towards an interest rate of, say, the average level for 1989 of 7.12 per cent (and a real rate of 4.53 per cent) the effects of German Unification meant converging to the July 1992 rate of 9.75 per cent (a real rate of 6.43 per cent).

To put EU interest rates in perspective, it is useful to contrast the interest rate response to, respectively, recession and the threat of recession in the US and Japan. In both countries short-term interest rates were substantially reduced: from 1989 in the US (from 8.11 per cent to 3.68 per cent in 1992 and a low of 3.17 per cent in 1993 – a real rate of 0.19 per cent); and from 1990 in Japan (from 7.72 per cent in 1990 to 2.98 per cent in 1993 and 0.5 per cent in the first three quarters of 1996 – a real rate of 0.2 per cent) (Datastream). In the US and Japan, therefore, counter-recessionary interest rate policy reduced rates to levels about 6 per cent lower than the German Lombard rate.

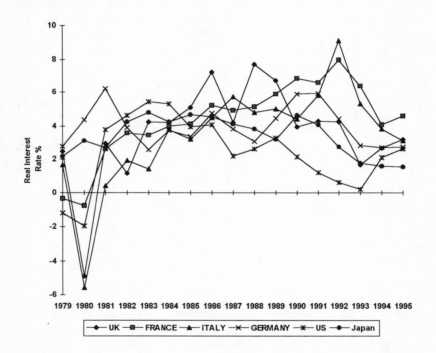

Note: * Calculated as the difference between the nominal interest rate (3-month Treasury discount rates and the 3-month Frankfurt interbank offered rate for Germany) and inflation (calculated from consumer price indices).

Source: Datastream (own calculations).

*Figure 8.9 Real interest rates of major currencies, 1979–1995**

This divergence in interest rates carried over to real interest rates. Figure 8.9 shows the evolution of real interest rates during the period of the EMS in the main EU economies – France, Germany, Italy and the UK – together with the US and Japan.

The period 1979–91 also covers the course of the business cycle (recession–boom–recession). From low (even negative) levels during the first recession and onset of recovery, the tendency of real interest rates during the 1980s boom was to rise. From 1989, however, there was a clear divergence between EU and non-EU economies. In the EU, real interest rates continued to rise even as EU members entered recession or were very close to doing so. In contrast, in the US from 1989 and in Japan from 1990, not only nominal rates but also real interest rates underwent substantial reduction to levels typically well below the EU norm.

Unification caused German short-term interest rates to set a high floor to both real and nominal interest rates within the EMS. Consequently, *to the extent that interest rates were higher than they otherwise would have been, German Unification exerted a deflationary influence throughout the EU.*

This is apparent from the cost to the UK of the interest rate consequences of German Unification. We can indicate the order of magnitude by applying published estimates of interest rate effects on UK GDP. These are readily available from the comparative studies by Church et al. (1988, 1989, 1990 and 1991) on leading macroeconometric models of the UK economy. In all the models 'the impact of interest rates on expenditure is now more powerful than in the past' (Church et al. 1991, p. 59). However, in 1991 it was still the case that, as the authors commented in their first survey, 'the results for interest rate simulations typically show very wide dispersion across the models, and often across different vintages of the same model' (Church et al. 1988, p. 78). For each model surveyed in the years 1988 to 1991, Table 8.1 gives the percentage change in GDP after one year in response to an unanticipated and permanent cut of one percentage point in short-term interest rates. The final column gives the mean GDP response.

In spite of dispersion across models and vintages of the same model, the mean GDP response is fairly stable – that is, a one percentage point cut in short-term interest rates generates an increase in GDP of 0.34 per cent (rounded) after one year. We can apply this average estimated interest rate effect to calculate the cost to the UK in 1991 of the interest rate reper-cussions of GEMSU. By 1991, the UK was in deep recession (real GDP fell by 2.2 per cent). Yet short-term rates of interest in the EU were 5.5–6 per cent higher than those prevailing in the US and Japan. Moreover, once released from the constraints of ERM membership in September 1992, UK short-term interest rates rapidly declined by about five percentage points (see Figure 8.7). In the light of this, we assume that in 1991 short-term nominal interest rates were at least 4 per cent higher in the UK than they

*Table 8.1   Interest rate simulation: percentage change in UK GDP after
              one year as a result of a one percentage point cut in nominal
              short rates*

	LBS	NIESR	HMT	BE	OEF	LU	CUBS	Mean GDP response
1988	0.36	0.67	0.38	0.24	0.15	na	0.15	0.325
1989	0.37	0.42	0.42	0.19	na	na	na	0.35
1990	0.22	0.50	0.45	0.18	0.40	na	na	0.35
1991	0.34	0.41	0.39	0.19	0.29	na	na	0.324

Key: LBS – London Business School; NIESR – National Institute of Economic and Social
Research; HMT – Her Majesty's Treasury; BE – Bank of England; OEF – Oxford
Economic Forecasting; LU – Liverpool University; CUBS – City University Business
School.

would have been in the absence of German Unification. In this case, *in
1991 the interest rate repercussions of GEMSU reduced UK GDP by about
1.4 per cent.*

8.1.6   Appreciation of EU Currencies

The divergence between high short-term interest rates in the EU and falling
rates in the US and Japan made the rate of return on holdings of EU
currencies increasingly attractive. In turn, this caused the EU currencies as a
group to appreciate against other major trading currencies. In the macroeconometric models, interest rates affect GDP not only through
their influence on consumption and investment expenditure but also
through their influence on the nominal and real exchange rates. Indeed,
the tendency is for interest rates and exchange rates to be jointly determined through an uncovered interest parity condition (Church et al. 1991,
p. 62). Because of this joint determination, no additional quantification is
needed: exchange rate effects have already been accounted for in the
interest rate effect.

8.1.7   Deflationary Impact on the EU

Interest rates and exchange rates within the ERM constituted a financial
transmission mechanism between the specifically German features of the
Unification shock – fiscal deficit, current account deterioration and
inflationary pressure – and the economies of Germany's EU partners.
Together, rising interest rates and appreciating exchange rates exerted a
significant deflationary influence on the economies of the EU: (1) higher

interest rates raised the cost of borrowing and thus depressed consumer spending (especially on consumer durables) and business investment; and (2) appreciating exchange rates reduced net exports.

The medium-term consequence of German Unification was to curtail private sector demand – that is, consumption, investment and net exports. Moreover, because higher interest rates increase the proportion of income needed to service existing debt, constraints on public expenditure were tightened. Membership of the EMS also ruled out independent monetary policy. With depressed demand and the traditional tools of macroeconomic policy precluded, German Unification exerted a significantly adverse medium-term impact on the rest of the EU. In the case of the UK in 1991, the beneficial trade effect was as much as 0.5 per cent of GDP and the interest rate cost about 1.4 per cent of GDP. Accordingly, our calculations suggest that *in 1991 the net German Unification effect on the UK economy was to depress GDP by about 1 per cent.*[6]

8.1.8 Implications for Monetary Cooperation in the EU

When the EMS is subject to an 'asymmetric shock' – that is, a situation in which EMS countries are affected in different (or even opposite) ways by economic developments – there is a strong case for realignment. In the early period of the EMS (up to 1983) there were a number of realignments precipitated by different rates of monetary growth and inflation. However, the biggest shock ever to hit the EMS is German Unification. This shock, moreover, was asymmetric.

Realignment – in this case, an appreciation of the DM against the other EMS currencies – could have had a number of beneficial effects for the rest of the EU.

1. Traded goods produced in Germany's EU partners would have gained price competitiveness. This would have translated more of the benefits of fiscal expansion in Germany into increased demand for EU goods.
2. DM appreciation would have had a counterinflationary effect in the German economy (imports becoming cheaper). With currency appreciation doing some of the work of counterinflation policy, the Bundesbank could have reduced interest rates. In turn, this would have enabled lower interest rates throughout the EU.

By the Summer of 1992, the case for realignment was apparent in the growing conflict between the Bundesbank's use of high interest rates to counter the inflationary consequences of fiscal expansion and the desire in the rest of the EU for renewed economic growth. As time went on, this conflict eroded the credibility of the ERM parities.

In the case of the UK, for example, the longer the recession and the greater the cost of maintaining sterling's ERM parities, the more open to doubt became the government's continued commitment to these parities as the 'cornerstone' of its economic policy. Economic fundamentals indicated high and rising costs associated with the government's commitment to sterling's ERM parities. After more than two years of recession, the UK still suffered from persistent trade deficits; and interest rates at least 3–4 per cent higher than justified by the condition of the domestic economy. The alternative was exchange rate realignment within the ERM. Accordingly, the credibility of the government's exchange rate commitment tended to weaken. Quite simply, it was becoming increasingly difficult to believe in a policy that promised indefinite recession. This made sterling's position in the foreign exchange market potentially volatile.

Increasingly, therefore, the logic of realignment contradicted the attempt of EU governments to set in place a 'hard EMS' (that is, an EMS without realignments) as part of the transition to monetary union. Against this background, the foreign exchange market required only a proximate cause to trigger speculation against sterling. In the event, in September 1992, this was provided by a 7 per cent devaluation of the lira. The consequence was that the realignment suggested by economic fundamentals was not negotiated and implemented within the ERM but, instead, forced upon the government as the result of a run on the pound and disorderly retreat from its previous policy commitments. In the Summer of 1993, a similar drama was played out with the French franc cast in the leading role. Finally, therefore, the contradiction between the realignment required to adjust to the asymmetric shock of German Unification and the hard EMS project was resolved by currency crisis and the reordering of the EMS. These events put an end to the hard EMS that emerged in 1987 – that is, the EMS as a system of fixed exchange rates preparatory to the irrevocable fixing of parities and full monetary union.

The repercussions of German Unification demonstrate that fixed exchange rate regimes of the 'hard' variety cannot survive large and sustained asymmetric shocks. This is a strong argument against any attempt to revive the hard EMS. Moreover, in the absence of massive enhancement of the EU's budgetary capacity (sufficient to compensate the losers from asymmetric shocks), or an unlikely conversion of the EU's citizens to wage flexibility and/or migration (sufficient to offset the output and employment effects of asymmetric shocks), the repercussions of German Unification also warn against monetary union.

The choice need not be between the alternatives of continuous exchange rate instability with a free foreign exchange market or occasional but costly upheaval under a fixed regime. Instead, a relatively greater measure of stability in the international trading environment could be secured by *a regime of fixed but adjustable exchange rates*. This would be to restore the EMS as it existed between its early turbulence and the attempt to harden it into a preparatory stage of monetary union.

8.2 CONSEQUENCES FOR GERMAN COMPETITIVENESS: THE OVERVALUATION OF THE DM

This section does not attempt a complete analysis of the impact of Unification on German competitiveness. Instead, we argue that changes in the external value of the DM should be prominent in any such analysis.

8.2.1 Tight Monetary Policy, Bundesbank Credibility and the Appreciation of the DM

GEMSU occasioned an unprecedented increase in government borrowing. Even before GEMSU, anticipated pressure on the capital market caused long-term interest rates to rise as market participants discounted the probable effects of Unification. First, anticipated inflation forced up the long-term *nominal* rate (to compensate investors for expected loss of capital value). Second, anticipated borrowing arising from reconstruction of the eastern economy and/or emigration was expected to change the demand and supply conditions for long-term capital and, hence, the long-term *real* interest rate. Consequently, between 1989 and 1990, the long-term nominal interest rate jumped from 7 to 8.8 per cent and the long-term real interest rate from 4.8 to 6.2 per cent.[7] In addition, upward pressure on long-term capital market rates was reinforced by the Bundesbank policy of raising short-term money market rates (see Figures 8.5, 8.7 and 8.9, and Section 8.1.4).

German monetary policy has been very tight. This is demonstrated by the relationship of short-term to long-term interest rates. In spite of upward pressure on capital market rates, Figure 8.10 displays evidence that the counter-inflation stance of the Bundesbank was sufficiently rigorous to invert interest rate yield curves in four of the seven years following 1988. In 1988, short-term rates began a rise of record duration, to be followed by reductions that were relatively cautious in international comparison. (See Figures 8.5 and 8.7 for comparison with UK interest rate reductions after the UK left the ERM in September 1992.) Under normal circumstances, because risk increases with the duration of loans, the longer the term the higher the interest rate (hence, the 'normal' yield curve). However, from 1988, and particularly in the aftermath of

Unification, the Bundesbank reinforced its reputation for monetary reliability – that is, adhering to its Statutes by giving priority to price stability – by unpopular rises in short-term interest rates (FT, 17 July 1992, p. 16). Figure 8.8 shows that German inflation rose substantially in the early 1990s. Investors understood that to some extent, German inflation reflected the once-and-for-all effect of price reform in eastern Germany: phasing out subsidy and deregulating non-tradable goods (in particular, rents, energy and transport) helps to explain why, in 1992, western inflation was 4.0 compared to 5.1 per cent for the whole of Germany; and, in 1993, 3.6 compared to 4.5 per cent (JG 1995, p. 21). Decisive, however, was the credibility secured by the Bundesbank in pursuing a tight monetary policy against both international and domestic opposition. This convinced investors that inflation would be brought under control and that the DM was secure as a low-inflation currency. In turn, the expectation of low inflation was reflected in lower long-term interest rates. Hence the 'inverted' yield curve: high short-term interest rates created the expectation of low inflation, thereby reducing the risk of investing in long-term DM-denominated assets as well as the rates necessary to ensure their purchase.

Relatively high and rising short-term interest rates induce investors to purchase and hold assets denominated in DM. Even when German rates began to fall, it may be hypothesized that Bundesbank credibility with respect to

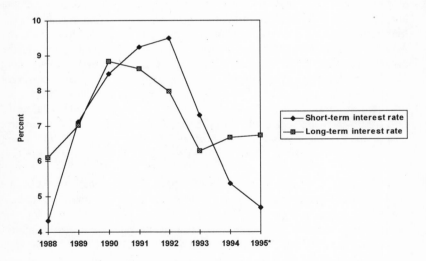

Note: * First three quarters.

Source: JG (1995, p. 356).

Figure 8.10   German short- and long-term interest rates, 1988–1995[*]

inflation perpetuated the attractiveness of the DM as a 'safe haven' for the world's liquidity. Of course, this cannot be ascribed wholly to Unification. In particular, we need to take into account the interest rate policy of the US Federal Reserve, associated wariness on the foreign exchange market of inflation and 'cheap dollars', and the consequent role of the DM as substitute for the US dollar. And, as we have seen, the tightening of monetary policy began in 1988. None the less, tightening rather than relaxing its monetary stance in unified Germany confirmed the reputation of the Bundesbank and the credibility of the DM as a low-inflation currency and, hence, reliable store of value. This was particularly the case, because exceptionally tight monetary policy was in part a 'punishment strategy' to offset the potentially inflationary effects of exceptionally loose fiscal policy and exceptional wage pressure which, in turn, were caused by Unification (see 1.9, above). Accordingly, Unification may be seen not as the sole cause but as a major factor in the appreciation of the DM.

Figure 8.6 charts the evolution of the external value of the DM since 1989: by the mid-1990s, the DM had appreciated by upwards of 20 per cent against the US dollar, had appreciated, depreciated and again appreciated against the yen, and remained stable against the EMS currencies. Against other currencies generally and in real terms the DM had appreciated by about 10 per cent. Another measure suggests a real appreciation of 20 per cent since 1990 ('Commerzbank Viewpoint': *The Economist*, 27 July 1996).[8] By the mid-1990s, appreciation and overvaluation of the DM were commonly identified as a source of competitive problems for German traded goods (JG 1995, pp. 61 and 131; *Economic Bulletin*, Vol. 33, No. 1, January 1996, p. 7; and Barclays Economics Department 1996, p. 5). However, judgements that a currency is under- or overvalued presuppose some measure of its appropriate value in terms of other currencies. Accordingly, we begin by presenting a simple method of estimating the appropriate or equilibrium level of the exchange rate.

8.2.2 Is the DM Overvalued? A Simple Method of Calculation

We calculate equilibrium exchange rates as bilateral rates compatible with macroeconomic balance.[9] Our method comprises two steps.

1. We identify the most recent year in which the two economies were closest to macroeconomic balance. Our proxy for macroeconomic balance combines relatively high-growth, low-inflation, unemployment close to the NAIRU, and a balanced current account.
2. Starting from this base year, we use time-series data to calculate the equilibrium exchange rate in each subsequent year. Two methods are used to perform these calculations.

a. The first takes into account the effects of inflation on the long-run equilibrium exchange rate in the manner suggested by the theory of relative purchasing power parity (PPP). In year t – the base year – we assume that the equilibrium (PPP) rate is given by the period average spot rate in this year. In each succeeding year – starting with year $t+1$ – the PPP rate is calculated by adjusting the previous year's PPP rate to offset the effects of different inflation rates.

b. The second takes into account not only the effects of inflation on the equilibrium exchange rate but also the additional effects of differential productivity growth. This approach is suggested by a productivity-modified theory of relative PPP. After the base year, each year's modified PPP rate – starting with year $t+1$ – is calculated by adjusting the previous year's modified PPP rate to offset the effects of *both* different inflation rates *and* different rates of productivity growth.

Choice of base year

The choice of base year is critical. The market average rate in this year provides an initial value for the long-run equilibrium exchange rate. Accordingly, this initial value influences the level of all subsequent calculated values of the equilibrium exchange rate. If the base year is not a year of macroeconomic balance for both economies, then the exchange rate in that year cannot be considered an equilibrium exchange rate. In this case, calculated rates for successive years will, likewise, not give equilibrium values.

By assumption, in the base year the market average nominal exchange rate gives the equilibrium exchange rate. To determine the year in which both economies were closest to macroeconomic balance, we establish a set of macroeconomic 'glee' indices for each economy. The year with the optimum mix of the standard macroeconomic performance criteria for the years 1960–89 is assumed to be the year closest to 'macroeconomic balance'. The components of the indices are as follows.

1. The measure of *unemployment* (U) is the deviation of measured unemployment from the Non-Accelerating Inflation Rate of Unemployment (NAIRU) (using estimates from Layard et al. 1991, p. 436). (This is to take account of changes in structural unemployment which, by definition, are independent of the exchange rate.) The series used for the indices is calculated as the actual rate of unemployment minus the NAIRU. Small percentage differences are better than large ones and negative percentages are best of all. (The cost of unemployment lower than the NAIRU should be picked up in higher inflation.)

2. *Inflation* is the percentage rise in consumer prices on the previous year.

3. *Annual GDP growth* is multiplied by −1 to be in line with the 'smaller the better' principle of inflation and unemployment.
4. *Current account* balance is measured as a percentage of GDP and also multiplied by −1 to be in line with the 'smaller the better' principle of the indices. Deficits and surpluses are treated symmetrically as percentage point deviations from current account balance.

The following four indices comprise the same four data series but with different weightings to reflect a range of relative priorities attached to the different macroeconomic performance criteria and to prevent one variable from driving the index.

$$\text{INDEX 1} = \frac{CPI + (2*GDP) + U + CA}{4}$$

$$\text{INDEX 2} = \frac{CPI + GDP + (2*U) + CA}{4}$$

$$\text{INDEX 3} = \frac{CPI + GDP + U + (2*CA)}{4}$$

$$\text{INDEX 4} = \frac{(0.5*CPI) + GDP + U + CA}{4}$$

where:

CPI = percentage change in consumer prices
GDP = percentage change in gross domestic product multiplied by −1
U = Registered unemployment rate minus the NAIRU
CA = Current account (percentage of GDP) multiplied by −1

In addition, for each country we calculated an aggregate of the four indices. In each case, we used a three-year moving average as a smoothing device in order to avoid selecting an outlier – that is, an annual value unrepresentative of the medium-run period – as the base year.[10] For all countries, the early 1960s emerged unambiguously as the era closest to the ideal of macroeconomic balance: 1962 in the UK and Germany (all four indices together with the aggregate); 1964 in the US (indices 1, 3, 4 and the aggregate; 1965 for index 2); and 1966 in France (indices 1, 4 and the aggregate; 1962 for index 2 and 1967 for index 3). In all cases, the individual and aggregate indices are consistent and the differences between years in this era are small compared with all later periods. Accordingly, the base year for each bilateral equilibrium exchange rate is identified as the lowest point of the mean of the two-country aggregate indices. Figure 8.11

plots these mean or bilateral indices and establishes 1962 as the base year for the DM/sterling and DM/FF together with 1964 for the DM/$US.

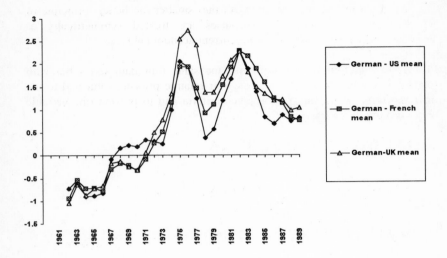

Note: * The lower, the closer to macroeconomic equilibrium in both countries.

Sources: CPI series: Maddison (1991, pp. 212–15); GDP: Maddison (1991, pp. 216–19); Unemployment (registered): Maddison (1991, pp. 262–5); Current Account: *European Economy* (various issues).

Figure 8.11   Mean macroeconomic indices*

PPP calculations

Once the base year is selected, we use two related theories of exchange rate determination to calculate the subsequent time-path of the equilibrium value of the exchange rate: (1) the theory of relative purchasing power parity; and (2) a productivity-modified relative PPP relation. Both theories are implemented for the DM/sterling rates. However, because of lack of availability of data and supporting econometric evidence on the influence of productivity growth differentials, only the first approach is implemented for the DM/French franc and DM/$US rates.

Relative PPP – or the 'inflation theory' of exchange rate determination – is the theory that over the long run the percentage change in the exchange rate equals the difference in inflation rates between the two currencies. Consequently, if one currency is subject to higher inflation than another, then its value in terms of that other currency must decline. According to relative PPP

$$\%\Delta ER = \%\Delta P^* - \%\Delta P^G, \tag{8.1}$$

where:

$\%\Delta E$ = percentage change in exchange rate (foreign currency per unit of domestic currency; for example, £s per DM 1);

$\%\Delta P^*$ = percentage change in foreign price level; and

$\%\Delta PG$ = percentage change in German price level.

PPP rates from the base year to 1995 are calculated from time-series data as follows. In the base year, the long-run equilibrium or PPP value is given by the nominal exchange rate. In succeeding years, the effects of the relative price changes on the PPP rate are lagged one year.

$$PPP_t = PPP_{t-1} + \frac{(\%\Delta CPI_{t-1}^* - \%\Delta CPI_{t-1}^G)PPP_{t-1}}{100} \tag{8.2}$$

where CPI is the consumer price index.[11]

By adjusting PPP for productivity differentials, real economy determinants as well as monetary determinants are introduced. De Grauwe (1989) developed a PPP model modified to take account of productivity differentials in the traded goods sector.

$$\%\Delta PPP^M = (\%\Delta P^* - \%\Delta P^G) + (1 - a)(\%\Delta q^G - \%\Delta q^*), \tag{8.3}$$

where

$\%\Delta PPP^M$ = change in the productivity-modified PPP rate;

a = the share of traded goods in the consumption basket;

$\%\Delta q^*$ = percentage change in productivity in the foreign economy; and

$\%\Delta q^G$ = percentage change in productivity in the German economy.

Beachill and Pugh (1996) have used cointegration techniques to estimate Equation 8.3 for three exchange rate series including the DM/sterling rate. The estimated equation for this rate is

$$\%\Delta ER = PPP + 0.32^*PDIFF, \tag{8.4}$$

where

$\%\Delta ER$ = percentage change in the exchange rate;

PPP = the inflation differential (UK–German); and

$PDIFF$ = the productivity growth differential in the traded goods sector (German–UK).

Equation (8.4) tells us that in the long run the exchange rate changes in proportion to the inflation differential and a little less than one-third of the productivity differential in the traded goods sector (that is, a 3 per cent difference in productivity growth would generate an exchange rate change of almost 1 per cent). In our estimation of productivity-modified PPP rates we used this coefficient. The productivity data used to arrive at these econometric estimations is also used in the following calculations.[12]

The productivity-modified DM/£ PPP rates (PPP^M) were calculated for the same period and according to the method used in the PPP calculations. Equation (8.5) differs from equation (8.2) by the extension to take account of differential productivity growth.

$$PPP_t^M = PPP_{t-1}^M + \frac{[(\%\Delta CPI_{t-1}^* - \%\Delta CPI_{t-1}^G) + (1-a)(\%\Delta q_{t-1}^G - \%\Delta q_{t-1}^*)]PPP_{t-1}^M}{100} \quad (8.5)$$

where $(1 - a) = 0.32$, from equation (8.4).

8.2.3 Over- and Undervaluation of the DM

We calculated equilibrium time paths for three bilateral DM exchange rates: PPP rates with respect to sterling, the US dollar and the French franc; and, in addition, a productivity-modified PPP rate with respect to sterling. Finally, we compared these calculated equilibrium rates with the actual period average bilateral nominal exchange rates in order to measure year by year the extent by which the DM was over- or undervalued. The results are reported in Figure 8.12.

Figure 8.12 reveals similarities in the pattern of DM under- and overvaluation. In the 1960s, lower inflation and/or higher productivity growth tended to increase German price competitiveness, while fixed exchange rates prevented an offsetting appreciation of the DM or depreciation of other currencies. Thus under the Bretton Woods system the DM was generally undervalued until, successively, sterling devalued (1967), the franc devalued (1968), and the US dollar floated (early 1970s). In the 1970s, floating exchange rates allowed Germany's inflation and productivity growth advantages to be more than offset by currency depreciation in the UK, US and France, causing the DM to be overvalued with respect to their currencies.

The tightening of monetary policy at the turn of the decade, first in the UK and then in the US led to an appreciation of sterling and the US dollar sufficient to make the DM undervalued against both currencies. DM undervaluation against sterling reached its maximum in 1981, declined steadily until 1986, but then persisted as preparation for ERM entry and then actual membership precluded the UK government from offsetting the competitive effects of higher inflation with currency depreciation. Following exit from the ERM in 1992,

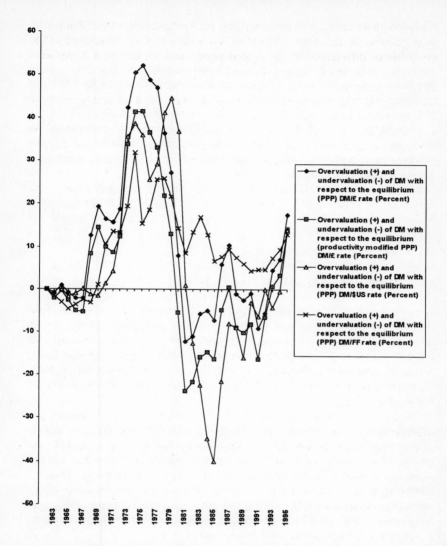

Sources: CPI series: Maddison (1991, pp. 212–15) and OECD, *Main Economic Indicators* (various issues); Productivity (1960–88): van Ark (1990, p. 372); Productivity (1989–92): calculated from (a) Manufacturing Output: OECD, *Main Economic Indicators* (various issues) and (b) Employment in Manufacturing and Hours of Work per Week in Manufacturing: International Labour Office, *Year Book of Labour Statistics* (various issues); Market (Nominal) Exchange Rate, Annual Average: *Financial Statistics* (CSO).

Figure 8.12   Under- and overvaluation of the DM against sterling and the French franc, 1962–1995 and the US dollar, 1964–1995 (percentages)

DM undervaluation was reversed. By 1995, overvaluation increased to, respectively, 14 per cent (PPP measure) and 18 per cent (productivity-modified measure). In the case of the US dollar, speculation boosted its appreciation so that by 1985 the DM was 40 per cent undervalued. Most of this was reversed by 1987. The remaining undervaluation of the DM was eliminated by the aftermath of Unification, with substantial overvaluation (14 per cent) appearing in 1995. In the case of the franc, from 1979 the Exchange Rate Mechanism (ERM) precluded higher French inflation being offset by overvaluation. From then on, and particularly with the onset of the 'strong franc' policy in 1983, the constraints of fixed exchange rates once again favoured relatively low-inflation Germany by reducing the overvaluation of the DM to less than 5 per cent between 1990 and 1992. However, the relaxing of ERM bands in 1993 allowed the DM to appreciate against the franc, steadily raising the degree of overvaluation from 7 per cent in 1993 to 13 per cent in 1995.[13]

8.2.4   Implications for the Price Competitiveness of German Traded Goods

One of the major problems associated with relative PPP calculations of the equilibrium exchange rate is the selection of a base year. However, our macroeconomic 'glee' indices give a transparent method of selection. Moreover, different weightings on the components of our indices, and even a radically different approach to defining the unemployment variable, make no significant difference to the choice of the base year. The length of time between the base year and the current period also gives rise to some concern. The greater the distance between the base year and the current period, the greater the scope for influences other than monetary changes to affect the long-run equilibrium exchange rate. For this reason, the productivity-modified PPP is to be preferred, because it accounts for real economy as well as monetary influences on the equilibrium exchange rate.[14] However, in the case of the DM/sterling rate, we take account not only of monetary influences (pure PPP) but also of real economy influences (productivity-modified PPP) and obtain broadly similar results with respect to the pattern of DM under- and overvaluation.

Analysis of three bilateral exchange rate series against equilibrium levels cannot give a global measure of the overvaluation of the DM. For this, we would need to calculate a trade-weighted or effective productivity-modified PPP rate for the DM against all the major trading currencies. This is not possible, however, because we lack comparable data and corresponding econometric estimates of the influence of productivity growth differentials on the necessary range of DM exchange rates. However, *our results are indicative of a general overvaluation.* We have analysed the three exchange rates that, respectively, determine the price competitiveness of German products with respect to its three major trading partners. In 1994, France accounted for 12 per cent of German exports and 11.1 per cent of imports, the UK for 8 per cent of exports and 6.2 per cent of imports, and the USA for 7.9 per cent of exports and 7.3 per cent of imports (JG 1995, p. 64). In relation to these three economies, accounting for almost 30 per cent of total German exports and 25 per cent of total imports, we have found that in round terms the DM was overvalued by between 10 and 20 per cent.

In assessing the competitive effect of DM overvaluation, we need to consider not only the extent of overvaluation but also the path by which it has reached its present value against the currencies of Germany's major trading partners. For the period since 1989 (the last complete year before Unification), Table 8.2 compares the maximum under- and overvaluation of the DM against the currencies of Germany's three major trading partners. Against sterling and the dollar, DM appreciation worsened the price competitiveness of German traded goods by about 30 per cent. In the case of the franc, the ERM has constrained DM appreciation and loss of competitiveness to be only a third as extensive.

Table 8.2   Changing value of the DM and its impact on German price competitiveness

	Over-/undervaluation of DM in relation to the £UK, $US and the FF (percentages)					
	Sterling (£UK)		Dollar ($US)		Franc (FF)	
	Productivity-modified PPP	PPP		PPP		PPP
1991	−9	−16	1989	−16	1990	+4
1995	+18	+14	1995	+14	1995	+13
Loss of price competitiveness	27	30		30		9

Figure 8.12 shows that this scale of under- and overvaluation of the DM is not unprecedented. In the 1970s, movements in the value of the DM were even more dramatic. However, we can surmise that overvaluation of the DM might be less tolerable now than in the 1970s. First, an increased number of rivals capable of supplying high-quality products has eroded quality differentials as a source of competitive advantage for German producers. Accordingly, as the offset of non-price competitiveness has declined so the loss of price competitiveness becomes more serious. Second, in the 1990s the competitive impact of currency appreciation has been compounded by an increase in both wage and non-wage labour costs. And, third, since the 1970s outward foreign direct investment has increased the proportion of company earnings that are

denominated in foreign currency and thus vulnerable to DM appreciation.[15] Against this background, the value of the DM must play a major part in any story about Germany's declining competitiveness. In the short run, this will not necessarily reduce Germany's trade surplus. This is because firms are defending market share by reducing profit margins (Barclays Economics Department 1996, p. 9). In the long run, however, reduced profitability will curtail investment which, in turn, will undermine price and non-price competitiveness alike.

NOTES

1. The argument proceeds mainly by means of applying basic economic concepts, providing evidence in the form of charts, and quantifying effects in a simple, transparent manner. For discussion of the underlying models, see Cobham (1997). An alternative is to use a multicountry econometric model. To anticipate, the result of our 'back of the envelope' approach is not far removed from the result of a study using precisely such a model. Andrew Hughes Hallet and Yue Ma estimated the costs of German Unification by modifying the IMF's MULTIMOD MODEL: 'The costs of financing the fiscal deficit, and of the close control of the money supply needed to control inflation ... are high interest rates and a small rise in the effective DM exchange rate ... they imply recessionary pressure on Germany's EC partner countries. Growth rates are 1–2 per cent lower than otherwise, implying that one-third of the costs of unification will be paid by Germany's EC partners' (Hughes Hallet and Ma 1992, p. 2). A similar result is obtained by Barrel (1997, p. 82).

2. Calculated from data in JG (1991, p. 315) and Datastream. From July 1990, trade data include the overseas transactions of eastern Germany – the former territory of the GDR.

3. The data is seasonally adjusted. This isolates the effect of GEMSU on the relative change of imports and exports. However, exports are measures f.o.b. (free on board) and imports c.i.f. (cost, insurance and freight). This means that Figure 8.2 is not quite accurate with respect to the respective levels of imports and exports.

4. The increase in UK exports to Germany was not a statistical artefact reflecting the incorporation of UK exports to the DDR. First, as mentioned above, these were incorporated into (pan-)German trade data in Q3 1990 and, hence, would not distort a step increase between Q3 and Q4. Second, they were simply too small: in the whole of 1989, for example, UK exports to the DDR amounted to just 0.045 per cent of GDP (trade data from EU 1991).

5. In the case of the UK, this concurs with the Bundesbank estimate of the contribution of the import pull accounted for by GEMSU to economic growth in Germany's EC partners: 'In the larger Community states – *France, Italy, United Kingdom* – the fillip to economic activity in 1990 and 1991 was somewhere in the order of ½ percentage point' (Deutsche Bundesbank 1992, p. 26; see also note 6, below).

6. This is a less sanguine conclusion about the repercussions of GEMSU on Germany's EU partners – at least as far as the UK is concerned – than that of the Bundesbank: 'On balance, over the last two years the demand-induced boost to growth generated by the German unification process clearly outweighed the possible interest-rate-related adverse effects on macroeconomic activity in the partner countries' (Bundesbank 1992, p. 22).

7. The long-term nominal rate is the yield on public bonds reported in the OECD's *Main Economic Indicators*. The long-term real interest rate was calculated as this nominal rate minus the weighted average of current and one-year lagged inflation (two-thirds and one-third, respectively) as measured by the Consumer Price Index (all households).

8. The real exchange rate (RER) is an index of domestic price competitiveness and is calculated as follows:

$$RER = ER \times \frac{P^*}{P},$$

where *ER* is the nominal exchange rate (units of domestic currency per unit of foreign currency), P^* is the foreign price level, and *P* the domestic price level. When *ER* is a trade-weighted average of bilateral exchange rates, and P^* and *P* trade-weighted consumer price indices, we have a real effective exchange rate (that is, a general index of the real external value of the DM or, equivalently, of the price competitiveness of German traded goods). This is the measure that suggests a 10 per cent appreciation since 1990. Alternatively, the nominal exchange rate can be corrected for foreign and domestic unit labour costs. This common measure of real external value suggests a 20 per cent appreciation of the DM between 1990 and 1996.

9. We would like to acknowledge joint work with Grant Lewis as the source of the following method and calculations.
10. The indices are purely ordinal: the only meaning of the scale is to indicate lower (better) and higher (worse).
11. The reasons for choosing CPI indices as the most appropriate for PPP calculations are given by Pentecost (1993, pp. 31–2).
12. Van Ark's (1990) data covers the period 1950–88. For the years 1989–95, we calculated productivity growth differentials from data on manufacturing output, persons employed in manufacturing, and average weekly hours worked in manufacturing.
13. These are all *real* overvaluations: inflation rates are fully accounted for in the calculation of our equilibrium rates.
14. Our productivity-modified PPP calculations suggested a 1990 ERM entry rate for sterling of DM 2.64. In line with the fundamental equilibrium exchange rate calculations of Williamson (1991) and Wren-Lewis et al. (1991), this suggests that sterling was overvalued against the DM at the time of ERM entry.
15. According to *The Economist* (11 September 1993, p. 102), 'about a quarter of listed German companies' earnings are translated from dollars'.

9. Conclusion .

From the vantage point of late 1996, we have discussed German Unification from the point of view of economic developments and problems in its first five years, some of its wider repercussions and, finally, medium- to long-term perspectives for its successful completion. In these final remarks, we first review the main lessons and policy implications. We then conclude with a discussion of the possibility that increasingly widespread changes in the conduct of industrial relations and collective bargaining in eastern Germany are encouraging similar changes in western Germany. If developments in the east are helping to initiate a process of institutional renewal throughout unified Germany, then not only is a self-sustaining process of growth and convergence in the east more likely but eastern innovations will contribute to renewed dynamism in the western economy.

9.1 WHY GEMSU HAD SUCH A DEVASTATING IMPACT: THE WEAKNESS OF THE DDR ECONOMY

Chapter 1 analyses the historically unprecedented and overwhelming shock to which GEMSU subjected the economy of the DDR, the consequent downward movement along the 'J-curve' of economic reform, and the corresponding fiscal consequences of Unification. In Chapter 2 we advance an explanation of why eastern producers were too weak to survive in an open market economy. We argue that an inability to handle product complexity created an inherent bias against innovation and restructuring that culminated in an adverse effect on economic performance. This hypothesis was supported by empirical data on production complexity and value added measurements in manufacturing industries and provides an explanation for the relative economic backwardness of the DDR. The data also confirm the superiority of western economies in their ability to handle increasingly complex production techniques. It is against this background that it becomes clear why after Unification eastern producers lacked the ability to compete.

9.2 SOURCES OF POLICY FAILURE (I): POLITICAL OPPORTUNISM

The next conclusions arise from Chapters 2 and 4. Both concern ways in which political expediency or opportunism can clash with and undermine longer-term policy aims.

In 1990 politics was in charge. In historical perspective, the cost has not been high for overcoming an alien ideology and uniting a country. Accordingly, criticism is directed not at the cost as such but rather at the denial, in the face of plentiful professional opinion to the contrary, that Unification would demand no sacrifice. This denial helped to achieve Unification by minimizing opposition in both west and east but also worsened subsequent conditions for successful reconstruction. Initial denial of the need for even modest sacrifices made it much more difficult to raise taxation and social contributions to finance Unification which, in turn, enlarged borrowing and by the mid-1990s created severe fiscal problems.[1] Similarly, until the mid-1990s the case for wage restraint was harder to make. Consequently, in the west, increased taxation and social contributions exerted downward pressure on profitability both directly and, via wage pressure, indirectly. And, in the east, after large initial wage increases precluded a low-wage, low-tech development path for east Germany, continued wage pressure ran counter to the growing need for moderation and flexibility. (According to our argument in Chapters 5, 6 and 7, wage moderation is necessary to allow rising productivity to be reflected in rising profitability and, hence, a self-sustaining process of investment and growth.) The lesson here is that political opportunism, in this case denying the economic consequences of political decisions, at best can impose additional costs and, at worst, jeopardizes the realization of the initial aim. At least, the immediate benefits of such opportunism, in this case the minimizing of opposition to Unification, should be weighed against the probable long-term costs.[2]

9.3 SOURCES OF POLICY FAILURE (II): POLITICAL MYTH

Willingness to pay for Unification through curtailment of living standards in east and west Germany alike was also weakened by a mythologized version of the 1948 currency and economic reforms. Essentially, this attributed the west German 'economic miracle' of the 1950s and 1960s to the 1948 reforms in a simple relationship of cause and effect. Unfortunately, in 1990 it was the mythologized version that influenced popular expectations about the impact of German Economic, Monetary and Social Union (GEMSU). Political debate was not informed by an understanding that the reforms of 1948 were undertaken in conditions entirely different to those of 1990. Consequently, easterners and westerners alike were unprepared for the extent of economic collapse and corresponding costs of Unification. For whereas the 1948 reforms played an enabling role in relation to unrealized potential, GEMSU ruthlessly exposed the lack of potential of the eastern economy as it was at the time of Unification. The problem with basing GEMSU, and popular support for GEMSU, on the mythology rather than the substance of 1948 was that eventually Germans would measure the actual outcome of Unification against the illusory promise of a new economic miracle. Consequently, neither easterners nor westerners were prepared for the costs of Unification. In turn, this increased the difficulty of securing consensus on sharing the burden. Again, the mythology of 1948 influenced expectations so as to minimize opposition to rapid Unification while jeopardizing the chance of securing the sacrifices necessary to secure its success in the long run. This suggests that while political myth can be an important source of political legitimacy, as an input into decision making it is a likely source of policy failure. Policy based on myth is unlikely to have the intended consequences.

9.4 POLICY DESIGN FOR TRANSITION: THE NEED TO SECURE CERTAINTY WITH RESPECT TO THE *ECONOMIC CONSTITUTION*

Chapter 1 compared transition in eastern Germany and other countries of the ex-Soviet bloc. Of fundamental importance to the transition process is the 'economic constitution'. This must include the legal foundations of private ownership, production and exchange; that is, contract and company law together with means of enforcement. Any uncertainty with respect to these fundamentals will impede investment and thus the ability to restructure. In eastern Germany, for example, until the principle of restitution was modified, uncertainty about ownership was *the* major obstacle to investment. In the appendix to Chapter 4, we use a recently developed theoretical framework to explain why it is not just the timing but also the eventual volume of investment that can be affected by uncertainty. Uncertainty causes investors to delay, which reduces the chance of a favourable outcome to the transformation process. In turn, pessimism with respect to the outcome of reform will deter investment. From this we conclude by emphasizing the need for policies designed to reduce uncertainties in the investment environment. First and foremost in the transition process it is necessary to secure certainty with respect to the economic constitution. In turn, this requires confidence in political stability and the underlying support of the population for reform.

9.5 INSTITUTIONAL DESIGN FOR TRANSITION: THE TREUHAND

The instrument of transition was the Treuhand (THA). This was a transitional institution in two senses. As the temporary owner of former state-owned firms its success in rapid privatization of its holdings enabled first its own dissolution and, second, the completion of eastern Germany's transition from socialism to capitalism. Eastern Germany's economic problems are now not those of transition but more those of a relatively backward region in a developed market economy. The achievements of the THA were remarkable first for the speed with which the THA was built up and run down and, second, for the scale and complexity of its operations – the privatization and restructuring of an entire economy. The methods of the THA were predicated on west German finance and so are of limited relevance to other transitional economies. The lessons here are more to do with institutional design: the operation of the THA and the architecture of its relationships with different levels of government as well as with management and unions in its subordinate firms. Finally, we maintain that scapegoating the THA misses the point that extensive deindustrialization and job losses were the result of 40 years of command economy and the terms of GEMSU. These constituted the ultimate and proximate causes of economic collapse rather than four-and-a half years of the THA.

9.6 LABOUR MARKET POLICY (I): ACTIVE LABOUR MARKET POLICIES NOT SUFFICIENT

Analysis of the post-Unification eastern and western labour markets in Chapter 5 has been a major influence on our policy conclusions. Productivity has figured prominently in this book and it is the dynamics of productivity-related issues that are at the heart of the German labour market. We learned that active labour market policies, including government training and work creation schemes, have not succeeded in overcoming mass unemployment in east Germany. This need not be a wholly negative conclusion. On the contrary, experiences in east Germany could prove to be a constructive phase in the evolution of policy design. They have certainly left their mark on proposals for German labour market and welfare reform. First, criteria for access to active labour market programmes have become more stringent. Second, the costs of Unification have forced painful decisions that hitherto had been avoided. In particular, in 1996 limited cuts in welfare benefits have been implemented together with more pressure on job seekers to find work. This adjustment was in the first instance a response to fiscal pressures but also corresponds to a school of thought in west Germany that relates unemployment less to inadequate skills on the part of the unemployed and more to inadequate incentives to find work.

9.7 LABOUR MARKET POLICY (II): WAGE MODERATION IS NOW NECESSARY

These were not the only lessons drawn from labour market developments in east Germany. Probably the most valuable lesson is that after a series of rather unsuccessful attempts to reduce mass unemployment by active measures it is time to retreat from the position that 'demand doesn't matter'. In the first place, a balance needs to be struck between moderate wage increases and continuous investment demand. We argue that wage restraint has become necessary to allow productivity to rise faster than wages in order for profitability to rise. Increased profitability of eastern enterprises is a necessary condition for domestically generated investment finance which, in turn, is the key to a convergence process that is self-sustaining rather than dependent on external support. The problem in east Germany is that as yet not enough of the labour force are employed in high-productivity jobs. Accordingly, high-wage, high-tech employers do not yet constitute a critical mass of profitable exporters capable of generating rising living standards while allowing inward transfers to diminish. Chapters 5, 6 and 7 suggest that marked post-Unification wage increase has provided a platform for rather modest pay adjustments in the foreseeable future. Above all, wage restraint is needed to boost profitability and, thereby, private sector investment. East Germany's problem is not lack of a skilled workforce, or even mismatch between available skills and jobs, but that there is still not enough equipment to employ the workforce at prevailing wage rates. In Chapter 7 we documented rapidly increasing productivity in east Germany. Consequently, in the absence of (real) wage increases, demand for labour can increase. In the medium to long term, as increased profitability provides both means and incentive to secure investment, increasing demand for labour will arise from the need for trained people to operate new equipment. However, without the means and incentive of profit, demand for labour will be weak and east Germany risks acquiring 'the best-qualified unemployed workforce in Europe'.

9.8 LABOUR MARKET POLICY (III): LEARNING-BY-DOING IN A 'HIGH-WAGE, HIGH-TECH' CONTEXT AN ALTERNATIVE TO CONVENTIONAL TRAINING POLICY

A final conclusion from Chapters 5 and 6 is that training policy is not the only way or even the best way of upgrading workforce skills. By securing investment undertakings and providing employment subsidies the THA secured high-wage, high-productivity jobs. Ironically, to do so it had to eliminate the high-wage, low-productivity jobs which GEMSU and its aftermath had inflicted on the THA. This links with a second line of argument from Chapters 5 and 6. We argue that in 1990–91 initial wage increases without regard for productivity constituted an instrument of 'creative destruction'. High wages precluded a low-wage, low-tech development path for eastern Germany in favour of a high-wage, high-tech convergence strategy designed to replicate the main features of the western economy in eastern Germany. Among the benefits of this strategy is that it maximizes the benefits of learning-by-doing: operating with the latest equipment and products presents new problems and, hence, quantitatively and qualitatively greater learning opportunities than operating with lower-level and familiar technology. This suggests that a high-wage, high-tech strategy provides a platform for continuously enhancing the skills of the workforce, which is an alternative to conventional training policy.

9.9 MONETARY UNION IN EUROPE (I): VULNERABLE TO ASYMMETRIC SHOCK

In Chapter 8 we discussed the impact of GEMSU on monetary cooperation in Europe. The main lesson from this experience is that European monetary cooperation within the EU is vulnerable to shocks that affect members in different ways. Once monetary policy is dedicated to an exchange rate target (under a fixed rate regime), or taken away from national governments (with a single currency), there are insufficient means of macroeconomic adjustment to counteract the possibility of simultaneous overheating in some countries (for example, Germany in the early 1990s) and recession in others (for example, the UK in the early 1990s). Within Germany, migration and massive fiscal transfers were possible, with the latter taking the burden of adjustment. Within the EU, neither is on the agenda. Moreover, the remaining possibility, adjustment via wage and price flexibility, remains a policy objective rather than an established fact. Consequently, EU members within a fixed exchange rate regime or a single currency may lack means with which to offset the impact of major shocks. To those who argue that German Unification was a unique event, we reply it is unlikely that history has seen the end of unexpected events that will expose the EU to asymmetric shock and the potential disruption of monetary cooperation.

9.10   MONETARY UNION IN EUROPE (II): DANGEROUS (1) TO ALLOW ECONOMIC INTEGRATION TO BE DRIVEN BY A POLITICAL AGENDA, AND (2) TO NEGLECT REAL ECONOMY CONVERGENCE

GEMSU was not an agreement between equal partners. Monetary union, for example, did not create a currency union – with a new currency for united Germany – but simply extended eastwards the DM along with west Germany's monetary and financial institutions. None the less, there are two further lessons for European monetary union. First, in proceeding to GEMSU and in fixing its terms – including the currency conversion rate – politics was the prime mover. Unqualified commitment to national unity was implicitly a commitment to support eastern Germany with fiscal transfers. In the EU, however, there is no such commitment to support members that might prove to be losers from a single currency. This could be a source of tension and instability among members of the EU. Here the lesson is that it would be dangerous to allow economic and monetary union in the EU to be driven by political pressure. As long as European solidarity remains weak relative to national solidarity and, correspondingly, the EU lacks significant fiscal capacity, it will be prudent for EU members to base decisions about the single European currency on the economic calculus of costs and benefits. Advancing towards monetary union according to a political agenda might go disastrously wrong in the absence of European ideals sufficiently robust to support the potential costs. Second, GEMSU warns of the possibly devastating consequences of economic and monetary union between low- and high-productivity countries. This points to the importance of an initial entry rate compatible with macroeconomic balance. None the less, for the entry rate to *remain* compatible with macroeconomic balance presupposes a high degree of real economy convergence. For example,

- the business cycle will need to be synchronized to avoid the problem that undermined the EMS in the early 1990s – namely, two or more member states requiring opposing interest rate policy;

- monetary transmission mechanisms will need to converge – so that interest rate changes have the same real economy effects throughout the currency union (Crockett 1994, pp. 174 and 182–3); and
- in the absence of wage and price flexibility, productivity growth rates will need to be similar to avoid trend changes in the price competitiveness of member states' traded goods (Beachill and Pugh 1996, pp. 21–7).

The lesson here is that convergence criteria for monetary union should include not only monetary criteria – as required by the Maastricht Treaty – but also real economy criteria.

9.11   GERMAN COMPETITIVENESS (I): THE IMPACT OF CURRENCY OVERVALUATION

In Chapter 8 we also discuss the impact of Unification on German competitiveness. In brief, between 1990 and 1992 extreme fiscal expansion and high wage increases were offset by an equally extreme tightening of monetary policy. In turn, as the Bundesbank raised short-term nominal interest rates, the DM became increasingly overvalued. Through this channel, therefore, one consequence of Unification for west Germany has been adverse pressure on the price competitiveness of German traded goods:

> Though workers took advantage of the unification boom to win big pay increases, they also worked more productively. In national currency terms, Germany's unit labour costs have risen by less than the industrial-country average since Unification, according to DIW. German unit labour costs have surged compared with those in other countries only because the D-Mark has appreciated sharply. (*The Economist*, 4 December 1993, p. 94)

9.12   GERMAN COMPETITIVENESS (II): INCREASING LABOUR MARKET FLEXIBILITY IN EASTERN GERMANY AN EXAMPLE FOR GERMANY AS A WHOLE?

Finally, we return to the theme of labour market flexibility identified in Chapters 5, 6 and 7 as the key to eastern growth and convergence. This is scarcely a new theme in policy prescription for the German economy. Yet mass unemployment in eastern Germany has made the issues of flexibility with respect to wages, working conditions and bargaining practices so acute that the necessary changes have already begun at enterprise level. This is important not only because it demonstrates a capacity for autonomous initiative in east Germany but also because we believe this to be the most important example of developments in eastern Germany acting as a catalyst for change in unified Germany as a whole.

9.12.1 Unification a Source of Systemic Renewal in Germany

At first, it seemed that Unification changed hardly at all the pre-existing institutions of the BRD. Transformation in eastern Germany meant taking over western institutions, standards and practices. In western Germany, Unification was not seen as an occasion for renewal. On the contrary, western confidence was reinforced. At worst, this bred arrogance and a corresponding inability to listen. This is apparent in policy error: for example, restitution rather than compensation was insisted on by the governing coalition of the west against the advice of the east's elected CDU government. Worse, are western attitudes that led Günter Grass to liken Unification to colonial occupation. Apparently, therefore, Unification was the opposite of the kind of crisis that brings renewal and a new beginning. None the less, by the mid-1990s there were signs that unified Germany might be more than an enlarged but unreformed Federal Republic. Unification intensified a number of systemic problems, particularly in public finance and in the labour market. Above all, labour market reform is becoming the central issue in public policy: first, because labour market compromise is central to the ethos and operation of the social market; and, second, because fiscal pressure arising from Unification combined with only sluggish recovery from recession has heightened German concerns over economic stability and competitiveness into a sense of crisis. In the 1990s, there has developed even within the unions a widespread feeling that the system of collective bargaining must change (Bastian 1996, p. 4).

9.12.2 New Initiatives in the German Labour Market: an Alliance for Jobs and Competitiveness

The German labour market encompasses institutions – of collective bargaining, codetermination and vocational training – which exert decisive influence on the cost and quality of labour and, hence, on competitiveness. This together with related concerns over competitiveness and mass unemployment – not only in eastern but, increasingly, also in western Germany – is the background to the *Bündnis für Arbeit* (alliance for jobs). This was an initiative in the tradition of social partnership whereby unions are to make collective bargaining concessions in return for employment security and job creation. It was proposed in November 1995 by Klaus Zwickel, President of Germany's largest trade union, IG Metall, endorsed by the German Trade Union Federation (DGB), and was welcomed by Chancellor Kohl. At the January 1996 Kanzlerrunde – tripartite talks between unions, employers and government representatives – it became the basis for a provisional but wider *Bündnis für Arbeit und Standortsicherung* (alliance for jobs and competitiveness) with the aim of halving unemployment by the year 2000 (French 1996, p. 9). If successful, the Alliance will transform both the process and outcome of collective bargaining. The proposal

1. promotes flexible working by cooperating with the tendency to decentralize negotiation from the level of unions and employers' associations to plant level partners, and
2. alters 'the focus of bargaining from income to employment security and job creation' (French 1996, p. 12).

Our final comments, therefore, concern the implication of Unification for labour market reform in Germany. We argue that reform has not been caused but has been catalysed by developments in eastern Germany.

The aim of promoting employment through collective bargaining is not new. In the late 1960s and 1970s there was the full-blown corporatism of 'concerted action'. Although formal corporatist institutions did not survive, the ethos of social partnership continued to ensure corporatist outcomes. For example, in the 1980s wage restraint allowed increased profitability, thereby facilitating an investment boom that helped to secure high-wage, secure jobs in the long run (see Table 7.7, above). Another such corporatist trade off in the 1980s was concessions on working time, promoted by IG Metall to compensate employees for higher stress and to create jobs, in return for more flexible working practices and correspondingly localized bargaining (French 1996, p. 4). By the 1990s, competitive pressure and structural changes in production processes were increasing pressure for flexible working as well as for plant-level bargaining as the means of delivering flexibility:

> This question of decentralization has become more important in the 1990s with the development of smaller production units and attempts by employers to introduce more flexibility and decentralization into the industrial relations system. These developments place increasing pressure on the centralized system ... which sets pay and working conditions for whole industrial branches. (French 1996, pp. 2–3).

Accordingly, in the *Bündnis für Arbeit und Standortsicherung*, 'it is recognized that collective bargaining is the key area where employment can be safeguarded and new jobs created'. In particular, the agreement recognizes that 'there needs to be greater flexibility within the system, allowing the extension of negotiating opportunities for plant-level partners' in order to achieve 'more flexible working time to reduce plant-level costs and increase competitiveness ... avoiding overtime wherever possible ... the extension of part-time jobs (with social insurance obligations) ... [and] ... focusing special attention on the long-term unemployed ... collective regulations, such as entry-level wages below collective rates in the chemical industry, must be used more. (cited in French 1996, p. 10).

In the first half of 1996, progress was made towards implementing these principles in collective agreements; for example, in the chemical industry, the railways, and the steel industry (see French 1996, p. 10).

9.12.3   Developments in East Germany a Catalyst

Although the aim of employment promotion was established in the 1980s, developments in eastern Germany catalysed the emergence of a strategy for realizing this aim. Developments in eastern Germany contributed to the Alliance by destabilizing the system of universal collective bargaining, thereby increasing pressure on unions and employers' associations to embrace reform as an alternative to progressive loss of membership and control.

In eastern Germany, mass unemployment and fear of further job loss, especially among skilled workers, has led to non-enforcement of collective bargains. Instead, company-specific deals are ignoring industry guidelines negotiated between unions and employers' associations. This is not the result of a government or employers' offensive against organized labour. Instead, subcontractual wages are often agreed at plant level by Works Councils and even endorsed unofficially at local level by the trade union. Traditional industry-wide collective bargaining is thus being undermined from within. So far, this trend has been widely reported in the business press even if it is too recent to be reflected in systematic data and research results. The following case study of a medium-size firm in Eisenach is typical.

[T]he east is the place to be – for workers who want to work and employers who want to hire them. The key ... is flexibility. If anything sums up what German employers want from work forces ... it is 'flexibility': the ability to run double and triple shifts a day when demand warrants. At MITEC, a classic metal-bending Mittelstand company that makes gear boxes, Militzer (the owner) gets a 38.5-hour week, three shifts a day, as well as an innovative pay plan that allows workers to take some of their compensation in the form of extra days off. He also can cut through the stultifying work rules so common in the west and have workers do different jobs when necessary – without a lengthy consultation with the Works Council ... His highly skilled workers ... have effectively ignored the IG Metall contract signed last year ... They give him the wage restraint and the flexibility he needs to keep the company competitive – and them employed. ('Lessons from the east: the Ossis know how to be flexible', *Newsweek*, 18 March 96, p. 21)

Labour market flexibility is being achieved in individual plants and offices. Throughout eastern Germany, flexibility over wages and working conditions is being achieved either by ignoring national agreements or by employers 'leaving the employers' associations – which tie them to minimum wages laid down in collective agreements – and negotiating their own agreements at plant level'. Indeed, in 1995, 'only a quarter of eastern companies in private hands were members of employers' associations' ('Survey on Germany', *The Economist*, 9 November 1996, p. 10). In turn, eastern practice is feeding back into western Germany: 'Under the ... Alliance for Jobs banner a flurry of company-specific accords have been agreed, each negotiated with in-house worker's councils and not the national union leaders' (Bastian 1996, p. 5).

In eastern Germany, the trend to localized bargaining is helping to restrain wage costs while flexible working favours productivity. This will gradually increase corporate profitability, which we have identified as the key to self-sustaining growth. By catalysing similar tendencies in western Germany, eastern developments may also make an independent contribution to institutional renewal in the German labour market. If so, Unification will have given rise not only to problems but also to part of the solution whereby Germany's social market economy can recover its previous dynamism.

NOTES

1. This is clear not only from the explosion of public sector debt but also in the uncertain handling of mounting fiscal problems evidenced, for example, by increased recourse to off-budget funds.
2. This criticism notwithstanding, we share the view of Sinn and Sinn (1992) that an admirable feature of German Unification was that it was achieved without an outburst of chauvinism. Appeal to nationalistic passions to secure sacrifices for Unification would have been a cure more dangerous than the disease.

Bibliography

Abelshauser, Werner (1983), *Wirtschaftsgeschichte der Bundesrepublik Deutschland* (1945–1980), Frankfurt am Main: Suhrkamp

Akerloff, George A., et al. (1991), 'East Germany in from the Cold: The Economic Aftermath of Currency Union', in William Brainard and George Perry (eds), *Brookings Papers on Economic Activity*, Vol. I, Washington: Brookings Institute.

Altvater, Elmar et al. (1980), *Vom Wirtschaftswunder Zur Wirtschaftskrise*, Berlin: Olle & Wolter.

Amable, Bruno (1993), 'Catch-up and convergence: a model of cumulative growth', *International Review of Applied Economics*, **7** (1), 1–25.

Arrow, K.J. (1962), 'The economic implications of learning by doing', *Review of Economic Studies*, **28** (3), 155–73.

Balasubramanyam V.N., M. Salisu and D. Sapsford (1994), 'Foreign direct investment and growth in EP and IS countries', *Lancaster University Department of Economics Working Paper*, EC18/94.

Balasubramanyam V.N., M. Salisu and D. Sapsford (1996), 'Foreign direct investment and growth: new hypotheses and evidence', *Lancaster University Department of Economics Working Paper*, EC7/96.

Balcerowicz, L. (1990), 'The Soviet-type Economic System, Reformed Systems and Innovativeness', *Communist Economies*, **2** (1), 3–24.

Banerjee, A.V. and M. Spagat (1991), 'Productivity paralysis and the complexity problem: why do centrally planned economies become prematurely gray?', *Journal of Comparative Economics*, **15**, 646–60.

Barclays Economics Department (1996), *Barclays Country Report: Germany*, March.

Barjak, F., G. Heimpold, M. Junkernheinrich, B. Loose and R. Skopp (1996), *Management-Buy-Outs in Ostdeutschland*, Halle: Gutachten im Auftrag der Bundesanstalt für vereinigungsbedingte Sonderaufgaben.

Barjak, F. and R. Skopp (1996), 'Ostdeutsche Management-Buy-Outs: Der Beitrag des Managements zum Unternehmenserfolg', *Wirtschaft im Wandel*, No. 9, 9–15, Halle.

Barrel, Ray (1997), 'German monetary union and its implications for the rest of Europe', in Jens Hölscher and Stephen Frowen (eds), *The German Currency Union of 1990*, New York: St. Martin's Press and London: Macmillan.

Barro, Robert and Sala-i-Martin, Xavier (1995), *Economic Growth*, New York: McGraw-Hill.

Barry, Frank and John Bradley (1994), 'Labour market performance in the EU periphery', *Centre for Economic Research Working Paper*, No. 3, March.

Bastian, Jens (1996), 'Soviel Bündnis war noch nie: the institutional architecture of an alliance for jobs', paper presented to the Institute for German Studies Conference, 'The German New Länder in Locational Competition', June.

Baumol, William, et al. (1989), *Productivity and American Leadership: The Long View*, Cambridge, MA: MIT Press.

Beachill, Bob and Geoffrey Pugh (1996), 'Monetary co-operation in Europe and the problem of differential productivity growth', paper presented to the April 1996 Conference of the Royal Economic Society.

Begg, Iain, and David Mayes (1994), 'Decentralised industrial policies', paper presented to the April 1994 Conference of the Royal Economic Society.

Beintema, Nienke and Bart van Ark (1993), 'Comparative productivity in East and West German manufacturing before reunification', *Centre for Economic Policy Research Discussion Paper*, No. 895, February.

Bergson, A. (1978), 'The Soviet economic slowdown', *Challenge*, **20** (6), January–February, 22–7,

Bischof, Robert, Gottfried von Bismarck and Wendy Carlin (1993), 'East Germany: scaling down', in John Heath (ed.), *Revitalising Socialist Enterprise*, London: Routledge.

Blien, U. (1994), 'Convergence or Mezzogiorno scenario? Some theoretical considerations on the empirical development of the labour market in eastern Germany', paper presented at Sixth Annual Conference of European Association of Labour Economists, Warsaw.

Bofinger, Peter (1997), 'The German currency union – a critical assessment: the impact on German monetary policy', in Jens Hölscher and Stephen Frowen (eds), *The German Currency Union of 1990*, New York: St. Martin's Press and London: Macmillan.

Boltho, Andrea, Wendy Carlin and Pasquale Scaramozzino (1996), 'Will east Germany become a new Mezzogiorno?', Mimeo, Magdalen College, Oxford.

Borchardt, Knut (1991), *Perspectives on Modern German Economic History and Policy*, Cambridge: Cambridge University Press.

Brada, J. (1978), 'Plan execution and the workability of Soviet planning: comment', *Journal of Comparative Economics*, **2** (1), March, 65–9.

Brakeman, Steven and Harry Garretsen (1993), 'The relevance of initial conditions for the German Unification', *Kyklos*, **46** (2), 163–81.

Brinkman C. and V. Gottsleben (1994), 'Labour market and labour market policy in the eastern part of Germany: new approaches and new links to structural policy', *Labour*, **8** (3), 505–20.

Broadberry, S.N. and R. Fremdling (1990), 'Comparative productivity in British and German industry 1907–37', *Oxford Bulletin of Economics and Statistics*, **52** (4), 403–21.

Bukharin, Nicolai (1971), *Economics of the Transformation Period*, New York: Bergman Publishers (original publication – Moscow, 1920).

Bundesanstalt für Arbeit (1992), *Amtliche Nachrichten der Bundesanstalt für Arbeit*, Nürnberg.

Bundesanstalt für Arbeit (1993), *Sozialversicherungspflichtige Beschäftigte im Bundesgebiet West Ende*, December, Nürnberg.

Bundesanstalt für Arbeit (1994), *Amtliche Mitteilungen der Bundesanstalt für Arbeit*, September, Nürnberg.

Bundesanstalt für Arbeit (1997), Mimeo (personal communication).

Burda, Michael and Michael Funke (1992), 'Trade unions, wages and structural adjustment in the New German states', *Centre for Economic Policy Research Discussion Paper*, No. 652, June.

Burda, Michael and Michael Funke (1993), 'Eastern Germany: can't we be more optimistic?', *Centre for Economic Policy Research Discussion Paper*, No. 863, December.

Carlin, Wendy (1989), 'Economic reconstruction in western Germany: the displacement of "vegetative control"', in Ian Turner (ed.), *Reconstruction in Post-War Germany: British Occupation Policy and the Western Zones, 1945–55*, Oxford: Berg.

Carlin, Wendy (1993), 'Privatisation and deindustrialisation in east Germany', University College, London: unpublished draft, August.

Carlin, Wendy and Colin Mayer (1992), 'Restructuring enterprises in eastern Europe', *Economic Policy*, No.15, October, 311–52.

Carlin, Wendy and Colin Mayer (1995), 'Structure and ownership of east German enterprises', *Journal of the Japanese and International Economies*, **9** (4), December, 426–53.

Carlin, Wendy and David Soskice (1997), 'Shocks to the system: the German political economy under stress', *National Institute Economic Review*, February, 1–20.

Church, K.B. et al., (1988, 1989, 1990 and 1991), 'Comparative properties of models of the UK economy', *National Institute Economic Review*, August.

Cobham (1997), 'The German currency union and the crises in the European Monetary System', in Jens Hölscher and Stephen Frowen (eds), *The German Currency Union of 1990*, New York: St. Martin's Press and London: Macmillan.

Cornelsen, Doris (1990), 'Die Wirtschaft der DDR in der Honecker-Ära', in *Vierteljahreshefte zur Wirtschaftsforschung*, No. 1, 70–79.

Crafts, Nicholas (1997), 'Golden years', *European Economic Perspectives*, No. 12, February, Centre for Economic Policy Research.

Crockett, Andrew (1994), 'The role of convergence in the process of EMU', in Alfred Steinherr (ed.), *30 Years of European Monetary Integration*, Harlow: Longman, Ch. 11.

Davies, Stephen and Richard Caves (1987), *Britain's Productivity Gap*, Cambridge: Cambridge University Press.

De Grauwe, P. (1989), *International Money – Post-War Trends and Theories*, Oxford: Oxford University Press.

Deutsche Bundesbank (1995), *Geschäftsbericht*.

Deutsche Bundesbank (1992), 'Impact of German Unification process on economic trends in Germany's European partner countries', *Monthly Report of the Deutsche Bundesbank*, July.

Deutscher Bundestag (1987), *Materialien zum Bericht zur Lage der Nation im geteilten Deutschland 1987*, Drucksache 11/11, Bonn.

Deutscher Gewerkschaftsbund (1992), 'Industrieller Berufsausbildung droht jetzt das Aus', *Gewerkschaftliche Bildungspolitik*, Düsseldorf, June.

Dickertmann, Dietrich and Siegfried Gelbhaar (1994), 'Treuhandanstalt: Theoretische Deutungsmuster ihrer Privatisierungstätigkeit', *Wirtschaftsdienst*, **74**, June, 316–24.

Diewald, M. and H. Solga (1995), 'Ordnung im Umbruch? Strukturwandel, berufliche Mobilität und Stabilität im Transformationsprozeß', paper presented at the 27th German Sociological Meeting, Halle, 3–7 April.

Dinenis, Elias and Michael Funke (1994), 'Factor prices, employment and investment in UK and West German manufacturing', *The Manchester School*, **LXII** (4), December, 412–24.

Dixit, A. (1993), 'Irreversible investment and competition under uncertainty', in Kaushic Basu et al. (ed.), *Capital, Investment, and Development*, Oxford: Blackwell.

Dixit A. and R. Pindyck (1994), *Investment Under Uncertainty*, Princeton, NJ: Princeton University Press.

Dobischat, R. and G. Neumann (1992), 'Qualifizierungs- und beschäftigungspolitische Perspektiven in den fünf neuen Bundesländern', *Gewerkschaftliche Bildungspolitik*, Düsseldorf, April.

Doeringer, P. and M.J. Piore (1971), *Internal Labor Markets and Manpower Analysis*, Lexington, MA: D.C. Heath & Co.

Domdey, K.H. (1997), 'Privatisation in the new Bundesländer: a critical assessment of the Treuhand', forthcoming in T. Lange and J.R. Shackleton (eds), *Germany: An Economy in Transition*, Oxford: Berghahn Books.

Dumke, Rolf H. (1990), 'Reassessing the *Wirtschaftswunder*: reconstruction and postwar growth in West Germany in an international context', *Oxford Bulletin of Economics and Statistics*, **52** (4), 451–91.

Dunn, Malcolm H. (1994), 'Do nations compete economically', *Intereconomics*, November/December, 303–8.

Economic Bulletin: German Institute for Economic Research (DIW), *Economic Bulletin* (Gower Press, monthly), various issues.

Economist (The), various issues.

Edwards, J. and Klaus Fischer (1991), 'Banks, finance, and investment in West Germany since 1970', *Centre for Economic Policy Research Discussion Paper*, No. 497, London.

Engelbrech, G. (1994), 'Unemployment among women in east Germany: consequences and ways out', paper presented at the Sixth Annual Conference of European Association of Labour Economists, Warsaw.

European Union (EU) (1991), *Basic Statistics of the Community*, Brussels.

Fischer, Wolfram et al. (eds) (1996), *Treuhandanstalt: The Impossible Challenge*, Berlin: Akademie Verlag.

Fitzroy, F. and M. Funke (1994), 'Skills, wages and employment in eastern and western Germany', *London Business School Centre for Economic Forecasting, Discussion Paper*, No. DP24–94.

Freiburghauser, D. and G. Schmid (1975), 'Theorie der Segmentierung von Arbeitsmärkten: Darstellung und Kritik neuerer Ansätze mit besonderer Berücksichtigung arbeitsmarktpolitischer Konsequenzen', *Leviathan*, **3** (3).

French, Stephen (1996), 'Bündnis für Arbeit: continuity and change in the collective bargaining policy of IG Metall', paper presented at the Association for the Study of German Politics Graduate Conference, 25 April 96.

Fritsch, M. and C. Werker (1994), 'Die Transformation der Unternehmens-struktur in Ostdeutschland', *Employment Observatory*, Brussels: Directorate-General Employment, Industrial Relations and Social Affairs, No. 13, December.

Frowen, S.F. and J. Hölscher (eds) (1997), *The German Currency Union of 1990 – A Critical Assessment*, New York: St. Martin's Press and London: Macmillan.

Financial Times (FT), various issues.

Gallik, D. et al. (1979), 'The 1972 input–output table and the changing structure of the Soviet economy', *Soviet Economy in a Time of Change*, Vol. 1, pp. 423–71, Compilation of papers, Joint Economic Committee, US Congress, Washington, DC.

Georgellis, Y. and T. Lange (1997), 'The effect of further training on wage growth in West Germany, 1984–1992', *Scottish Journal of Political Economy*, **44** (2), 165–81.

Giersch, Herbert et al. (1992), *The Fading Miracle: Four Decades of Market Economy in Germany*, Cambridge: Cambridge University Press.

Gladisch, D. and L. Trabert (1995), 'Geschlechtsspezifische Differenzierung der Erwerbsbeteiligung', *Wirtschaft im Wandel*, April, Institut für Wirtschaftsforschung, Halle.

Görzig, B. (1991), 'Produktion und Produktionsfaktoren in Ostdeutschland', *Dokumentation*, Deutsches Institut für Wirtschaftsforschung (DIW), Berlin.

Görzig, B. and M. Gornig (1991), 'Produktivität und Wettbewerbsfähigkeit der Wirtschaft der DDR', *Beiträge zur Strukturforschung*, No. 121, Berlin.

Gomulka, S. (1986), *Growth, Innovation and Reform in Eastern Europe* Brighton: Wheatsheaf Books.

Gordon, D.M. (1972), *Theories of Poverty and Underemployment*, Lexington, MA: Lexington Books, D.C. Heath & Company.

Gowan, Peter (1995), 'Analysing shock therapy', *New Left Review*, No. 213 September–October, 3–60.

Gröner, Helmut and Silke Baumann (1994), 'Die Kontroverse um die Erhaltung industrielle Kerne in den neuen Bundesländern', *Beitrag zum 27. Internationalen Forschungsseminar: Ökonomische Erfolge und Mißerfolge der deutschen Wiedervereinigung – Eine Zwischenbilanz*, Radein, February.

Grosser et al. (1990), *Soziale Marktwirtschaft*, Stuttgart: W. Kohlhammer.

Grünert, H. and B. Lutz (1995), 'East German labour market in transition: segmentation and increasing disparity', *Industrial Relations Journal*, **26** (1), 221–40.

Härtel, Hans-Hagen (1994), 'Abwicklung der Treuhandanstalt', *Wirtschaftsdienst*, **74** (12), December, 600.

Härtel, Hans-Hagen and Reinald Krüger et al. (1995), *Die Entwicklung des Wettbewerbs in den neuen Bundesländern*, Baden-Baden: Nomos.

Harris, J.R. and M.P. Todaro (1970), 'Migration, unemployment, and development: a two-sector analysis', *American Economic Review*, **60**, 126–42.

Hax, Herbert (1991), 'Privatisation agencies: the Treuhand approach', Kiel Institute for the World Economy, unpublished draft.

Hickel, Rudolf and Jan Priewe (1994), *Nach dem Fehlstart: Ökonomische Perspektiven der deutschen Einigung*, Frankfurt am Main: Fischer.

Hitchens, D., K. Wagner and J.E. Birnie (1993), *East German Productivity and the Transition to the Market Economy*, Aldershot: Avebury.

Hoffmann, Lutz (1993), *Warten auf den Aufschwung*, Regensburg: tv Transfer-Verlag.

Hofmann, Peter and Kurt Stingl (1990), *Marktwirtschaft in der DDR*, Berlin: Rudolf Haufe.

Hughes Hallet, Andrew and Yue Ma (1992), 'East Germany, West Germany, and their Mezzogiorno Problem: An Empirical Investigation', *Centre for Economic Policy Research – Discussion Paper*, No. 623, February, London.

Hughes Hallet, Andrew and Yue Ma (1993), 'East Germany, West Germany, and their Mezzogiorno problem: a parable for European economic integration', *The Economic Journal*, **103** (417), 416–28.

Hughes Hallet, Andrew and Yue Ma (1994), 'Real adjustment in a union of incompletely converged economies: an example from East and West Germany', *European Economic Review*, **38**, 1731–61.

Huster, Ernst-Ulrich et al. (1973), *Determinanten der westdeutschen Restauration 1945–1949*, Frankfurt am Main: Suhrkamp.

Institut der Deutschen Wirtschaft (iwd), *Informationsdienst*, Köln; various issues.

Jahresgutachten (JG) (1990) (1991) (1992) (1993) (1994) (1995) (1996) – full title: *Unterrichtung durch die Bundesregierung: Jahresgutachten 1991/92 des Sachverständigenrates zur Begutachtung der gesamtwirtschaftlichen Entwicklung*; also for (1992/93), (1993/94), (1994/95), and (1995/96), Bonn: Deutscher Bundestag.

Kaser, Michael (1995), 'Post-communist privatisation: has the Treuhand model helped?', Lecture in the Open Seminar Series of the Institute for German Studies, University of Birmingham, January.

Kay, John (1993), *Foundations of Corporate Success*, Oxford: Oxford University Press.

Klös, H.-P. (1993), 'Labour markets in Eastern Europe and east Germany: challenges for labour market policy', *Employment Observatory*, Directorate-General Employment, Industrial Relations and Social Affairs, Brussels, No. 7.

Klodt, Henning (1994), 'Wieviel Industrie braucht Ostdeutschland?', *Die Weltwirtschaft*, No. 3, 320–33.

Knoll, J.H. and U. Sommer (1992), *Von der Abgrenzung zum Beitritt: Erwachsenenbildung/Weiterbildung in der Bundesrepublik Deutschland und der Deutschen Demokratischen Republik vor und nach der Wende*, Serie Beruf und Bildung, Expert Verlag.

Kolb, J. (1995), 'Lohnrückstand und Arbeitskostenvorteile in Ost-deutschland', *Wirtschaft im Wandel*, No. 7.

Konietzka, D. and H. Solga (1995), 'Two certified societies? the regulation of entry into the labour market in East and West Germany', paper presented at the European Science Foundation Workshop on 'Transition in Youth: Comparisons over Time and across Countries', Oostvoorne, Netherlands, 22–25 September.

Kornai, J. (1980), *The Economics of Shortage*, Vols. I and II, Amsterdam: North-Holland.

Kornai, J. (1986), 'The soft budget constraint', *Kyklos*, **39**.

Kornai, J. (1990), *The Road to a Free Economy*, New York: Norton.

Kramer, Alan (1991), *The West German Economy, 1945–1955*, Oxford: Berg.

Kühl, J. (1993), 'Zur Veränderung der arbeitsmarktpolitischen Instrumente seit 1990', in H. Bosch, H. Heinelt and B. Reissert (eds), *Arbeitsmarktpolitik nach der Vereinigung*, Berlin: Edition Sigma.

Landes, David S. (1969), *The Unbound Prometheus: Technological Change and Industrial Development in Western Europe from 1750 to the Present*, Cambridge: Cambridge University Press.

Lange, T. (1993), 'Training for Economic transformation: the labour market in eastern Germany', *British Review of Economic Issues*, **15** (37), October, 145–68

Lange, T. (1996), 'Labour's unemployment strategy: panacea or placebo?', *International Labour Market Occasional Papers*, No. 1, Aberdeen and Berlin.

Lange, T. and K. Maguire (1996), 'Rethinking the state we are in: lessons from Germany and East Asia', *International Labour Market Occasional Papers*, No. 3, Robert Gordon University Aberdeen and IWVWW Berlin.

Lange, T. and J. Atkinson (1995), *Employment Prospects for Older Workers to 2030*, Institute for Employment Studies, University of Sussex.

Layard, R., S. Nickell and R. Jackman (1991), *Unemployment: Macroeconomic Performance and the Labour Market*, Oxford: Oxford University Press.

Levine, H. (1982), 'Possible causes of the deterioration of Soviet productivity growth in the period 1976–80', in *Soviet Economy in the 80s: Problems and Prospects*, Vol. 1, Joint Economic Committee, US Congress, Washington, DC, pp. 153–68.

Maddison, Angus (1982), *Phases of Capitalist Development*, Oxford: Oxford University Press.

Maddison, Angus (1991), *Dynamic Forces in Capitalist Development*, Oxford: Oxford University Press.

Manove, M. (1971), 'A model of Soviet-type economic planning', *American Economic Review*, **61** (3), June, 390–406.

Maurer, Rainer (1994), 'Die Exportstärke der deutschen Industrie – Weltmarktspitze trotz technologischen Rückstands?', *Die Weltwirtschaft*, No. 3, September, 308–19.

McCombie, J. and A. Thirlwall (1994), *Economic Growth and the Balance of Payments Constraint*, London: Macmillan.

Nicolai, W. (1993), 'Three years transformation process in the new federal states in Germany: results and problems on the macro and microeconomic level', paper presented at the EADI VIIth General Conference on 'Transformation and Development: Eastern Europe and the South', 15–18 September, Technical University Berlin.

Nicolai, W. (1997), 'The role of small and medium enterprises in the new Federal States', in T. Lange and J.R. Shackleton (eds), *Germany: An Economy in Transition*, Berghahn Books, forthcoming.

O'Mahony, Mary (1992), 'Productivity and human capital formation in UK and German manufacturing', *National Institute of Economic and Social Research Discussion Paper*, No. 28.

OECD, *Main Economic Indicators* Paris: OECD, various issues.

OECD (1989), *Employment Outlook*, Paris: OECD.

OECD (1993a), *OECD Economic Surveys: Germany 1993*, Paris: OECD.

OECD (1993b), *Employment Outlook*, Paris: OECD,

OECD (1995), *Germany: OECD Country Report*, Paris: OECD.

Owen-Smith, Eric (1994), *The German Economy*, London: Routledge.

Pentecost, Eric (1993), *Exchange Rate Dynamics*, Aldershot: Edward Elgar.

Porter, Michael (1990). *The Competitive Advantage of Nations*, London: Macmillan.

Powell, R.P. (1977), 'Plan execution and the workability of Soviet planning', *Journal of Comparative Economics*, 1 (1), March, 51–76.

Priewe, J. (1994), 'Long-term socio-economic prognoses for the new Lander', *Employment Observatory*, Brussels: Directorate-General Employment, Industrial Relations and Social Affairs, No. 13, December.

Priewe, J. and R. Hickel (1991), *Der Preis der Einheit*, Frankfurt am Main: Fischer.

Pugh, Geoffrey (1993a), 'The economics of German Unification', *Greenwich Papers* (formerly Thames Papers in Political Economy), No. 1, Summer 1993, London: Greenwich University.

Pugh, Geoffrey (1993b), 'Problems of economic transformation in eastern Germany: an overview', *British Review of Economic Issues*, 15 (37), October, 119–44.

Pugh, Geoffrey (1994), 'The economic consequences of German Unification for the EC', Centre for European Research in Economics and Business, *Working Paper*, No. 4, Staffordshire University Business School.

Pugh, Geoffrey (1997), 'The investment diversion effects of German Unification', in Jens Hölscher and Stephen Frowen (eds), *The German Currency Union of 1990*, New York: St. Martin's Press and London: Macmillan, 1997.

Pugh, Geoffrey and David Carr (1993), 'The monetary consequences of German Unification', *Economics and Business Education*, 1, Part 1(3), Autumn, 116–23.

Quiang, Y. and Ch. Xu (1990), 'Innovation and financial constraints in centralised and decentralised economies', Mimeo, London School of Economics.

Redding, Stephen (1996), 'The low-skill, low-quality trap: strategic complementarities between human capital and R&D', *Economic Journal*, **106** (435), March, 458–70.

Ricoy, Carlos J. (1991), 'Cumulative causation', in J. Eatwell, M. Milgate and P. Newman (eds), *The New Palgrave Dictionary of Economics*, Vol. 1, London: Macmillan, pp. 730–5.

Robinson, P. (1995), 'The limits of active labour market policies', *Employment Policy Institute Economic Report*, **9** (6).

Rodrik, Dani (1995), 'Getting interventions right: how South Korea and Taiwan grew rich', *Economic Policy*, No. 20, April, 53–107.

Roth, Karl Heinz (1990), 'Nach dem Anscluss', in *Konkret*, September, 10–15.

Schenk, Karl-Ernst (1994), 'Treuhandanstalt: Unerfüllbare Erwartungen der Kritiker', *Wirtschaftsdienst*, **74** (4), 174–6.

Schmieding, Holger (1991), 'Die Ostdeutsche Wirtschaftskrise: Ursachen und Lösungsstrategien', *Kiel Institute for the World Economy, Working Paper*, No. 461.

Schultze, Charles L. (1987), 'Saving, investment, and profitability in Europe', in Robert Z. Lawrence and Charles L. Schultze (eds), *Barriers To European Growth*, Washington, DC: The Brookings Institute.

Sengenberger, W. (1987), *Struktur und Funktionsweise von Arbeitsmärkten: Die Bundesrepublik Deutschland im internationalen Vergleich*, Frankfurt am Main: Campus.

Shackleton, J.R. and T. Lange (1993), 'Training in Germany: a dissident view', *Economic Affairs*, June, 16–21.

Shackleton, J.R., L. Clark, T. Lange and S. Walsh (1995), *Training for Employment in Western Europe and the United States*, Aldershot: Edward Elgar.

Siebert, Horst (1991a), 'German Unification: the economics of transition', *Kiel Institute of World Economics, Working Paper*.

Siebert, Horst (1991b), 'Uniting Germany', *Economic Policy*, No. 13, October, 287–340.

Siebert, Horst (1992), *Das Wagnis der Einheit: Eine wirtschaftspolitische Therapie*, Stuttgart: DV.

Siebert, Horst (1994), 'Integrating the eastern Länder: how long a transition?', *Kiel Discussion Papers*, No. 229, April.

Siebert, Horst et al. (1991), 'The transformation of a socialist economy – lessons of German Unification', *Kiel Institute of World Economics, Working Paper*, No. 469.

Sinn, Gerlinde and Hans-Werner Sinn (1992), *Jumpstart: The Economic Unification of Germany*, Cambridge, MA: MIT Press.

Smyser, W.R. (1993), *The German Economy*, Harlow: Longman.

Snower, D. (1994a), 'Converting Unemployment Benefits into Employment Subsidies', *Centre for Economic Policy Research (CEPR), Discussion Paper*.

Snower, D. (1994b), 'Why people don't find work', *Centre for Economic Policy Research (CEPR), Discussion Paper*.

Socialist Economic Bulletin (1991), No. 4, May.

Soos, K.A. (1984), 'Apropos the explanation of shortage phenomenon: volume of demand and structural inelasticity', *Acta Oeconomica*, 3–4.

Statistisches Bundesamt (1993a), *Wirtschaft und Statistik*, Wiesbaden.

Statistisches Bundesamt (1993b), *Zur wirtschaftlichen und sozialen Lage in den neuen Bundesländern: Sonderausgabe*, Wiesbaden, April.

Statistisches Bundesamt (1995), *Volkswirtschaftliche Gesamtrechnung*.

Statistisches Bundesamt (1997), Mimeo (personal communication).

Thimann, C. (1993), 'Why is investment in eastern Germany so unexpectedly slow?', paper presented at the April 1993 Royal Economic Society Conference, University of York.

Tober, Silke (1997), 'Monetary reform and monetary union', in Jens Hölscher and Stephen Frowen (eds), *The German Currency Union of 1990*, New York: St. Martin's Press and London: Macmillan.

Treaty of 18 May 1990 (1990) – full title: 'Treaty of 18 May 1990 between the Federal Republic of Germany and the German Democratic Republic establishing a Monetary, Economic and Social Union', in *The Unity of Germany and Peace in Europe*, Bonn: Press and Information Office of the Federal Government.

Treuhandanstalt (THA) (no date, no place of publication), *The Chance of the 1990s: Investing in Eastern Germany*.

Treuhandanstalt (THA) (1991) (no place of publication), *Promoting the New Germany*.

Treuhandanstalt (THA) (1993), 'Kommunalisierung', *Monatsinformation der THA*, December.

United Nations (1995), *Statistical Yearbook*, New York: United Nations.

van Ark, Bart (1990), 'Comparative levels of manufacturing productivity in post-war Europe: measurement and comparisons', *Oxford Bulletin of Economics and Statistics*, **52** (4), 343–73.

Vassilakis, Spyros (1991), 'Learning-by-doing', in J. Eatwell, M. Milgate and P. Newman (eds), *The New Palgrave Dictionary of Economics*, Vol. 3, London Macmillan, pp.151–2.

Vickers, John and George Yarrow (1988), *Privatisation: An Economic Analysis*, Cambridge, MA: MIT Press.

Vierzehnter Bericht (1996), 'Gesamtwirtschaftliche und unternehmerische Anpassungsfortschritte in Ostdeutschland: Vierzehnter Bericht', *Wochenbericht*, **63** (27).

Wochenbericht (WB) – weekly report of the Deutsches Institut für Wirtschaftsforschung, Berlin.

Welfens, P. (1992), *Economic Aspects of German Unification*, Berlin: Springer Verlag.

Williamson, J. (1991), 'FEERs and the ERM', *National Institute Economic Review*, August, 45–50.

Wolff, Edward (1991), 'Capital formation and productivity convergence over the long term', *American Economic Review*, **81** (3), 565–79.

Wood, Adrian (1995), 'How trade hurt unskilled workers', paper for the International Economics Study Group Conference on 'Trade and Unemployment', September.

Wren-Lewis, S., P. Westaway, S. Soteri and R. Barrell (1991), 'Evaluating the UK's choice of entry rate into the ERM', *The Manchester School*, **LIX** Supplement, June, 1–22.

Youthaid and National Association of Teachers in Further and Higher Education (NATFHE) (1993), *Credit Limits: A Critical Assessment of the Training Credits Pilot Scheme*, January.

Zwölfte Bericht (1995): full title: 'Gesamtwirtschaftliche und unternehmerische Anpassungsfortschritte in Ostdeutschland: Zwölfte Bericht', *Wochenbericht*, **62** (3), January, 72–98.

Index